W9-DCG-494

CLIFF BUTLER – BUTLER CONSULTING AND RETIRED VICE CHAIRMAN OF PILGRIM'S PRIDE CORPORATION, MOUNT PLEASANT, TEXAS

"Bill Helming's new book presents the prophesy of (1) the economic judgment for the excesses we have wreaked upon America's economy and (2) the pathway out of the wilderness of economic depression through knowledge and change in our way of thinking and investing. This is required reading for your economic future."

☆ ☆ ☆ ☆ ☆ ☆ ☆

Keep Smiling and God Bless

By the Author

Bill Helming	Date

This book was written during the seven months of
June-December, 2009
and published in early January of 2010

ISBN #978-0-615-34497-3

By

Bill Helming
Bill Helming Consulting Services
bhelming@comcast.net

This book was printed by

J and J Printing
16701 West 116th Street
Lenexa, Kansas 66219
(913) 491-4774

Jim and Jane Ferguson, Owners
(913) 643-0385
jim@jjprint.com

About the Author
Bill Helming

For more than 40 years, Bill Helming has been forecasting U.S. and global macroeconomic trends. He is an independent thinker and considered by many to be a futurist. Bill is a highly respected U.S. *big picture* economist and expert with one of the most accurate and impressive long-term forecasting, macroeconomic and beef industry track records in the U.S. today. He accurately forecasted the 1981-82, 1990-91, 2000-01 and the 2008-09 recessions. In 1980-81, well in advance of these events happening, he forecasted the sharp decline in the farm economy and farm and ranch real estate prices, the substantial moderation in the long-term trend towards disinflation, plus lower trending crude oil prices and interest rates.

Bill became the first Chief Economist for the National Cattlemen's Beef Association (NCBA) in 1965. He also was the founder and first general manager of "CattleFax" in 1968 (the highly respected national database, market outlook, analysis and research organization of NCBA). In 1974, Bill began an agribusiness consulting service that is still going strong today. Bill Helming Consulting Services is located in Olathe, Kansas and focuses on the U.S. and global macroeconomic and Ag sector outlook, including the outlook for cattle, hog, chicken, grain and crude oil prices, interest rates, inflation versus deflation, the U.S. dollar, employment, etc. Bill has been self-employed since 1974 and writes a quarterly and highly valued macro-economic and Ag sector outlook report called *AS I SEE IT*. He has clients and subscribers all over the U.S.

Bill is also well known and highly respected as a farm and livestock economist and agribusiness consultant. For the 14 years from 1977 to 1991, he produced a syndicated daily radio program (The Helming Report) for over 350 farm and Ag radio stations that aired three to four times a day (five days a week). He has been prominently and regularly featured in major beef industry and trade publications such as *BEEF* magazine, as a key source for information on the Ag sector and his macroeconomic forecasts. He spends most of his time consulting and working closely with the U.S. large-scale cattle feeding industry

A

in the high plains mainstream cattle feeding region and gives a number of speeches each year on the long-term U.S. economic outlook.

Bill worked for 22 years, with the help and input of many people across the U.S., to craft and advance a complete federal income tax code replacement, known as *The BEST Plan*. *The Broad Economic Simplification Tax*, bill S.1921, was introduced in the U.S. Senate by Senators Jim DeMint and Lindsay Graham of South Carolina on October 26, 2005.

Bill recently became chairman and CEO for the newly-formed and privately-owned large-scale cattle feeding company (Rolling Plains) that began operations in the first quarter of 2010. He is the founder of the company whose headquarters is in Olathe, Kansas. Within eight years, Rolling Plains fully expects to become one of the largest cattle feeding enterprises in the U.S. Bill is uniquely qualified to lead and to serve as Rolling Plains' chairman and CEO.

Bill grew up on a feedyard and cattle ranching operation in southern California in the 1950's. He graduated with honors and received BS and MS degrees in Agriculture Economics from the University of Nevada, Reno (1964-1965). Bill received the University's Centennial Alumnus Award in 1988 from the Board of Regents for "**Outstanding Graduate of the University for the Past 100 Years.**" He is married to Kathleen and they live in Olathe, Kansas.

A

Acknowledgements

When I think about the people that I want to thank and acknowledge for their encouragement, support and help in writing this book, there are many people who quickly come to mind. Going back many years, some of these special people include my mom and dad, Barbara E. Helming and Oscar C. Helming, Jr., my two brothers, Jim and Bob, my two sons, Troy and Nathan, my father-in-law, Jim Jones, Teresa Islas and family, some of my University of Nevada at Reno professors, the late Bill House, a Kansas rancher and a highly respected and successful beef cattle industry leader and a very good friend, plus my many clients, subscribers and friends, some of whom strongly encouraged me to write this book.

It took me the seven months of June-December, 2009 to write this book. I could not have done it nearly as well or as quickly without the excellent help, encouragement, ideas and editing skills of four people. I extend my heartfelt thanks and most sincere appreciation to the following very special people:

- *Kathleen Helming*, my loving wife, gave me very extensive encouragement and ideas on the content of this book. Prior to our meeting, she had been doing secretarial work for a college and moved on to a real estate company where, over time, she became its office operations manager. Based on her interest, we had many conversations about the economy. She told me that she began to understand much more clearly why the companies she worked for had been in such challenging times during the 1970s and 80s, which were times of serious inflation. When I began to write this book, she said, "Remember, people will be extremely helped by understanding that it is normal for our capitalistic system to have up and down periods – they will be inclined to plan ahead." Kathleen helped to ensure that the book would be easy to read and understand. I credit her for the title of the book and for the many easy ways to express the complicated subjects covered in each chapter.

- *Paulette Boyt*, my business assistant for the past five years, is one of the several people who strongly encouraged me to publish this book. She is also one of three people who made very good use of her excellent editing skills. She also conducted extensive research in order to compile the data to create the figures throughout the book.

  Paulette worked countless hours on this book, and without her dedication, skills and hard work, it would not have become a reality.

Paulette attended business school in the 1960s. She worked as a legal secretary in the 1960s and 1970s, then at the IBM corporate headquarters and Sprint in the 1980s. She was also the office manager for Heartland Community Church in the 1980s. In 1989, she began her own professional secretarial services company, PDQ Word Processing. She is now an independent contractor through her business and does multiple tasks for me.

- *Tamara Cutler*, my daughter, is a very talented person on many fronts, including being an excellent writer. She lives with her husband, Jeff, and their 11-year old twins, Adair and Gage, in East Lansing, Michigan.

Tamara performed a very valuable and important role as the second key person who thoroughly edited this book from cover to cover. She has made a very helpful contribution to the finished product and was a real inspiration and source of encouragement to me in getting this book successfully completed.

Tamara graduated from the University of Colorado in 1991, Magna Cum Laude with a B.S. degree in Business Administration. She worked in sales and marketing for Baxter International from 1991-1996, becoming a senior marketing manager in the Chicago area. She has worked for the Stryker Corporation from 1996 to the present time. While with Stryker, Tamara has been (1) Sales Planning and Development Manager, (2) National Account Manager, (3) Director of National Accounts and (4) currently Vice President of Healthcare Systems U.S.

- *Gene Meyer* is the third editor on this book. I have known Gene for about 34 years. He has been a successful business journalist for most of his working life. His 37-year career includes very significant experience at the *Wall Street Journal, Commodity News Services, Inc.* and *The Kansas City Star* newspaper. He worked for the *Kansas City Star* for 26 years (1983-2008). Gene is now a self-employed business and news writing consultant. While with *The Star*, Gene generated about *145* to *150* byline stories annually on deadline to help readers interpret multiple types of economic and financial news, tax laws, stock markets, insurance trends and stories concerning finances on a personal level.

Gene performed a very valuable and important role as the third pair of eyes to review this book. He also thoroughly edited this book from beginning to end. His writing skills have contributed a great deal to the readability of this book and I am very grateful for his contributions. Gene received a B.S. degree in journalism and international studies from Iowa State University, Ames, Iowa, in 1972.

B

Table of Contents

Introduction

When Johnny came marching home following World War II, the United States took a deep breath, stood up to its full height and made the determination to become strong and mighty again based on hard work and the principles of freedom and capitalism. The U.S. and world economy truly hit bottom in the 1930's. After the war, we began to focus on renewing, rebuilding and increasing the prosperity of our great nation. In the approximately 64 years since 1945, the United States has experienced some significant economic bumps and slumps and several wars and skirmishes. But overall, as a nation, we have continued doggedly on a path of growth, prosperity and improved living standards for most Americans. We put the Great Depression of the 1930's long behind us. Most people believed such times could never happen to our country again. As a nation, we thought we were invincible and that things would be different going forward. Perhaps we were wrong. Perhaps we needed to review our history books. Perhaps we should have reminded ourselves that *what goes up eventually comes down* regarding our economy and the long-term boom and bust 60- to 80-year business cycle. Perhaps we forgot that history does repeat itself.

This book is written for my fellow Americans and is intended to help you to better understand why the U.S. economy is facing a *modern day* depression that began in 2008 and 2009 and a *new normal* that will continue through 2010-2014 and beyond. My hope is that those who read this book will have a head start on dealing with the very challenging economic times ahead and will take advantage of opportunities that will present themselves.

Most people alive today have *not* experienced the difficulty of an economic depression in their adult lives. However, almost everyone generally knows what a recession is. Most Americans know that recessions usually last for less than a year. Short-lived recessions and generally good times are what most people today consider as normal, particularly if they exclude the serious and painful financial and economic conditions in 2008 and 2009 regarding the loss of jobs and the loss of wealth in their homes' values and their life's savings.

Economic depressions last for years. I wrote this book to help as many Americans as possible to understand and plan for a *new normal*. This *new normal* will include much slower economic growth, higher unemployment, lower income levels and higher taxes through at least 2020 than most Americans expect. The stage is set. Most Americans will be surprised, frustrated and angry at what our country is going to be facing economically, financially, politically and otherwise in the next five to 10 years. The years 2008 and 2009 represent an important wakeup call. The real storm is ahead of us in the 2010-2014. *My*

C

recommendation is to hope for the best, but plan for the worst. Knowledge is power, and if you know what is coming, you can plan accordingly. I encourage you to review Chapter 10, which highlights my recommendations of what to do and what not to do in the wake of what I expect to happen in 2010 - 2014.

The economic and financial market forecasts, analysis and conclusions contained in this book are sobering and perhaps frightening for many people. However, I believe they are realistic and likely to play out as presented between now and the year 2014 and beyond.

Since our federal government congressional, administrative and Federal Reserve Board policies and actions can and do have positive or negative impacts on our U.S. economy, Chapter 9 in this book explores the negative impact that the massive recent increases in our national debt, spending, budget deficits and coming higher taxes are going to have on our economy and on the American people in the next five to 10 years and beyond. The federal government bailout and economic stimulus programs will not work as advertised. These socialistic policies and trends will end up making economic conditions significantly worse and will substantially delay much needed improvement in economic growth and in new net job creation during the next five years and beyond.

Finally, I wrote this book to present my perspective and outlook of the economic times we live in to a much larger portion of the U.S. population, so that more people can potentially benefit from my analysis and forecasts. Some of my clients and the readers of my quarterly outlook reports for the past 38 years have strongly encouraged me to write this book so that more people may be better informed and prepared. My desire is that you find this book on our economy and financial matters interesting, easy to comprehend and helpful to you, your family and to your business.

Chapter 1
Depressions vs. Recessions
What's the Difference?

In 2007, the U.S. economy began to slow significantly, mostly because of a persistent drop in real estate prices and related problems. Optimists spoke of a "soft landing" for those whose jobs and investments would be affected. But on November 12, 2007 and again on December 14, 2007 and March 7, 2008, I told my clients and subscribers across America[1] to "be prepared for one of the most challenging, serious and painful U.S. economic recessions that we have experienced since World War II." Again on June 16, 2008, I told them to "be prepared for a U.S. *modern day* economic and financial depression within the 2008 and 2014 time period."

This chapter explains the major differences between recessions, depressions and long periods of economic stagnation. It also outlines my definition of a U.S. *modern d*ay economic depression and why I believe it will happen in 2008-2014. Only two depressions in U.S. history have lasted longer than the one coming now.

Recessions vs. Depressions and/or Prolonged Periods of Economic Stagnation

U.S. recessions and depressions or prolonged periods of stagnation share *one very common characteristic. Both are typically associated with much slower than normal growth.* Within each, there is some negative growth, along with some positive and sub-par growth. Net average annual growth rates typically are positive, but below normal, for each over periods of one to three years.

There are important differences too:

- Recessions typically last for months and rarely more than one year.
- Depressions or prolonged periods of stagnation typically last far longer, usually for seven to 10 years.

Figures 1.1 and 1.2 provide a summary and a historical perspective of U.S. economic recessions versus depressions or prolonged periods of stagnation from 1930 through 2007, plus my summary forecasts for 2008 through 2014.

It is important to understand that *the rate of growth is the single most important factor that determines relatively good versus bad times.* It is what

---

[1] Bill Helming's quarterly *AS I SEE IT* newsletter

determines whether significant numbers of jobs are created or lost. Generally speaking, when the average annual rate of growth in the U.S. is *3.0%* per year or higher, a lot of new jobs become available and unemployment falls. Likewise, when the rate of growth in the U.S. is *2.0%* per year or lower, large numbers of jobs are lost and unemployment rises. These trends and numbers are valid and reliable on an annual basis, but not on a monthly or quarterly basis. Consequently, the growth numbers that really matter are year-to-year average annual comparisons of growth measured by the Gross Domestic Product, or GDP. GDP is broadly defined as the total dollar value of all the goods and services produced in the United States. We will look more closely at what it can tell us later in this chapter.

Figure 1.1
Summary of the Major Differences between a Recession and a Depression

Recessions	Depressions and Periods of Stagnation
1. On average, they occur once every five to seven years.	1. Typically they occur once every 60 to 80 years or every 1.5 to 2.0 generations.
2. Typically they last for only months and less than one year.	2. Typically they last for seven to 10 years and sometimes longer.
3. Typically the unemployment rate ranges between *4.2%* and *8.7%*.	3. Typically the level of unemployment ranges between *9.5%* and *18%*.
4. Typically the rate of sub-par economic growth is a positive *1.0%* or *2.0%* for *six* to *16 months* with two or more quarters of negative growth followed by positive and normal economic growth soon afterward via a **V**-shaped downturn and recovery.	4. Typically the rate of sub-par economic growth is a positive *1.0%* to *2.0%* with periodic quarters or years of negative growth for a period of *seven* to *10 years* via an **L**-shaped downturn and a much slower than normal recovery.
5. Typically the rate of CPI inflation moderates, but price inflation continues, i.e. disinflation.	5. Typically you see CPI price deflation, zero inflation or very low inflation rates for five to seven years or longer.
6. Short interest rates (the fed funds rate) decline only moderately for most recessions and usually for about one year and then start trending higher again.	6. Short interest rates (the fed funds rate) decline sharply towards the zero level and stay there for an extended period of time (for several years).

7. Typically the depth of the downturn is moderate and lasts for one year or less before significant recovery starts.	7. Typically the depth of the downturn is much greater and more painful for a period of years, including large numbers of bank, business and consumer bankruptcies and failures.
8. Most asset classes, i.e. the stock markets, real estate values and commodity market values, continue increasing, level off or decline only moderately for a period of months with only modest amounts of wealth being lost.	8. Almost all asset values, including the stock market, real estate and commodities decline substantially, resulting in trillions of dollars of lost wealth over a period of several years or more.

Source: This summary was created by the author.

Figure 1.2
The Three U.S. Depressions Since 1800 and the Eleven U.S. Recessions Since 1940, including:
- The Duration in Months and Years
- The Unemployment Rate
- The Actual and Forecasted GDP Growth

Depressions and Recessions	Dates	Duration in Months from Peak to Trough	Dura-tion in Years	Rate of GDP Growth	Unem-ployment Rate*
A. Depressions:					
1. Depression of 1807**	1807-1814	---	7	---	---
2. Long Depression**	1873-1896	---	23	---	---
3. Great Depression**	1930-1939	---	10	1.32	18.3
Average	---	---	*13.3*	*1.32*	*18.3*
B. Recessions:					
1. Recession of 1945-1947**	1945**	8	1	-1.1	5.5
2. Recession of 1948**	1948-1949	11	1	2.0	4.9
3. Recession of 1953**	1953-1954	10	1	2.0	4.3
4. Recession of 1957**	1957-1958	8	1	0.5	5.6
5. Recession of 1960**	1960-1961	10	1	2.4	6.1
6. Recession of 1969**	1969-1970	11	1	1.5	4.2
7. 1973 oil crises recession**	1973-1975	16	2	2.7	6.3
8. Recession of 1980**	1980	6	1	-0.2	7.1
9. Recession of 1981-1982**	1981-1982	16	2	0.3	8.7
10. Early 1990's recession**	1990-1991	8	1	0.9	6.2
11. Early 2000's recession**	2001-2003	8	1	1.7	5.5
Average	---	*10.2*	*1.2*	*1.2*	*5.9*

C. The Author's Forecasts

1. The 2008-2009 recession*** (began 4th quarter, 2007)**	2008-2009	---	2	-1.25 to -1.75	7.5
2. The 2008-2014 depression***	2008-2014	---	7	1.5 to 2.0	---
3. The 2010-2012 depression***	2010-2012	---	3	---	11.0

*Source: The U.S. Department of Labor for 1930-1939 and for the *11* recessions and for 2008. The unemployment rate for 2008-2009 of *7.5%* is based on *actual* average unemployment numbers for calendar year 2008 of *5.8%* and on the author's forecast for calendar year 2009 of *9.2%*, wherein the *actual* unemployment number for the first 11 months of 2009 was *9.2%*, ranging between a low point of *7.6%* in January, 2009 and a high point of *10.2%* in October, 2009. **The author's forecast for the average annual U.S. unemployment rate for the 2010-2012 time period is within the *10.5%* to *11.5%* range**. The author's forecast for the monthly **peak** unemployment rate in the 2010-2012 time period is close to *12%* and possibly higher.

**Source: National Bureau of Economic Research and Wikipedia for list of recessions and depressions in the U.S.

***Source: The estimates for the 2008-2009 U.S. recession and for the 2010-2014 *modern day* depression are made by the author, Bill Helming. The actual rate of GDP growth was *3.82%* for the 1940-2007 time period and was *1.32%* for the 1930-1939 time period.

In December of 2007, the beginning of the 2008-2009 Great Recession, the number of Americans that were unemployed was *7.5 million* with a corresponding unemployment rate of *4.9%* according to the U.S. Bureau of Labor Statistics. As of December, 2008, there were *8.924 million* American men and women unemployed. As of November, 2009, there were *15.4 million* Americans unemployed with a corresponding unemployment rate of *10%*. For the 24 months from December, 2007 through November of 2009, the number of Americans who lost their jobs increased by *7.9 million* or *106%* in two years!

What is "Normal?"

An annual average growth rate of *3%* to *4%* per year is normal for the U.S. A *5%* to *6%* per year rate is excellent. Growth in those ranges encourages the creation of many new jobs each month and generally improving wages and employee benefits. Rates in the *1%* to *2%* yearly range or lower are sub-par and much *slower than normal*. Rates in this range result in many people losing their jobs, reduced wages and employee benefits. When the U.S. economy contracts and rates fall below 0%, as we experienced in much of 2008 and 2009, the result is a very large number of job losses and reduced incomes and employee benefits for many people.

Figure 1.2 gives you important information and history on the three U.S. depressions since 1800 and the 11 recessions since 1940 through 2007. It includes their duration in months and years, plus the average annual unemployment rate during the Great Depression in the 1930's and for the 11 recessions, plus the average annual actual and forecasted GDP growth from 1930-2014.

There are several other important factors that distinguish depressions from recessions, including their frequency and the course of their paths to recovery (see Figures 1.3, 1.4, 1.5, 1.6 and 1.7).

Depressions and extended periods of stagnation occur as part of long-term 60 to 80-year *boom* and *bust* cycles. *What goes up eventually comes down* in the U.S. economy. Also, *what goes down eventually goes back up*. The key difference between a recession and a depression is the rate of growth and the length of time it takes before *normal* growth begins again. A depression is the *bust* phase of a *long-term* business cycle. The *boom* part of a cycle occurs when an economy generally goes up for 60 to 80 years. The *bust* cycle is when that same economy eventually comes down and grows only at a much reduced rate for seven to 10 years. This has been historically true and will continue to be true in the future.

Recessions are much shorter. A recession typically lasts for less than a year, not the seven to 10 years typical for a depression. This downturn, followed by a relatively quick recovery usually follows a **V**-shape pattern, as shown in Figure 1.3. Recovery typically takes place during the approximately six to 12 months following the deepest part of the **V**. We've seen this **V**-shaped pattern in the last 11 U.S. recessions that have occurred during a broader long-term business cycle boom since about 1940. Therefore, it is easy to see, after the economy tipped in late 2007 into the current recession, why many people expected we would soon have a relatively quick rise back to a *normal* economy. I don't believe this will be the case, for reasons we will explore in Chapters 3, 4 and 5.

Figure 1.4 shows the usual **L**-shaped path of a U.S. downturn and recovery during seven to 10 years of a depression or long stagnation following a very serious, painful and much longer than normal recession. The **L**-shaped pattern simply means that once the economy hits its low point, it stays relatively flat and recovers very slowly instead of quickly returning to normal. **It takes years as opposed to months for the economy to really get back on track and back to *normal* in an L-shaped downturn and recovery**. This is what typically happens during the *bust* phase of the long-term, 60- to 80-year business cycle.

This is not what most Americans today are expecting or planning on. However, the **L**-shaped downturn and recovery is very likely what will play out within the combined 2008-2014 time period. I believe the odds of this happening are *90%*.

Figure 1.3

Illustration of the Typical V-shaped U.S. Downturn and Recovery over a 6- to 16-month Time Period During and Following Periodic Recessions within the 60- to 80-year Boom Period of the Long-term Business Cycle

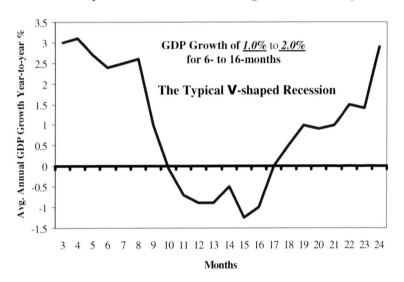

Source: Illustration created by the author.

Stagnation does *not* mean stagflation. A stagflating economy generally is one that is growing flatter and more slowly than normal while unemployment and inflation rates remain above normal. In a *stagnating* economy, as I define it in this book, growth rates are even further below normal and unemployment is even higher. Consumers are saving more money than usual, which drops consumer spending far enough below normal to cut inflation – measured by the Consumer Price Index – to nearly zero or even to create deflation. This is simply another way to describe and define a five- to 10-year **L**-shaped downturn and recovery as illustrated in Figure 1.4. This is in contrast to a **V**-shaped downturn and recovery that generally lasts for a period of months and usually less than a year.

Figure 1.4
Illustration of the Occasional and Typical **L**-shaped U.S. Downturn and Very Slow Recovery over a 10-year Period During and Following a *Modern Day* Depression or Prolonged Stagnation Period (over a Seven- to 10-year Bust Period) of the Long-term 60- to 80-year Business Cycle

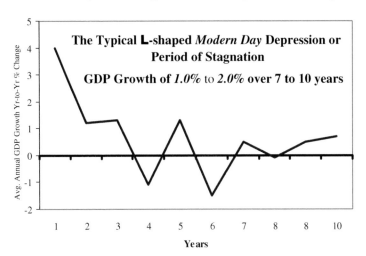

Source: Illustration created by the author.

We will look more closely at some causes of periodic stagnation in Chapters 4 and 5. Some good examples include stagnation that occurred in Japan for 14 years from about 1992-2005 and in the U.S. during much of the Great Depression years or for 10 years during the 1930's.

Gross Domestic Product grows at an average annual rate of *1.0%* to *2.0%* in an essentially flat, very slow **L**-shaped recovery period as shown in Figure 1.4. Even in the higher end of that range, between *1.5%* and *2.0%* per year, these numbers will result in no new job growth, a continuation of job losses, and much higher-than-normal unemployment numbers for several years.

Green, Yellow and Red Light Zones – Why the GDP Matters

Figure 1.5 shows differences among GDP growth rates in what I describe as *green, yellow* and *red light zones*. The *green light zone* is a boom period, during which GDP grows *3.0%* to *6.0%* annually for several years. The *yellow light zone* represents a recession, during which GDP growth rates slow to *1.0%* to *2.0%,* usually for 12 months or less. *Yellow light zone* recessions also may be periodic, as when GDP contracts for two or more quarters within a six- to 16-month period. The *red light zone* is a depression, in which GDP growth rates slow to an average annual *1.0%* to *2.0%* for seven to 10 *years.* GDP growth may

7

even be negative in one or more red light zone depression years, when economic output falls short of a year earlier.

New job creation is very positive in the green light zone. Significant job losses produce higher unemployment in the yellow light zone. In a red light zone, major job losses push unemployment rates to yearly averages of *9.5%* to *12.0%* or higher for several years.

Figure 1.5
The Illustration of Positive and Slow Average Annual Gross Domestic Product (GDP) Growth via Green, Yellow and Red Light Zones

GDP Growth Categories	Range in GDP Growth by Zone		
	Green Light Zone	Yellow Light Zone	Red Light Zone
1. Real positive GDP Growth for years	*3% to 6%* (Boom period persisting for many years)		
2. Slow GDP Growth for months		1% to 2% (Recessions if they persist for 6 to 16 months)	
3. Slow GDP Growth for years			*1% to 2%* (Depressions and stagnation periods if they persist for 7 to 10 years)

Source: Illustration created by the author.

Figure 1.6 shows the differences that GDP rates make on employment. Between *125,000* and *300,000* **new jobs per month are created** when the economy grows *3%* to *6%* annually during *green light zone* booms. Between *75,000* and *200,000* **jobs per month are lost** in *yellow light zone* recessions. Those **losses grow to between *200,000* and *600,000* jobs per month** in the *red light zones* of depression/stagnation.

8

Figure 1.6

The Illustration of Major New Job Growth, Significant Job Losses and Major Job Losses via Green, Yellow and Red Light Zones for Different GDP Growth Rates for Months versus Years

Rates of GDP Growth	Gains and Losses of Jobs		
	Green Light Zone	Yellow Light Zone	Red Light Zone
1. A *3% to 6%* growth rate over many years (boom period)	The creation of *125,000* to *300,000* new jobs per month		
2. A *1% to 2%* growth rate for 6 to 16 months (recessions)		The loss of *75,000* to *200,000* jobs per month	
3. A *1% to 2%* growth rate for 7 to 10 years (depressions)			The loss of *200,000* to *600,000* jobs per month

Source: Illustration created by the author.

Figure 1.7 summarizes the rate of GDP growth, the average level of unemployment and the length of four significant economic events we are examining. Those are the 1930s depression, the last economic *boom* period from 1940 to 2007, the 11 economic recessions that took place between 1940 and 2007 in the U.S., and my forecasted *modern day* depression and period of stagnation in 2008-2014.

The *bust* phases of longer-term business cycles stem primarily from two causes: financial *excesses* and major changes in birth rates over time. We will discuss in Chapter 3 how changing birth rates, and particularly the appearance of the 1946-1964 *baby boom* generation affect longer-term cycles. But first, let's look at the role financial excesses play.

Financial excesses, such as incurring too much debt or accelerating the use of credit to pursue prosperity more quickly, can cause the creation of major asset or financial bubbles that inevitably collapse. Farmland, single family home prices, commercial and industrial real estate, energy prices, technology stocks and easy credit are just some of the bubbles that have bloomed and burst in our recent lifetimes.

Figure 1.7

The Rate of Growth in Gross Domestic Product (GDP), the Level of Unemployment and the Duration in the Number of Years or Months for the Last Depression in the 1930's, the Last Boom Period from 1940-2007, the last 11 Recessions between 1940 and 2007, the 2008-2009 Serious U.S. Recession and the Next *Modern Day* Depression in the 2008-2014 Time Period

Summary of the Most Recent Bust and Boom Periods in the U.S.	Rate of GDP Growth	Rate of Unemploy-ment	Duration in Months/ Years
A. The *bust* period during the Great Depression from 1930-1939.	*1.32%*	*18.3%*	10 years
B. The *boom* period from 1940-2007 or for 1.70 generations (assuming 40 years in a generation).	*3.82%*	*5.3%*	68 years
C. The 11 recessions that took place between 1940 and 2007 in the U.S.	*1.2%*	*5.9%*	10.2 months
D. The author's forecast for the 2008-2009 serious, deepest and longest lasting recession since the Great Depression (1930s).	*-1.25%* to *-1.75%*	*7.5%*	24 months
E. The author's forecast for the next *modern day* depression and stagnation period during the 2008-2014 time period, with the most serious, painful and financial pressures coming during the three years 2010-2012.	*1.75%** (1.5% to 2.0%)	*11.0%*** (10.5% to 11.5%)	7 years

*Author's forecasts. You can expect and should plan on the GDP growth rate to be within the *1.5%* to *2.0%* range for the seven years of 2008-2014. The level of monthly unemployment will likely peak at about *12%* during the year of 2012.

The author is forecasting the average annual rate of unemployment to be 11% within the 2010-2012 time period and falling within the range of *10.5%* to *11.5%*. Plan on the level of U.S. unemployment remaining **above the *9.5%* to *10%* level for the 2010-2014 time period and perhaps longer.

Long-term market boom and bust cycles typically last 30 years in commodity markets and the farm economy. The last previous bust phase of this cycle in the U.S. occurred in the mid 1980s, which I forecasted in the early 1980s. Now another bust in the farm economy, farmland values and agriculture commodities is coming, and at the same time as the economic bust phase of the overall U.S. 60- to 80- long-term economic and business cycle. The last time this happened was in the 1930s during the Great Depression that lasted for 10 years.

Again, there have been 11 recessions in the United States since 1940, not including the current 2008-2009 recession. The average time from the peak of the cycle to its trough for these recessions was 10.2 months and their average duration was 1.2 years, according to the National Bureau of Economic Research (NBER), an independent economic group that determines when U.S. business cycles officially begin and end. Individually, the recessions were as short as six months, in 1980, or as long as 16 months, in 1981-82. Unemployment rates averaged *5.9%* during those 11 recessions, compared to an average *5.3%* during the 68-year 1940-2007 boom during which those recessions occurred. Unemployment was highest during the 1981-1982 recession, at *8.7%,* and lowest during the 11-month 1969-1970 recession at *4.2%.* (More details are shown in Figures 1.2 and 1.7)

NBER defines a recession as a decline in a country's gross domestic product (GDP) or negative real economic growth for two or more successive calendar quarters, plus important changes in industrial production, sales, real income, generally rising levels of unemployment, as well as other related economic and financial conditions that it takes into account. Those include the supply, use, demand and costs for the factors of production, consisting of capital and labor, plus new technology, innovation and productivity gains or losses.

The key figure in calculating recessions or depressions remains the gross domestic product, or GDP. GDP is the total dollar amount of all goods and services produced and purchased in the United States, and all goods and services that the U.S. exports. *Goods* include, for example, new homes, cars, tools, equipment, home and office furniture and furnishings, food and supermarket purchases, fuel, clothing, electronic devices, medicine and drugstore purchases and many other tangible items. *Services* include medical services, accounting, consulting, cleaning, legal services, travel charges, utilities, sporting events, dining out, movies, theater and other entertainment. The GDP numbers used in this book are *real* GDP numbers, which means they have been adjusted for inflation. This is the common practice by business and government officials who use and publish these types of numbers.

The growth rate economists talk about is normally the percentage of increase or decrease in the GDP from the previous year. GDP growth is created by all the money consumers and businesses spend and invest, all the money government spends, all the money that foreign buyers spend for goods and services produced here, and the inventory value of all the things that are still waiting to be sold. Buying and importing goods and services that we don't produce in the U.S. diminishes GDP growth. That is why any surge in the import of 70% of the crude oil we use, for example, has a negative impact on our quarterly and annual GDP numbers in the U.S.

The GDP growth rate is one of the most important indicators of the economic health or the lack thereof in any country. There are other very important indicators too. One is the level and duration of rising or falling unemployment, which measures change in how fast and how many people are finding or losing jobs. Another is the rate of productivity gains in creating and making available goods and services in our economy or in other economies in the world. If the GDP is growing at *3%* to *6%* per year, so will business activity and new company startups, jobs, personal incomes and business and corporate profits, investment, risk taking and tax revenues. If the GDP slows down and falls below *2.0%* per year, businesses start making fewer new purchases or investments in new plants, equipment and inventories. They also stop or substantially reduce hiring new employees or even reduce jobs as they wait to see if the economy will improve and by how much and when. Consumers, in turn, reduce their spending too, either because they have less money to spend or they simply become more cautious and GDP growth slows further. Among other things, this also results in reduced tax revenues.

The U.S. is largely a consumer driven and spending economy. Consumer spending today accounts for close to *70%* to *71%* of the GDP. When people significantly increase spending and reduce savings, those actions have a very positive impact on all phases of the economy. The reverse is also true. When people significantly reduce or stop spending money and start saving more, the GDP rate slows down substantially or even goes negative as it has in major periods of 2008 and 2009, and this has a major negative impact on all phases of the economy for months or even years. The result is either a serious recession or depression depending on how long GDP is negative or how much slower than normal the GDP growth rate is and for how long. In short, the most important economic indicator is the rate and level of gains in new jobs or the loss of jobs. *What really counts are jobs and the incomes resulting from those jobs.*

GDP growth slows in a recession, businesses stop expanding, employment falls, unemployment rises, and housing and other real estate prices and stock market prices generally decline. It is clear from this that the U.S. has been in a serious, very painful and much longer lasting recession than normal since the fourth quarter of 2007 through 2008 and 2009. According to the NBER, the 2008-2009 U.S. recession is already the longest on record by far since 1940.

I estimate that the *combined* GDP number for 2008 and 2009 will end up being within the range of a *-1.25%* to a *-1.75%*. This means the U.S. economy, on balance, shrank *1.25%* to *1.75%* in 2008 and 2009. The officially recorded GDP rate changes for each quarter of calendar year 2008 are *-0.7%, 1.5%, -2.7%* and *-5.4%*, resulting in a total change of *0.4%* for the full year. Growth rates in calendar 2009 are officially recorded at *-6.4%, -0.7%* and *2.2%* for the first, second and third quarters, respectively. I estimated that the official GDP number for the year 2009 will contract by *-2.5%* to a *-3.0%*.

Bottom line, the performance of the U.S. economy in 2008-2009 was the most painful, serious and longest lasting recession since the Great Depression in terms of economic contraction, job losses, declining wages and reduced employee benefits, and loss of wealth in real estate and stock markets. By 2014, if not sooner, I believe the NBER will likely classify the downturn of 2008-2014 as a depression, or at least a period of major stagnation and the period of 2008-2009 as the *Great Recession*.

Many experts and economists say that recessions occur only when GDP is negative for two or more consecutive quarters. But for all practical purposes, recessions begin when several quarters of slowing, but still positive GDP growth affect jobs and incomes. Often, when average annual GDP growth is below *2.0%*, a quarter of negative growth will occur, followed by several quarters of positive growth, and then another quarter of negative growth. In many cases, the NBER will classify this as a recession.

I agree with this analysis and line of thinking. The dot.com stock market crash and subsequent downturn in 2000 is a good example. This was not a recession in technical terms because the GDP contractions, in the third quarter of 2000 and the first and third quarters of 2001, were not consecutive. However, anyone who lived through that period knows that it felt like a recession and that jobs and incomes were negatively affected. And in fact, GDP growth did not rise above *3%* until the third quarter of 2003. The NBER classified the 2001-2003 time period as a recession lasting a total of eight months.

A review of the data and our history books will show that recessions last for a few months and typically for less than one year. Depressions, on the other hand, last somewhere between seven and 23 *years*. Besides being much longer than recessions, depressions are more severe. Depressions feed and grow when falling demand forces businesses and consumers to cut debt, write down or write off obligations that cannot be paid, and suffer the loss of substantial wealth in real estate, the stock market or other major assets. Spending slows dramatically when this contraction occurs, prolonging and increasing the downturn as jobs are lost and banks, businesses and consumers fail in growing numbers.

This is what we will see unfold over 2010-2014 beyond what we have already seen in 2008 and 2009. We will look more closely at the reasons why in Chapters 3, 4 and 5.

Depressions are always associated with major and very serious deflation of prices and asset values and zero or very low inflation rates that tend to be long lasting in terms of years. We've already seen early symptoms of prolonged deflation and major declines in home, commercial and industrial real estate values, falling commodity and stock market prices, lower interest rates and other financial indicators. These deflationary forces will likely persist until at least 2014 and even longer.

Price and asset value deflation is much more modest or essentially nonexistent during recessions and usually lasts for a number of months, not years. Depressions are the *bust* phase of a long-term 60- to 80-year business cycle. The *boom* phase of a long-term business cycle generally lasts for *1.5* to *2.0 generations* (assuming one generation equals 40 years) within the cycle, but may be punctuated with periodic recessions, such as the 11 *bumps in the road* that the U.S. experienced during 1940-2007.

Unemployment always rises in both recessions and depressions. Historically, however, it is much higher and longer lasting during depressions and long periods of stagnation. For example, unemployment rates averaged *18.3%* during the Great Depression and *peaked at 25%* in *1933*. In comparison, average annual unemployment rates never topped *8.7%* and averaged *5.9%* during the 11 recessions between 1940 and 2007. (See Figure1.2)

I believe that over the 2010-2012 time period, the average annual unemployment rate in the U.S. will be close to *11.0%* or almost double the average of the 11 recessions between 1940 and 2007 of *5.9%*, and that growing numbers of those who do have jobs will be working for reduced incomes and benefits, i.e. the underemployed. I estimate the combined unemployment rate for 2008-2009 will be *7.5%* as shown in Figure 1.2 (*5.8%* in 2008 and *9.2%* in 2009), before climbing to an annual average of about *11.0%* for 2010-2012.

I believe the *peak* U.S. unemployment number in the years of 2010 to 2012 will be close to *12%*, or *18.6 million* men and women who will have lost their jobs. I estimate that *average* U.S. unemployment for 2010-2012 will be between *10.5%* and *11.5%*. These unemployment numbers will be much higher than those experienced in the past 11 recessions and significantly higher than most people are expecting and planning for today. These numbers do not include the much larger numbers of men and women who have given up looking for a job or who are greatly under-employed as discussed in Chapter 5.

Figures 1.2 and 1.7 give you my estimates of the 2008-2009 recession, which I believe will be the early stages of a 2008-2014 U.S. *modern day* depression and period of stagnation. The three official depressions the United States has experienced so far lasted an average *13.3* years. I am confident that the fourth U.S. overall economic depression will occur within the 2008-2014 time period and last about seven years. I believe the years 2010-2012 will be the most painful, for reasons we will explore further in Chapters 3, 4, 5 and 6.

During the Great Depression, the GDP grew an average *1.32%*, veering between a minus 13% in 1932 to a positive 13% in 1936. The economy shrank in five of the years of the Depression; in 1930, 1931, 1932, 1933 and 1938, and by 8.6%, 6.4%, 13.0%, 1.3% and 3.4%, respectively, as measured by 2000 dollars. It also grew in five of the years; in 1934, 1935, 1936, 1937 and 1939, by 10.8%, 8.9%, 13.0%, 5.1% and 8.1%, respectively.

Most Americans know that recessions happen in our country periodically. We know that some recessions are relatively mild, as in 1969-1970. Some are significantly more painful and serious, as in 1981-1982. The differences are shown in Figure 1.2. We also know that growth, employment, wages, the stock market and home values typically go back up to positive growth levels or back to *normal* shortly after a recession ends. These are the **V**-shaped downturns and recoveries we saw in Figures 1.1 and 1.3.

Each U.S. depression and recession has been generated by financial excesses or shocks to the economy, plus other forces such as major changes in monetary policies by the Federal Reserve Board, changes in birth rates and the impact of wars. Prior to the Great Depression, for example, there was excessive credit growth, leverage and easy credit terms by banks in the 1920s. This led investors to borrow and speculate in real estate and stocks, which produced bubbles in those markets. As with all financial and asset class bubbles, these reached their bursting point. Many banks failed. Many investors lost most of their wealth. This caused major *runs on the banks* in the 1930's.

Does this sound similar to what we generally experienced during the booms in technology stocks, farmland values, commodity prices, home real estate and easy credit before 2008? The answer, of course, is yes. History does repeat itself.

The United States has experienced three depressions in 208 years of history since 1800. Based on the data and work of the NBER, outlined in Figure 1.2, the first U.S. depression began in 1807 and lasted seven years. The second began in 1873 and lasted 23 years. The third began in 1930 and lasted 10 years to 1939. I believe the fourth U.S. depression began in 2008 and will last approximately seven years or through 2014. The more serious pain will very likely be experienced by *all* Americans in 2010-2012 for reasons that are outlined here and will be discussed more fully in Chapters 3, 4, 5, 6 and 10.

During the 1930s, the Federal Reserve tightened monetary policy substantially, which raised interest rates and reduced the growth in the money supply. This ended up making things worse and prolonged the Great Depression *bust* phase in the long-term business cycle about 80 years ago. In 2008 and 2009, the Federal Reserve, the U.S. Treasury and Congress adopted a policy of *too big to fail* for banks, automobile companies, Wall Street investment banking firms, insurance companies and others. Japan adopted the same policy between 1992 and 2005. This proved to be a major mistake and a flawed policy there. It will likewise prove to be a seriously flawed policy for the U.S. in 2010- 2014 for reasons that will be discussed in Chapter 5.

The United States' longest depression, which lasted 23 years between 1873 and 1896, stemmed from major changes that had to and did take place throughout the United States, and especially the South, after the Civil War. Similar, but milder changes also occurred after World Wars I and II, the Korean War and the Vietnam War. Over the past *200* years, wars have had both positive and negative consequences on U.S. economic growth, on jobs, wages, and on businesses, as well as federal government spending, debt accumulation, on budget deficits and taxes collected.

The painful and serious 16-month recession of 1981-82 was primarily caused by the 1973 oil crisis and the Iranian Revolution in 1979 that in turn caused a very sharp 1979-1980 increase in worldwide crude oil, gasoline and diesel fuel prices and the energy crisis. The energy crisis led to record high levels of U.S. inflation (the monthly CPI reached *13.5%* in 1980). The Federal Reserve raised short-term interest rates sharply, putting prime rates in the *17%* to *21%* range to blunt those inflationary forces, which was a key factor that caused the 1981-1982 U.S. recession and sharply higher levels of unemployment from 1981 through 1983.

> **The difference between the *horsepower* of a GDP growth rate of 3% to 4% or greater and a GDP growth rate of 1.0% to 2.0% or less is like the difference between the *horsepower* of both a large semi tractor trailer truck and a Volkswagen pulling a heavy load.**

A depression is typically a severe economic downturn. It is a major slowdown in the rate of GDP growth that lasts for a number of years with substantial increases in the level of unemployment that stays higher than normal for a period of several years.

The difference between the *3.82%* GDP growth rate for the U.S. during the 1940-2007 boom and 11 recessions and a growth rate of *1.5%* to *2.0%* that I am forecasting for 2008-2014 is huge. This represents a decline of *55%* from the boom to the bust. In comparison, a similar decline in growth to the growth rates of the Great Depression would be *66%* (*3.82%* **versus** **1.32%**). The Great Depression of the 1930s lasted 10 years. Total output fell from a peak $103 billion to a low $35 billion in the 1930's and the dollar value of world trade declined by 65%. A decline in the U.S. growth rate to between *1.5%* and *2.0%* in 2008-2014, which I am forecasting, would confirm this as a *modern day* depression and a period of stagnation.

Comparing the power of the U.S. economy growing at a positive *3.82%* rate to the power of the U.S. growing at a slower, lower, but still positive *1.5%* to *2.0%* rate is like comparing the *horsepower* of an eight-cylinder, diesel-powered 18-wheeler tractor trailer to the *horsepower* of a six-cylinder, gasoline-powered Volkswagen pulling the same fully-loaded 30-foot trailer. Both can move forward, but the Volkswagen is going to move very slowly compared to the larger and much more powerful 18-wheeler. The 18-wheeler's increased horsepower, GDP growth rates between *3%* and *6%*, will result in the creation of significantly more new jobs, higher incomes, increased investment and higher tax revenues. The Volkswagen's limited power, GDP growth rates between *1.5%* and *2.0%,* results in very painful job losses, rising and much higher than normal unemployment, reduced incomes and benefits, reduced investment, lower tax revenues, massive annual budget deficits and a sharply rising national debt and debt servicing interest expense.

According to history, a depression is not only long term, but also deep. A good picture of the difference between a recession and a depression would be to compare the walls of the Grand Canyon to the banks of the Mississippi or Missouri Rivers.

The official U.S. Department of Labor unemployment rate for calendar year 2008 is *5.8%*. My forecast for calendar year 2009 is *9.2%*. This results in a two-year combined unemployment rate estimate of *7.5%*. The 1981-1982 recession helped push combined monthly unemployment rates for the three years 1981-1983 to *8.9%.* Even so, the economy grew a combined *0.3%* in calendar years 1981 and 1982. I estimate that combined growth for calendar years 2008 and 2009 will drop to within the *minus 1.25%* to *minus 1.75%* range for these two years. I also expect the level of unemployment in the 2010-2012 time period to be within the *10.5%* to *11.5%* range, much higher than the actual level of unemployment of *8.9%* for the three years 1981-1983.

Historically, depressions have occurred about 60 to 80 years apart in the United States, or every *1.5* to *2.0* generations, assuming that a generation is 40 years. The length of time between the nation's third depression, the 1930s Great Depression, and the 2008-2014 fourth depression that I believe is now upon us will be about 75 to 80 years. This amounts to about two generations since the last depression. Depressions do not happen very often, but when they do, they come as a real shock to most people. This is because few people living today have experienced a depression in their adult lives. But almost everyone has some experience with recessions. They sense generally that recessions typically last for less than a year (average of *10.2* months for the last 11 recessions as shown in Figure 1.2). Based on this past experience and what most people consider to be *normal*, many people today understandably think that the U.S. economy, employment, wages, incomes, home values and the stock market will begin to improve relatively soon and follow an accustomed **V**-shaped downturn and recovery path back to the long-term positive 1990-2007 trend line in GDP growth. This is not, however, what is going to likely happen over the next five to 10 years. Depressions and periods of substantial stagnation last for a number of years. I believe the odds are high that 2010-2014 will be very difficult and painful for most people, for our economy and for our country.

What is a *Modern Day* Depression?

Thinking of this coming period as a *modern day* depression is appropriate for several reasons. First, most adults today in America can neither relate to nor realistically be expected to understand what a depression really is, i.e. what really happened 75 to 80 years ago or to sense firsthand the great differences between a recession and a depression which are described in Figures 1.1 through 1.7.

In the case of the coming *modern day* depression, there will be a *new normal*. This book presents the reasons why I believe that we will not return to the *normalcy* we have known and experienced in the 68 years of the general *boom* period from 1940-2007. Consumer spending, household wealth, employment, borrowing capacity and incomes will be much less than normal in 2008-2014, for reasons we will discuss in Chapters 3, 4 and 5. Rates of consumer saving, taxes, budget deficits and unemployment will rise to and remain at much higher levels than we are accustomed to and for a much longer period of time, even years. This is *not* what normally happens during and after a typical, relatively short-lived recession. This is, however, what typically happens in a depression lasting five, seven and 10 years or longer. This is one reason why I use the term *modern day* depression.

The term *modern day* is useful because the U.S. economy and the depression coming in 2008-2014 will be shaped by forces far different than ones in the 1930s. Past major financial excesses by 78 million baby boomers, followed by their reduced spending and increased savings now, by itself will be

18

a force powerful enough to wreak changes greater than we've seen in any of the 11 recessions since 1940, but generally not as severe as Americans experienced in the Great Depression during the 1930s.

For example, on November 14, 2008, I told my clients and subscribers[2], "I fully expect that the level of U.S. unemployment will reach the *10%* to *15%* range within the 2009-2014 time period." This is a much higher level of unemployment than both the *5.9%* average we experienced in the past 11 recessions since 1940 and the average *5.6%* average for the 68 years from 1940 to 2007, but lower than the average *18.3%* level of unemployment in the 1930s or the high water mark of a *25%* unemployment rate in 1933.

During the 1930s Great Depression, almost *35%* of all people and families in the United States lived on farms or ranches. Today no more than *2%* to *3%* do. This is a major difference. More than one-third of all U.S. citizens and families in the 1930s had food to eat and a place to live, even without much income, because they lived on farms or ranches. Today this is obviously not the case. Thus, I call it a *modern day* depression and a period of major and long lasting stagnation.

We were a part of the global economy in the 1930s, but nothing like the global economy we have today, 75 to 80 years later. For starters, populations are much larger now than at the turn of the last century in 1900 and in the 1930's. The total U.S. population in 1900 was about *77 million* and *123 million* in 1930, compared to around *306 million* as of January, 2009, according to the U.S. Census Bureau. This represents an increase of *183 million* people or *149%*, in the total U.S. population in the 80 years from 1930-2009 and *229 million* people, or *289%* in the 109 years since 1900. This U.S. Census Bureau data shows us that the year-to-year increase in the U.S. population over the past 80 years was *1.87%* per year and that the average annual increase in the U.S. population over the 109 years from 1900 to 2009 was *2.10%* per year.

These U.S. population numbers and increases include U.S. births and the substantial increases in the number of people immigrating into the U.S legally and illegally over the years. The rate of increase in the total world population has been even faster since 1900. Almost all economies worldwide are very much connected today and affect each other by our different cultures, wage rates and import/export trade. For example, substantial portions of the U.S. manufacturing industry and businesses have been effectively exported to other countries where labor costs are much lower. Our banking, financial systems, stock markets, currency valuations, economic growth, consumer spending, as well as our government monetary, fiscal and trade policies are all very much intertwined

---

[2] Ibid

and highly reliant on each other more today than was the case in the 1930s. This is a further reason why I use the term *modern day* depression.

Information, data and news travel around the world today far more quickly than it did 75 to 80 years ago. In those days, there was no television, internet, cell phone, or other devices to connect us to the global village. This difference alone makes it a *modern day* depression.

The U.S. stock market has not yet discounted a *modern day* depression, as defined in this chapter, which will substantially reduce corporate profits beyond what most people in 2009 and early 2010 are expecting and planning on. It has also not yet discounted the substantially higher level of unemployment that usually occurs in a depression compared to what normally is the case in a recession. These and a number of other key points of interest are discussed in Chapters 3, 4, 5, 6 and 10.

The major Timeframe Differences between Depressions and Recessions

Figure 1.8 shows graphically, in the form of a bar chart, the startling differences between the time involved with economic depressions (years), compared to the time involved with recessions (months). The typical time involved with depressions is seven to 10 years. The typical time involved with recessions is months and less than one year. In many ways, these are like the differences between night and day or a three mile road race, compared to a *26.2* mile marathon. The difference is huge as you can easily see in Figure 1.8. You might be able to run a three mile race without a lot of preparation, but you wouldn't attempt to run a 26.2 mile marathon without being well prepared.

In 1930, *88%* of our total U.S. national income was consumed in the private sector and *12%* of our total national income was consumed in the public sector, by federal, state and local governments, on a combined basis and based on data from the U.S. Commerce Department's Bureau of Economic Analysis. What this means, as shown in Figure 1.9, is that in 1930 *88%* of all U.S. wage earners worked for and received paychecks from businesses, institutions and organizations in the private sector of our economy, while *12%* of all U.S. wage earners worked for and received their paychecks from the federal, state and local governments. In 2007, based on the same Bureau of Economic Analysis source of the data referenced above, *57%* of all U.S. wage earners worked for and received their paychecks from the private sector and *43%* of all U.S. wage earners worked for and received their paychecks from the public sector. This is a very important change in *78* years. My estimates for the year 2014 are also shown in Figure 1.8 and are discussed in Chapter 9. By 2014, I fully expect that about *50%* of all U.S. wage earners will be working for and will receive their paychecks from the private sector and *50%* of all wage earners will be working for and will receive their paychecks from the public sector. This will be bad news and negative for the U.S. economy in the years ahead and will, among other things, contribute to major stagnation for at least the next five to 10 years. This is well covered in Chapter 9.

Figure 1.8
Length in Months for Three Actual U.S. Depressions, 11 Actual Recessions and the Fourth Forecasted Depression by the Author

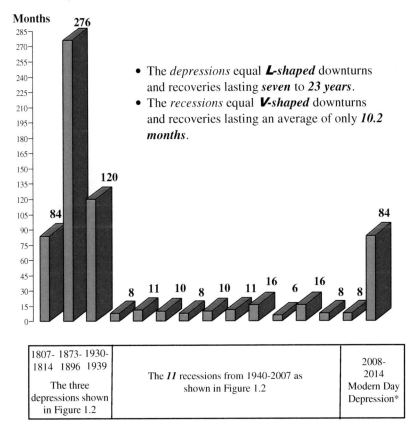

- The *depressions* equal **L-shaped** downturns and recoveries lasting *seven* to *23 years*.
- The *recessions* equal **V-shaped** downturns and recoveries lasting an average of only *10.2 months*.

1807-1814 1873-1896 1930-1939 The three depressions shown in Figure 1.2	The *11* recessions from 1940-2007 as shown in Figure 1.2	2008-2014 Modern Day Depression*

*Forecasted by the author

Source: National Bureau of Economic Research and Wikipedia for list of recessions and depressions in the U.S.

The dramatic increase in the proportion of our national income consumed by the private sector during the 78 years from 1930 through 2007 is another reason why I use the phrase *modern day* depression for the 2010-2014 time period. The much larger proportion of our national income, compared to the 1930s Great Depression, being made up of and consumed by our federal, state and local governments has both positive and negative implications for the 2010-2014 time period and beyond. For example, on the *positive side*, unemployment likely will be less severe in 2008-2014 than it was in the 1930s because of a significantly larger number of men and women who work for and get their paycheck from government, and specifically from our consumer and business tax dollars. In addition, the existence of and the changes in the Social Security, Medicare, food stamp, unemployment insurance and other related *safety net* federal, state and government programs funded by our tax dollars tend to make the economic pain somewhat less now and moving forward than in the 1930s or 80 years ago.

Figure 1.9
The Percentage of the U.S. National Income that was consumed by the Private Sector versus the Percentage that was consumed by Federal, State and Local Governments in 1930, 1947 and 2007

This is a Scary and Negative Trend for the U.S. from 1930 to 2007, including for the 2008-2014 Time Period

Years	The Percentage of our Total U.S. National Income that was Consumed by the Two Sectors	
	Private Sector*	Federal, State and Local Governments**
1930	88	12
1947	78	22
2007	57	43
2014***	50***	50***

*People who work for and own businesses and who receive their paychecks and income from the private sector.

**People who work for and who receive their paychecks from federal, state and local governments in the public sector.

***The years 2008-2014 are estimated by the author. The *50%* and *50%* are specifically for the year 2014.

Source: The Bureau of Economic Analysis, the U.S. Department of Commerce Washington, D.C.

On the *negative side*, the private sector in 2007 represented *57% of the national income* instead of *88%* back in 1930 and this represents a decline of *36%*. This is one of the reasons why, as part of the *new normal*, U.S. GDP growth will be significantly slower over 2008-2014 and unemployment will stay higher than has been normal previously. Historical and recent data clearly show

22

that sustainable and positive long-term growth and new job creation come much more from private sector businesses (particularly from small business) and from private sector institutions and organizations. Growth and new job creation primarily come from private sector businesses investing new capital, from increased entrepreneurship, from expanding existing small businesses and starting new small businesses, finding ways to increase productivity levels, innovation, creativity, the development and use of new technology, taking risks, making a profit and hiring more full-time and/or part-time employees.

Bottom line, the U.S. depends heavily on the private sector for growth and for new job creation or capitalism. Depending on federal, state and local government spending for growth and new job creation or socialism generally fails and produces far inferior results. These and related key points are discussed in Chapter 9. This is another reason why I use the term *modern day* depression.

Chapter 2
The Long-Term 60- to 80-Year Boom and Bust Business Cycle

History shows clearly that the U.S. economy has had both boom and bust periods over the past 208 years since 1800. So have all of Western and Eastern Europe and Japan. The chance of these cycles (usually lasting 60 to 80 years) continuing for another 200 years or more is very high. This chapter explores the roots of these long-term cycles and why they occur.

Wikipedia defines economic cycles as *fluctuations that occur around a long-term growth trend, and typically involve shifts over time between periods of relatively rapid economic growth (expansion or boom) and periods of relative stagnation or major decline (contraction, recession or depression).*

One good thing about these cycles is that the boom phases span relatively long periods of time, typically *1.5 to 2.0* generations, assuming that a generation consists of 40 years. *One bad thing* is that memories fade after 60 to 80 years, so that when an inevitable bust phase begins, it is very easy to mistake it for another one of those shorter and less severe recessions that are *road bumps* during the longer boom.

Figure 2.1 shows the long-term boom and bust business cycles that the U.S. has experienced since the end of its longest ever depression in 1896, *23 years*. Beginning in 1897, the economy boomed for *33 years*, until 1930. Gross Domestic Product (GDP) grew an average **3.52%** annually during those 33 years, despite several recessions that are normal *bumps in the road* during such expansions. Then came 1930 and the beginning of the last officially recognized *bust* period in U.S. history, the Great Depression. GDP growth rates during the 10 years from 1930 to 1939 slowed to an annual average **1.32%** crawl, producing major up and down swings in growth and pushing the average unemployment rates to a painful **18.3%**. The economy began another long-term boom in 1940. Growth during that boom period would continue until 2007, shaking off 11 recessions to expand at an annual average rate of **3.82%** for the entire *68 years*.

I predict that the next *bust* period for the U.S. will be within the seven years of 2008-2014. It could potentially last longer than seven years. The rate of average annual growth during this period will slow to a positive, yet painful **1.5%** to **2.0%** rate, not even half the boom time rate that many of us today think of as normal. I refer to this next bust period as a *modern day* depression and stagnation period. This will be a time when the American people will be adjusting to a *new normal*. Why that will happen and what it means is discussed in more detail in Chapters 3, 4, 5 and 6.

Figure 2.1
What Goes Up Eventually Comes Down
Prepare for a Serious and Painful
U.S. *Modern Day* Depression, Stagnation and a *New Normal* in 2010-2014

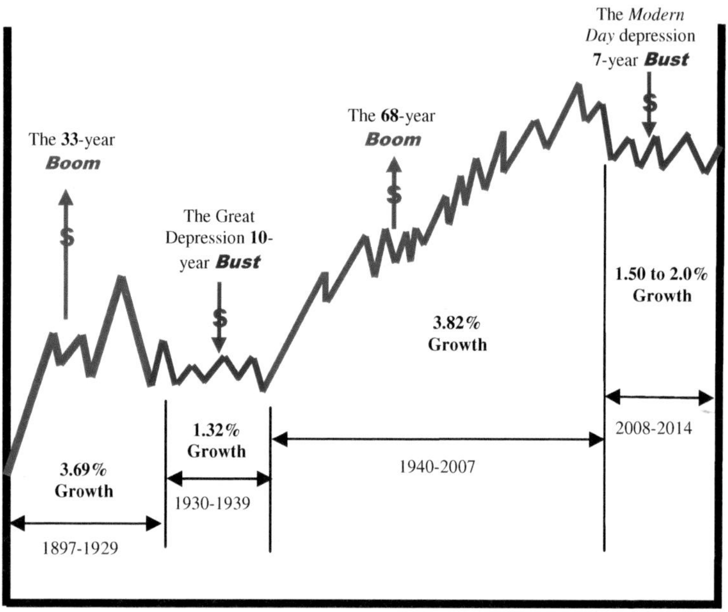

The *Modern Day* depression 7-year **Bust**

The **68**-year **Boom**

The **33**-year **Boom**

The Great Depression **10**-year **Bust**

1.50 to 2.0% Growth

3.82% Growth

1.32% Growth

3.69% Growth

2008-2014

1940-2007

1930-1939

1897-1929

A Period of 118 years

Source: Illustration by author.

The nation's most recent 68-year economic boom began in the World War II years of 1940-1945 and ended in 2007 or about 1.70 generations later. Most students of our economy, including me, believe that if it were not for the war, the 1930s Great Depression would likely have lasted longer than 10 years. Nonetheless, the U.S. generally experienced very significant and positive growth overall during 1940-2007, an average annual growth rate of *3.82%* per year as you can see in Figure 2.2. But the path was not uniformly smooth.

GDP growth was a very rapid average *13.8%* per year during the 1940-1944 during the heart of World War II, rising 8.8%, 17.1%, 18.5%, 16.4% and 8.1%, respectively, for the five years of 1940 to 1944. The U.S. economy actually shrank -1.1%, -11.0% and -0.9%, respectively, in the immediate postwar years of 1945, 1946 and 1947. And during the 50 years from 1957 through 2007, the growth rate slipped to *3.34%* per year, still healthy, but down *13%* from *3.82%* average for the 68-year boom. It slipped even further following the 1981-1982 recession to *15%* below the boom-long average, or *3.26%* per year during the 25 years 1983-2007.

Figure 2.2
The U.S. Year-to-Year Percentage Change in the Real Gross Domestic Product (GDP) for the Years 1940-2007 Based on 2000 Dollars

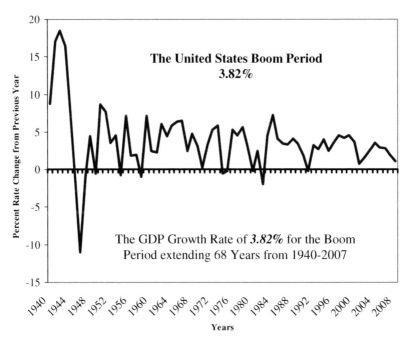

Source: U.S. Department of Commerce, Bureau of Economic Analysis, Washington, D.C.

Relatively short, modest recessions such as the 11 that occurred between 1940 and 2007 are *speed bumps* or *bumps in the road* of generally upward trending growth. They are typically caused by *blips* in the economy, such as brief slowdowns in consumer spending, the negative reaction by consumers and businesses to escalating interest rates orchestrated by the Federal Reserve Board, reduced industrial production, brief gluts of inventories or market shocks such as the 1973-1975 OPEC crude oil crisis or the collapse of the dot-com bubble in 2001-2003.

Booms collapse for bigger reasons. These collapses result from long-building financial excesses or significant changes in birth rates or a combination of these causes. In Chapters 4 and 5 we will see how consumers, families, businesses and governments, all living and borrowing way beyond their means, particularly during 1990-2007, undermined the longer 1940-2007 boom cycle. But now, we need to consider the true scope of the challenges we face.

Because long-term business cycles typically span *1.5* to *2.0* generations, people in all walks of life tend to forget about the last serious bust that occurred 60 to 80 years ago. Also, many people convince themselves that *things are different now*. They believe for many reasons that another depression in the U.S. just could not happen again. Thus, when the *bust* phase of the long-term business cycle happens, it comes as a real surprise to many people.

Most people develop a mindset that recessions do not last very long and that *things will get better and back to normal soon*. That is what happened during the 11 recessions since 1940. In the back of our minds we are sure this low period will pass soon and *we'll be off to the races again*. Consumers and business owners historically have acted on this belief by borrowing more money, spending more, and saving less. And sure enough, economic growth, employment, asset values and the stock markets improved. After repeating and experiencing this process over many years and reaping positive results each time, it is easy to see how most Americans can get pretty comfortable dealing with the recessionary *bumps in the road*. What many people do not realize, while this is going on, is that recessions do not end major financial excesses or weaken forces such as longer-term changes in birth rates. These forces continue building slowly and create financial bubbles that cannot be sustained and will eventually burst. *All asset bubbles eventually burst because they are not sustainable. What goes up eventually comes down.* This is the very nature and essence of our free market and capitalistic system in the U.S. This is why we also know that what goes down will eventually bottom out and begin slowly to go back up again as discussed at the end of Chapter 10.

Americans lead very busy lives. Most wage earners live from paycheck to paycheck, saving little and owing much as they work to raise and educate their children and to provide food and a home for their families. In many families, both parents have jobs or single parents work more than one job. They struggle to make ends meet. They struggle harder when rising unemployment or lowered wages and benefits make already difficult conditions even more painful.

This is why I have written this book. We, as Americans and as a nation, are generally not prepared for what very likely will happen over the next five years or longer, or the human and financial suffering that will result from a *modern day* depression or stagnation. The last thing on most of our minds are the consequences of a years long period of much slower than normal growth, rising and persistently high unemployment, declining wages and benefits, and higher taxes. These will be a surprise to many. They will be a hardship as well.

Most of us do not think about the historical reality that *what goes up eventually comes down*. It is very difficult for people to consider and become comfortable with a long-term change and the *new normal* that will result. I hope this book will help you and all Americans who read it to become more aware of the major economic changes I'm outlining and that it will help you and others to better prepare for these changes. *Being forewarned is being forearmed.*

Consider just one set of expectations that will not be realized because we are now at the beginning of a long-term economic change. Federal government *economic stimulus* and *bailout* programs created in 2008 and 2009 will not result in turning the U.S. economy around or creating more net new jobs or the higher incomes that were promised. Why that will not happen is discussed in Chapter 9. Later in this chapter, we will look at some recent history in Japan, a country which tried similar remedies and failed. The many Americans who believe the federal government can and will *fix* our economy will be greatly shocked and disappointed over the next several years to discover that the 2008-2009 *stimulus* and *bailout* plans and programs actually end up making things much worse and cause economic stress to drag on for much longer than otherwise would have been the case.

Most people who want something to be done really well, quickly, efficiently and cost effectively would not ask or want the government to do it. History is very clear that these federal government programs do not pan out as advertised by politicians and senior government employees. However, our taxes, our very rapidly increasing national debt and the interest on that debt will be going up for the next 10 years and far beyond because of *bailout* and *stimulus* spending. When Americans realize that *bailout*, *stimulus* and debt accumulation are not only failing, but making their lives worse, they will begin to spend even less and save more. This already is happening and will result in further, very significant problems in 2010-2014 in the U.S. Within the next five years, most Americans will come to realize that we are not in a normal, short-lived recession and we all will be adjusting to a *new normal*, i.e. *modern day* depression in the 2010-2014 time period.

2008-2014 Forecast

I believe the economic and financial conditions are now clearly present for a very painful and serious bust and the U.S. will experience its fourth and *modern day* depression in 2008-2014. I believe the odds of this happening are *90%*. The rate of GDP growth between 2008 and 2014 will very likely be, at best, in the *1.5%* to *2.0%* range averaging close to *1.75%*. This compares broadly to a twice-greater *3.82%* rate of growth during the 68-year boom of 1940-2007 and to a *1.32%* rate during the Great Depression. There is not much difference between a growth rate of *1.32%* and *1.50% to 2.0%*, but a major difference between a growth rate of *3.82%* and *1.50% to 2.0%* per year.

The differences between our recently ended *3.82%* long-term boom growth rate, the Great Depression *1.32%* rate and the *1.50%*, *1.75%* or *2.00%* I forecast for 2008-2014 is obviously huge (see Figures 2.2 and 2.3). The *horsepower* analogy in Chapter 1, comparing the power of an 18-wheeler and the power of a Volkswagen pulling the same load tells the magnitude of the difference. The *green/red light zone* comparisons show the consequences in job creation, job loss and rate of economic growth as discussed in Chapter 1. We will examine reasons behind the impending bust in Chapters 3, 4 and 5 and how a *new normal* in the economy during the bust will affect you.

GDP grew an average *1.32%* annually during the Great Depression years of 1930-1939 as shown in Figure. 2.3. Again, I believe the best we can realistically expect in 2008-2014 is a slightly higher annual average rate of *1.5%* to a *2.0%*, or approximately half or less of the annual average *3.82%* achieved in the 68-year boom since 1940. Such a dramatic drop in growth will produce huge increases in job losses and huge decreases in incomes, consumer and business spending, and tax revenues for five to 10 years.

Figure 2.4 shows a remarkable achievement in American economic history. In the 77 years beginning in 1930, GDP grew from about *$900 billion* near the depths of the Depression to more than *$13 trillion* based on 2005 dollars, as reported by the U.S. Department of Commerce, Bureau of Economic Analysis. Much of what made this possible is based on the principles of freedom and freedom of choice, free markets, capitalism, competition, hard work, increased productivity, innovation, new technology, entrepreneurship, the global economy and a sound and strong U.S. dollar that was widely held and respected as the reserve currency of the world.

Now, unfortunately, larger and very expensive government meddling in the private sector and the obvious socialism on many fronts is putting the outlook and future economic health, growth and well being of our country into serious doubt moving forward. We will look more closely at this important subject in Chapter 9, but first let us look at how such attempted solutions worked in Japan.

Figure 2.3
The Year-to-Year Percentage Change in the Real Gross Domestic Product (GDP) during the Great Depression for the Ten Years of 1930-1939 Based on 2000 Dollars

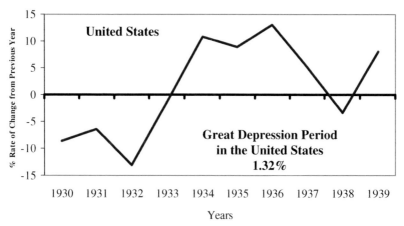

Source for Figures 2.3 and 2.4: U.S. Department of Commerce, Bureau of Economic Analysis, Washington, D. C.

Figure 2.4
The Real Gross Domestic Product (GDP) for the 80 Years from 1930-2009 Based on Billions of 2005 Dollars

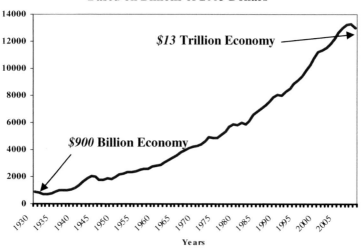

What we can Learn from Japan

The second largest economy in the world, Japan, experienced a serious, painful, 15-year modern day depression and prolonged stagnation and a *new normal* between 1992 and 2006. Easy credit, excessive debt, excessive speculation and over leveraging in the booming 1970s and 1980s produced huge bubbles in the country's real estate and stock market that burst in the early 1990s. Home, commercial real estate and land prices in Japan declined about *60%* from 1992 to 2006. Condominium prices declined *65%* to *70%* in the same 15-year period. The Japanese stock market, **the Nikkei, dropped *80%* from about *38,000*** in 1990 into the *7,600-8,000* range 14-15 years later in 2005-2006.

Japan's excesses in 1971-1991 seem very similar to the excesses of the United States in 1990-2007, of course. But there are other parallels too. Japanese banks were very slow to write down, write off or acknowledge the major declines in the value of stock and real estate values on their balance sheets and financial statements, just as U.S. banks have been doing. Also, Japan adopted an economic and financial policy that held that many financial institutions were *too big to fail*. This proved to be a big mistake and a flawed policy for them. Simply stated, this policy did not work for Japan. I believe a similar *too big to fail* policy adopted by the U.S. in 2008 and 2009 for banks and other private sector companies will in the next several years prove to be a seriously flawed and bad government policy here too. This same *too big to fail* policy will also fail in the United States.

Figure 2.5 shows important economic trends in Japan between 1971 and 2007. During the *21* years from 1971 to about 1991, real GDP in Japan grew *4.08%*. This was a great *boom* period for Japan. Then from 1992 to 2007, the average growth slowed to *1.24%* for a period of *16* years. This was the *bust* period for Japan.

The decline in the rate of growth in Japan from *4.08%* **per year to *1.24%* per year** represents a *70%* decline. Contraction that severe over so many years clearly puts Japan into the *bust* phase of their long-term business cycle and into a *modern day* depression and period of stagnation.

During the *32* years of 1960 to 1991, the average rate of unemployment in Japan was *1.82%* as shown in Figure 2.6. These were generally *boom* years for Japan. During the 16-year *bust* in 1992-2007, unemployment rose to *3.91%* or *115%* **higher.** Again, there are parallels in the U.S. economy.

As we discussed in Chapter 1, the *normal* unemployment rate in the United States was *5.3%* during the 68 years of the 1940-2007 boom. I predict that the U.S. unemployment rate will rise to about *11.0%*, a *108%* increase, during the *modern day* depression I am forecasting for the U.S. in 2008-2014. While that is not as high as the **18.3%** unemployment rate during the 1930-1939 Great Depression, it is essentially the same kind of increase Japan experienced in 1992-2006 relative to rising unemployment. In other words, I expect the rate of increase in U.S. unemployment during the coming *modern day* depression to be similar to what Japan experienced in 1992-2006.

Figure 2.5
The Year-to-Year Percentage Change in the Real Gross Domestic Product (GDP) for the 37 Years of 1971-2007

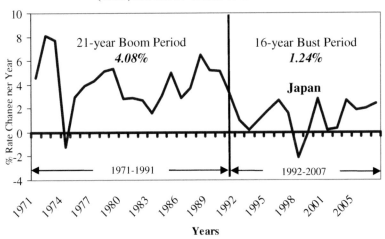

Source: Organization of Economic Co-Operation and Development (www.oecd.org), located in Paris, France

Figure 2.6
The Year-to-Year Percentage Change in the Unemployment Rate for the 48 Years of 1960-2007

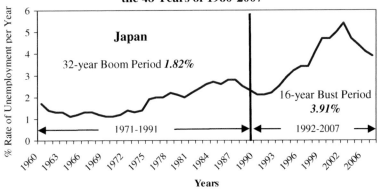

Source: Bureau of Labor Statistics - International

33

Economic, cultural and political differences between the U.S. and Japan make precise comparisons between the two economies difficult. A statistic called the *full employment level* provides one example. The full employment level is basically a residual unemployment rate that remains after everyone who wants a job has one.

Full employment levels typically are thought to be reached in the U.S. where workers prize jobs that they believe will enrich both their wallets and the economy and when unemployment falls to between *4.5%* and *5.5%*. In Japan, where workers are more likely to prize work for the sake of work even if it is less productive, the number drops to between *1.5%* and *2.5%*. Such differences make precise comparisons more complicated, of course. However, they go to the heart of the concept of productivity, which shapes answers to such questions as how economies fight depressions, who recovers from them and how fast.

Despite the burst in asset bubbles, major job losses and the very low GDP growth that Japan has experienced since 1992, the country's economy is relatively efficient, well diversified and competitive. Japan, with its well-educated work force and high levels of saving and investment rates, today ranks about *eighth* among *133* countries in the world in productivity according to the World Economic Forum's *Global Competitiveness Report* for 2009-2010. The U.S. ranked *first* on the list for many years until 2009 when escalating economic weaknesses slipped it to just below Switzerland. Yet a Japanese government effort in the 1990s to revive that country's economy and create job growth basically failed. Their *stimulus* and *bailout* programs did not work. Economic growth in Japan from the early 1990s through 2005 was much slower than was the growth in many other major industrial nations at that time, including the United States. Such results are very typical in the bust phase of long-term 60 to 80-year business cycles in the U.S., Japan and Europe. The same thing happened in the 1930s when U.S. *bailout* and *stimulus* programs also fell far short of the promises made by the politicians. Remember, it was World War II that got the U.S. economy back on track during the 1940-1945 time period.

The Power of Productivity

There are a number of important reasons why the U.S. leads the world in productivity gains today, except for Switzerland. These include our freedoms, our free market and competitive market system, the American work ethic, our capitalistic system, entrepreneurship, innovation, new technology and the millions of small and medium sized businesses in the United States. Creating businesses, taking calculated risks with privately raised capital to pursue higher profits and to provide higher incomes and improved benefits for wage earners has over time steadily increased the productivity of fulltime and part time workers in the United States.

New ideas, innovation and rapidly changing new technology play major roles in the impressive gains in productivity and leading position we hold compared to the world's other major economies. In general, when you adjust the relatively high U.S. wage rates for the higher productivity achieved by providing better goods and services faster, the effective cost of goods and services produced here is far more competitive with that which is produced in China, Mexico or other countries, than many people realize today. But we must continue to have further significant gains in year-to-year productivity for the U.S. to remain generally cost competitive. I believe the prospects of this happening are good. Continued advances and growth in new technology, innovations and new and improved ideas on many fronts will be a major driving force in the years ahead for America and our economy.

However, the much lower wages in other parts of the world have forced some U.S. industries and businesses to move their manufacturing to other countries. Examples of these would include clothing, shoes, toys, steel production, automobiles, televisions, radios, greeting cards and carpeting. But U.S. costs remain competitive for many others, including most food production, healthcare, financial services, chemicals and many kinds of technology companies.

The high level of U.S. productivity keeps us cost competitive in some businesses and industries. But, in others we have to either move production to other parts of the globe where labor costs are much less or import various products from places such as China, Japan, Mexico or South Korea for prices that are significantly *below* production costs for the same products here. This typically benefits U.S. consumers and many of our businesses. *This is why we will continue to live in a truly global economy of major imports and exports.* The U.S. imports, for example, **70%** of the crude oil it uses because it chooses to produce less than it consumes. We could produce a much higher percentage of our oil consumption by drilling and pumping offshore, but we do not do so because that activity is *politically and sharply* restricted.

Based on the *Global Competitiveness Report for 2009-2010* for the productivity for 133 countries across the globe, the *top 10* are listed and ranked below:

1. Switzerland	6. Finland
2. United States	7. Germany
3. Singapore	8. Japan
4. Sweden	9. Canada
5. Denmark	10. Netherlands

U.S. workers are among the most productive in the world. This has been true for many years. In fact, up until the 2009-2010 period as reported by the World Economic Forum, the U.S. ranked number one for many years.

Productivity gains are improving fast in China and much of the rest of Asia. Productivity is measured by comparing annual hours worked per person to the value of all goods and services produced. Annual working hours per person employed are higher in the United States and are significantly higher than for most European economies. The growth of our economy and our improved standard of living are a direct result of our increasing levels of productivity per worker. By the way, China and Mexico rank *29* and *60*, respectively, out of the total *133* countries in terms of productivity per employee hour today. High productivity levels in the United States have contributed significantly and will continue to contribute positively to a relatively strong U.S. dollar and its continuation as the reserve currency in the world for many more years. High productivity also contributes significantly to the U.S. also having the highest standard of living in the world.

Japan has about a *$4.8 trillion* economy (2009) and is the second largest economy in the world. Since the U.S has a *$13 trillion* economy (2009), this makes our economy *2.7* times larger than that of Japan. By 2011 or 2012, the Japanese economy will likely be the third largest economy in the world. China will then become the second largest economy in the world.

As a result of the real estate and stock market bubbles bursting in Japan as discussed above during the 1990s and during 2000-2005, the Japanese economy experienced a serious, painful and long-lasting *modern day* depression and stagnation period. *What goes up eventually comes down.* This happened in 1992-2005 in Japan just as it happened in the United States during the Great Depression years. Consumers, banks and businesses in Japan are continuing their financial deleveraging. This process will take at least 10 or more years to run its course in the United States. Because Japan and China depend heavily on exports and the U.S. and other countries to buy their products, much slower than normal U.S. growth over the next five to 10 years will be bad news for Japan and China as well as for many others in the world, including Canada and Mexico.

Birth rates have been declining significantly in Japan. As we will see in Chapter 3, their birth rate has been at *1.3* for a long time, substantially under the replacement rate of *2.1* children, which means two parents must have two children in order to replace themselves in the population. Therefore, Japan has an aging population and will continue to experience a general decline in consumption by consumers for at least 30 to 50 years. These conditions already have contributed significantly to Japan's economic slowdown, including the bursting of the country's real estate and stock market bubbles in 1992-2005. This turned out to be a painful process for the Japanese, who have had no choice but to adopt a *new normal.*

This is now happening and will continue to happen in the U.S. for at least the next five to 10 years. Also in Chapter 3 we will see the important impact of the *baby boomers'* impending 15- to 20-year shift toward spending less, investing less, saving more and downsizing. We will examine in Chapters 4 and 5 how the bursting of our U.S. real estate, stock market and commodity market bubbles between 2008 and 2014 will result in trillions of dollars in lost wealth and equity in the U.S. Like Japan, America will be experiencing and adjusting to a *new normal* in 2010-2014. This will be a painful experience for most Americans.

The long-term boom and bust cycle is alive and well. An historical review of economic ups and downs in Europe, Japan and the United States makes it clear that the prospects of major and prolonged busts will continue to occur in the years ahead. Most people today are not really aware of or concerned about the last U.S. bust *80* years ago. In addition, most people today, including most economists, have many reasons why they believe another such depression will not happen in the United States in the future.

Summary

I believe the odds are **90%** that the U.S. economy will experience within the 2008-2014 time period a painful and serious *modern day* depression, bust and period of stagnation. Growth will be much slower than normal and unemployment will be higher than normal for the full period and possibly beyond 2014. There are many reasons why consumer spending will be much less than normal and why consumer savings will be higher than normal during these years.

These trends will be heavily affected by the continued bursting of home, commercial, industrial, farm and ranch real estate asset bubbles in the U.S. over the next five years, the continued bursting of U.S. stock market bubbles over the next several years and reduced spending and investing, plus increased savings by the *78 million baby boomers* for the next 10 years or more. These trends will result in trillions of dollars of lost wealth in the U.S. Higher taxes, damaging government policies, sharply rising national debt and out-of-control government spending will all contribute to a period of economic bust, *modern day* depression and stagnation over the next five years of 2010-2014. The U.S. consumer cannot and should not be counted on to bring the rate of U.S. growth back to normal within the next five years. The odds of this happening are very low.

What goes up eventually comes down in boom and bust periods. What goes down eventually goes back up in the U.S. and other economies. The major question for the U.S. is how soon and how much recovery we will see.

Chapter 3
The Impact of Birth Rates and Demographics on Consumer Spending and Economic Growth

Population trends have a major impact on consumer spending, economic growth and long-term boom and bust business cycles in the U.S. and around the world. Most economists do not take into account how changes in birthrates and population growth have important and predictable, as well as good and bad consequences for the economies in which they occur. In this chapter, we will focus on how *78 million baby boomers* born between 1946 and 1964, along with changing trends in annual births in the U.S., Europe and Japan, will continue to alter economic power and how they will define the economic normal in the next *50* years and beyond.

Based on data from the U.S. Census Bureau, the Department of Labor and the recently published book, "The Great Depression Ahead" by Harry S. Dent, Jr., (page 44 of Chapter 2, published in January, 2009):

- A new generation is born about every 40 years.
- Consumer spending of that generation peaks between the ages of 46 and 50 in the United States. To be conservative, I am using the *average peak spending year* for U.S. consumers to be when they reach age 50.

Figure 3.1 shows how U.S. birthrates have fluctuated significantly since the early 1900s. Birthrates dropped significantly, from above *3.0* per woman (per family) in 1910 to below *2.0* just a mere 30 years later in 1940. Birthrates then shot higher, to *2.38* during the *baby boom* years of 1946-1964 before resuming their decline through the mid 1970s to their currently stabilized level around *1.4* and *1.6*. Thus, for more than *43* years following one of the most remarkable surges in population in U.S. history, parents on average have been producing only 1.5 children to replace themselves in the workforce. This will have a profound impact on the U.S. and world economies for decades to come.

There are several reasons why birthrates increased significantly during the 1946-1964 baby boom era. The Great Depression was long over, World War II was won and, for the first time in the adult lives of many young Americans then, confidence blossomed. Soldiers returned from the war, married and had families. The norm for most parents in those days was to have three, four or five children. There was great optimism about the future and, for about 18 years, having larger families was a part of this optimism.

Figure 3.1
The Birthrates in the United States for the 98 Years of 1910-2008

Birthrates per Woman

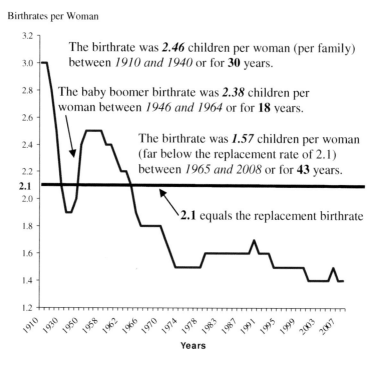

The birthrate was *2.46* children per woman (per family) between *1910 and 1940* or for **30** years.

The baby boomer birthrate was *2.38* children per woman between *1946 and 1964* or for **18** years.

The birthrate was *1.57* children per woman (far below the replacement rate of 2.1) between *1965 and 2008* or for **43** years.

2.1 equals the replacement birthrate

Years

Source: U.S. Department of Health and Human Services, National Center for Health Statistics, Washington, D.C.

There also are several reasons why U.S. birthrates began declining significantly after 1964.

- First, the overall economic growth rate generally was positive during the *boomer* period. It is a statistical fact that as a family's income goes up they tend to have fewer children. This was the overall case during 1965-2007.

- Second, family breadwinning patterns changed. During these years, many more women entered the workforce and hence many more families became two-income homes. This became an absolute necessity for many couples. Sharply rising inflation rates in the 1970s and early 1980s, for example, forced families to find more ways to increase their income in order to meet their weekly and monthly living expenses.

Consequently, women began having fewer children and choosing to work outside the home. This alone helped reduce the birthrates in the last 43 years. Couples also wanted to give their children a better life than they had experienced, but they found the cost of bringing children into the world, caring for them and providing a better education was not as feasible with larger families. Birth control pills also played a key part in reducing the number of children born after the mid 1960s.

- Third, education changed. Among adults in 1947 who were 25 years old or older, 33% had a high school diploma and 5% had a college degree, according to the U.S. Census Bureau. By 2004, among those who were 25 years old or older, 85% had a high school diploma and 28% had a college degree. In other words, as education improved, individual and family incomes improved, and more couples wanted to either have fewer children or none at all. GI Bill educational benefits following World War II also had an important and positive impact on more men and women going to college and hence having fewer children from the mid 1960s forward.

An estimated *58 million baby boomers* will still be living by the year 2030[3]. They will be between 70 and 90 years old and 55% of them will be women. By that same year, 2030, there will be 2.1 workers for each Social Security beneficiary when all *baby boomers* are at the age of 66 or older. As of 2006, there were 3.3 workers for each Social Security beneficiary[4].

Most consumers hit their annual spending peaks at age 50. That happened around 2005 for *baby boomers,* counting from the 1955 center of the boom. These same *baby boomers* will be spending considerably *less* during 2007-2022, compared to their peak spending years during the 1980-2007 time period. This already is having a major impact on economic growth that will continue for the balance of this 15-year period. These trends will contribute to the *new normal* for at least the next 10 years.

The *78 million baby boomers* accounted for about 26% of the total U.S. population as of February 1, 2009[5]. This is a large number and high percentage of the total U.S. population that will be for the next decade or more spending much less, saving much more, working or wanting to work for more years and downsizing their personal lifestyle. As of January, 2006, the U.S. Census Bureau estimated that there were about *8,000 people turning 60 each day*. Members of this statistical *pig in a python* began entering their *retirement* years in 2008.

---

[3] Social Security Administration
[4] Ibid
[5] Ibid

Their impact on the economy will, as you can imagine, have a major negative impact on GDP growth, home, commercial and farm real estate market values, the stock markets, rising unemployment and reduced wages, incomes and benefits over the 2010-2022 time period. The power of this population shift will come as a real shock to many people, because in general we do not think much about birthrates in the United States or in other countries of the world as an important part of the economic equation. The truth is that these population trends are a very significant driver of GDP growth, consumer spending, saving rates, and other forces that shape our economy and financial markets.

On the positive side, these same *baby boomers* increased their spending significantly during the 1980s and 1990s and continued to spend through about 2005-2007. This increased spending helped enhance GDP growth, home, commercial, industrial, farm and ranch real estate values, new job creation, U.S. stock markets and the overall standard of living and incomes for most Americans. In an important way, this *pig-in-a-python* spending and investment by the *baby boomers* also contributed heavily to the real estate, stock market and commodity market *wealth bubbles* and boom in the 1990s and in 2000-2007. These *wealth bubbles*, like all economic and financial bubbles, however, were not sustainable. They began bursting in 2006-2009 from their bloated weight and size, much like what happened in Japan during 1992-2005, as we saw in Chapter 2.

The loss of wealth in the U.S. will continue and greatly worsen in 2010-2014 and perhaps beyond. This will be one of the forces driving an ongoing reduction in spending and investment and an increase in saving by the *baby boomer* generation between 2007 and 2022. These developments are a direct and predictable result of birthrates peaking out in 1955, the peaking out in consumer spending 50 years later and the slowing down of that spending now. This will continue over the next 15 to 20 years. These trends will play out regardless of federal, state or Federal Reserve policy actions now or in the future, just as they did in Japan and Europe.

Changing birthrates in the U.S. over the years are certainly not the only contributing factor to long-term economic boom and bust business cycles. However, changes over time in birthrates do have an important impact on the longer-term 60- to 80-year boom and bust cycles.

Figure 3.2 shows the total number of births per year in the United States for the 98 years of 1910-2008. This figure clearly shows the substantial increase in births during the *18 baby boomer years* from 1946-1964 and the sharp decline in births from the early 1960s to the mid 1970s. Beginning in the mid to late 1970s and continuing to the early 1990s, total annual births increased before peaking out again. Bottom line, U.S. birthrates have fluctuated substantially over the last

100 years. These fluctuations have had and will continue to have a major impact, both positive and negative, on the rate of economic growth and spending by consumers and families. Birthrate trends will continue to help shape the size and severity of U.S. and global ups and downs for years to come.

Figure 3.2
The Total Number of Births per Year in the United States for the 98 Years of 1910-2008

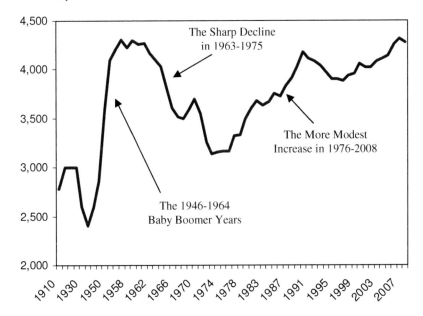

Source: U.S. Department of Health and Human Services, National Center for Health Statistics, Washington, D.C.

Figure 3.3 shows the U.S. annual resident population from 1900 to 2009 by year. The total resident population numbers, according to the U.S. Census Bureau, grew from about *77 million* people in 1900 to about *306 million* in 2009. This represents an average annual increase in the U.S. population of *2.10%* per year or a *296%* increase in population since 1900.

The Magic of 2.1

Populations in most countries in the western world are **not** growing unless, as in the United States, large numbers of people are migrating there legally or illegally. According to the U.S. Census Bureau and other independent sources, maintaining a steady population requires a birthrate of *2.1* children per woman (per family) over two or more generations[6]. In Western Europe the birthrate currently stands at about *1.5* or *30%* below what is needed to avert population loss over time. At that rate, *70* to *80* million fewer Western Europeans will be spending or contributing to the region's economic growth in the next *30* years than there are today. Germany's present birthrate is about *1.3* and in Italy and Spain, it is about *1.2*. Rates that low will reduce the working population by *30%* in *20* years, which will have a profound negative impact on the workforce and on rates of consumer spending and on economic growth in those countries. Their tax bases will also decline significantly. Low and declining birthrates and population trends in Western Europe are the same or even more severe in all of Eastern Europe, including Russia.

Figure 3.3
Total Annual Resident Population from 1900 to 2009 by Year
for the United States

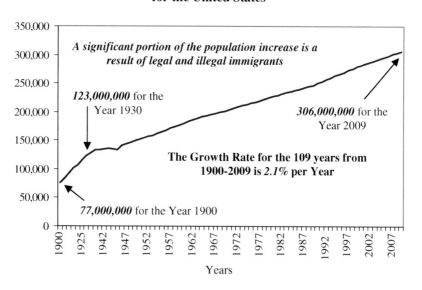

Source: U.S. Census Bureau – The 2009 Population Statistical Abstract, Table 2

---

[6] Ibid and Herbert Meyer via a paper he presented in 2008 to the World Economics Forum in Switzerland titled, "A Global Intelligence Briefing for CEO's." Herbert Meyer served during the Reagan Administration as special assistant to the Director of Central Intelligence and Vice Chairman of the CIA's National Intelligence Counsel.

When you don't have young workers to replace the older ones, you have to import them. European countries are currently importing Muslims into their populations as workers. Today, Muslims comprise *10%* of the population of France and Germany and the percentage is rising rapidly because they have higher birthrates. Many Muslim immigrants are not choosing to integrate into the culture of their host countries and this is proving to be a major political problem and challenge in Western Europe.

Japan, the world's second largest economy, began many years ago implementing policies to reduce birthrates, mainly because of its limited land mass and already large population. At its current *1.3* birthrate, Japan will lose up to about *60 million* people over the next *30* years. Unlike Europe and the United States, Japan does not allow large-scale immigration. Instead, the Japanese are slowly shutting down. Japan has already closed about *2,000* schools, at the rate of *300* a year. Japan is also aging very rapidly. By 2020, *20%* of the Japanese people will be *70* or older.

Despite a spectacular increase in U.S. annual birthrates during the 1946-1964 baby boom, the longer term U.S. average annual birthrate since 1900 has been about *1.87,* which is below the replacement rate of 2.1. Our birthrate for the past *43* years of 1965 through 2008 dropped even further, to *1.57* as shown in Figure 3.1. And in an increasingly multicultural America, birthrate changes within that overall drop reinforce the likelihood of a protracted decline in spending and saving. Birthrates among Caucasian Americans, who historically have controlled the largest shares of wealth and spending power in the U.S., are much lower than among the nation's Hispanic and Asian populations. Thus, as the Caucasian percentage of the U.S. population continues to shrink, as the U.S. Census Bureau projects in Figure 3.4, the level and rate of spending by consumers also will be slowly declining for a good many years.

Western civilization seems to have forgotten what many other societies understand. *You need kids to have a healthy society.* Children are huge consumers. They grow up to become spenders and taxpayers. If the U.S. birthrates in the last *35 to 40* years had remained the same as post-World War II, there would be relatively few Social Security and Medicare problems today or for the next *20 to 30* years.

After World War II, the U.S. instituted a *$600* tax credit per child. The idea was to enable mom and dad to have *four* children without being troubled by taxes. This led to a baby boom, which became a huge consumer market and turned into a huge tax base. Matching that incentive in today's dollars, however, would cost *$12,000* per child. So, the U.S. tax base will decline and consumer spending will also moderate significantly during the next 15 to 20 years, compared to the previous **30** years, as *78 million baby boomers* downsize, spend less and save more.

Figure 3.4

Past, Present and Projected Population Numbers and the Percentage Makeup of the Total Population for the United States by the Major Race Categories for the Years 2000, 2010, 2020, 2030, 2040 and 2050

(Population Numbers shown in Millions)

Population Categories by Race	2000	2010	2020	2030	2040	2050
Whites alone (not including Hispanics)						
Numbers	195,729	201,112	205,936	209,176	210,331	210,283
Percent of Total Pop. Rounded	69	65	61	58	54	50
Hispanic (of any race)						
Numbers	35,622	47,756	59,758	73,055	87,585	102,560
Percent of Total Pop. Rounded	13	16	18	20	22	24
Blacks alone						
Numbers	35,818	40,454	45,365	50,442	55,876	61,361
Percent of Total Pop. Rounded	13	13	14	14	14	15
Asians alone						
Numbers	10,684	14,241	17,988	22,580	27,992	33,430
Percent of Total Pop. Rounded	4	5	5	6	7	8
All other races*						
Numbers	4,272	5,373	6,758	8,331	10,162	12,220
Percent of Total Pop. Rounded	1	1	2	2	3	3
Total U.S. Population						
Numbers	282,125	308,936	335,805	363,584	391,946	419,854
Percent of Total Pop. Rounded	100	100	100	100	100	100

*Includes American Indians and Alaskan natives alone, native Hawaiians and other Pacific Islanders alone.
Source: U.S. Census Bureau, 2004, "U.S. Interim Projections by Age, Sex, Race, and Hispanic Origin"

China and India's populations are currently growing. Both countries are very large consumers of oil, energy, steel, chemicals, food and other items now, and will be even bigger consumers in the next 10 to 20 years. Both also face profound population challenges as well. China, like Japan, has a *closed-door* immigration policy that will lead to significant aging and a decline in spending starting in about 12 to 15 years. India, however, is on the verge of many years of higher consumer demand and increased spending; **52%** of that nation's total population is *under 20 years of age.*

In both China and India, there is a preference for boys over girls and both now have the technology to know the gender before birth. Families in these countries are aborting many of the girls. As a result, in each of these countries there are about *70 million* boys growing up who will never find wives. Nature, when unhampered, produces about *103* boys for every *100* girls[7]. In some provinces in China and India, however, the ratio is 128 boys to every 100 girls. This will create a potentially explosive situation politically, economically and otherwise in the years ahead.

Population increases in many countries, including the United States, will and must come from immigration. In Western and Eastern Europe, the primary increase in immigration is from the Muslim world. In the United States, the sharp increase in immigration has been primarily coming from the Hispanic, Asian and Muslim populations. Muslims also are the biggest contributors to a significant increase in immigration in Canada, and particularly that nation's eastern urban regions. These population mixes and changes in birthrates and demographic trends have major and serious economic, political, social and religious implications for all the countries that are affected, during the balance of this century and beyond. The implications for our children, our grandchildren and our great grandchildren are mind boggling. The world, as most of us have known it, is changing right in front us. *Prepare for a very new normal.*

What Drives a Declining Birthrate?

Europe and Japan, two of the world's major economic engines, aren't merely in a recession or long period of slower than normal growth and stagnation; they are *shutting down* because of major reductions in birthrates in their countries. This will have a major impact on the world economy longer term that is already beginning to be felt. Why are the birthrates so low? One reason is a direct correlation between the abandonment of a traditional religious society, with what usually is associated with strong family values, and a drop in the birthrate. Christianity in Europe, for example, is becoming irrelevant. Church attendance of any kind in Europe is declining significantly.

A second major reason is economic. When fewer people are working to support a larger number of retired people, it puts a huge tax burden on a smaller group of workers. As a result, many young people delay marriage and having children. Once this trend begins, the downward spiral only grows. Formerly cherished traditions are abandoned when the spiral grows. In Europe and Japan, one of those traditions was raising more children in larger families.

---

[7] U.S. Census Bureau

With birthrates in the U.S., Japan and all of Western and Eastern Europe being considerably below the replacement level of *2.1*, consumer consumption, spending and GDP growth will be significantly less than what society was accustomed to when the birthrates were at or above replacement level. This *new normal* also means that in the years ahead the level of unemployment will be at significantly higher levels than before and that business profits will be lower than the historical *normal* numbers were in the past.

Low population replacement levels will also cause companies and businesses to find more ways to reduce costs and improve productivity. This in turn will contribute to general price deflation, zero inflation or very low inflation. Wages, pensions and other benefits will increase only slightly, if at all. Some may go down. There will be less demand for office buildings, shopping centers, strip malls, homes, apartments, automobiles, hotels, plane travel, restaurants and other services. This is a picture of the coming *new normal* which is driven in no small way by the important changes in birthrates that are reshaping the economies of the U.S., Japan and Europe.

These lower birthrates will substantially increase the federal, state, city and county tax burden on all consumers and businesses and particularly on the younger members of societies around the world. The increased tax burden in the United States will accelerate even more rapidly because of massive increases in federal government spending and debt service obligations in 2008, 2009 and far beyond. Higher taxes mean less consumer spending and less business investment moving forward. Growth will slow, fewer new jobs will be created and living standards will be moderated for growing numbers of people in America, Japan and Europe. These trends will go far to establish a *new economic and financial normal* in the United States, Japan, Western and Eastern Europe in the years ahead.

Changing birthrates and some historical distributions of economic power also will help shape economic trends in the U.S. As shown in Figures 3.4 and 3.5, the U.S. Census Bureau projects that by 2050, the total Caucasian population of the U.S. will drop to no more than *50%*, down from *69%* in 2000. Hispanic and Asian shares of the population are projected to nearly double during these 50 years, primarily because both groups have birthrates and immigration rates that are higher than for Caucasians. Historically though, Caucasians have controlled the major wealth, investment and spending power in the U.S. This will change significantly over at least the next 10 to 20 years. That means their inclination to spend less and save more in a slowing economy will disproportionately slow GDP growth and consumer spending over the next 10 to 20 years. That in turn will push both unemployment and savings rates higher for all groups in the next 10 years and help prolong the bust phase of the long-term business and economic cycle.

Figure 3.5
Past, Present and Projected Population Numbers and the Percentage makeup of the Total Population for the United States by the Major Race Categories for the Years 2000, 2010, 2020, 2030, 2040 and 2050

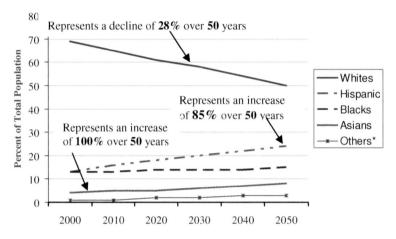

*Includes American Indians and Alaskan natives alone, native Hawaiians and other Pacific Islanders alone.
Source: U.S. Census Bureau, 2004, "U.S. Interim Projections by Age, Sex, Race, and Hispanic Origin"

Summary

These longer-term population and demographic trends will have important economic, spending, investment and wealth effects on our economy for many years into the future. The economy will continue to grow more slowly than it did from 1940-2007. Our society will become more multicultural, reflecting differences among birthrates in the Caucasian, Hispanic, black, Asian and Muslim portions of our population[8]. In addition, the numbers of immigrants that already have or are expected to come to the U.S legally or otherwise in the next 40 years will be largely Hispanic, Asian and Muslim people. These changes represent an important part of the *new normal* regarding reduced consumer spending, wealth accumulation, economic growth, job creation and incomes. They present new and very real challenges to our notions of capitalism versus socialism and of an expansive government versus escalating debt and higher taxes. These trends obviously have very important short- and long-term political implications. We will examine some of the major economic and political issues they present in Chapter 9.

---

[8] Ibid

Chapter 4
What Caused the U.S. Economic Downturn in 2008 and 2009? The 2008-2009 Great Recession

This chapter discusses how easy credit, pyramiding debt and yielding to a temptation to spend as if there were no tomorrow all came together in the Great Recession of 2008-2009 to create a fertile environment that has produced the most serious and longest lasting U.S. economic downturn since the Great Depression in the 1930s. My objective here is to help you better understand why and how our economy has arrived at this point, why 2008-2009 will end up being the early stages of a long-term 2008-2014 *modern day* depression, and why and when recovery comes years from now, it will follow the **L**-shaped downturn and recovery pattern discussed in Chapter 1 and **not** the quick **V**-shaped economic downturn and recovery as most people expected in 2009 and early 2010.

Living far Beyond our Means in the U.S. Created major Financial and Asset Bubbles, particularly in 1990-2007

All financial and asset bubbles can be counted on to eventually burst. The only question is, when. Two hundred years of history in the United States, Japan and Europe is clear on this point. What specific financial and asset bubbles am I talking about relative to the 2008-2014 time period? Real estate, stock market, commodity market and credit default bubbles.

A *bubble*, in this book, occurs when the value of an asset rises, often slowly and for years, to a point where the increased value can no longer be sustained. It stops going up and finally bursts. Then the value drops sharply, normally much faster than it increased and often for years. Think of a large balloon. Blowing the balloon up will make it inflate. But, blowing it up past its limits will cause it to burst. Home and condominium prices, commercial, industrial, farm and ranch real estate values, the stock market and most of the world's major commodities all have bubbled and have burst in our recent past.

Physical balloons burst quickly as shown in Figure 4.1. But in the real economy, as we will see in Chapter 7, this deflation can take years, during which it is measured by CPI price deflation, near zero inflation rates and/or much slower than normal increases in consumer prices.

Figure 4.1
What Goes up Eventually Comes Down

Hard and Financial Asset Values Inflate over Time and then these same Asset Values finally Burst and Begin the Deflating Process

This is What has and will Happen during the 2008-2014 Time Period

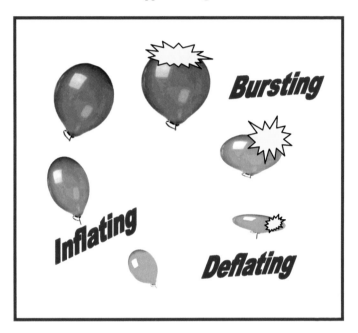

Major long-term Financial and Hard Asset Bubbles can be Accurately Anticipated and Forecast

Most economists, financial advisors, stockbrokers, investors, business owners, managers, bankers, government and Federal Reserve Bank employees, politicians and consumers do not believe that major and long-term financial and hard asset bubbles can be accurately anticipated and forecast. The primary reason is because they do not know about, believe in or take seriously the long-term 60- to 80-year economic boom and bust business cycle. But as we saw in Chapter 2, these cycles do exist and have for hundreds of years in Japan, Eastern and Western Europe and the United States.

I do believe in long-term boom and bust business cycles. I have found that studying them carefully has been very helpful to me and to my clients, subscribers and friends for the past 40 years. The first and most important key to

52

look for is one or more of the major financial and hard asset *excesses* that show up about every **60** to **80** years in our overall economy and in other economies around the world. They also show up once about every *30* years in our farm economy and for most commodity markets.

Those intervals are approximate, however. History shows that the specific number of years between major boom and bust cycles fluctuates over time.

For example, the span from the beginning of the *first* U.S. economic depression in 1804 to the beginning of the *second* depression in 1873 was *67 years*. The similar span from the beginning of the *second* depression in 1873 to the beginning of the *third* depression, the Great Depression, in 1930 was a shorter *57 years*. Now, the interval from the beginning of the Great Depression to the *fourth* and *modern* day depression that I am forecasting for the 2008-2014 time period is *78 years*. So, for the purposes of this book, I am using a practical range of *60 to 80 years* from cycle to cycle.

As discussed in Chapter 1, *60* to *80 years* is long enough for most people to forget what happened one full cycle earlier. In addition, the 60 to 80 years gives most people time to develop one or more reasons why they believe another depression cannot or will not happen again. Many people simply say *things are different now.*

In two of my *AS I SEE IT* economic and Ag sector outlook update newsletter reports[9], I told clients that I strongly believed there would be **four** economic and financial market bubbles bursting within the 2008-2014 time period. They were (1) the housing, commercial, industrial, farm and ranch real estate bubbles, (2) the commodity market bubbles, (3) the stock market bubbles and (4) the private debt and credit default bubbles. These bubbles grew and are bursting simply because most of us have been living far beyond our means for a long time. In the November 14, 2008 report, I also warned clients that because of these bursting bubbles, they should plan for a serious, deep, painful and prolonged U.S. and global economic contraction and *modern day* depression. That depression began in the last half of 2008. I also told them to plan for a powerful deflation of prices and asset values over at least five to seven years or longer and substantially higher levels of unemployment, reaching the *10%* to *15%* range within the 2010-2014 time period.

Balloons lose air in fractions of seconds if they pop or in minutes or longer if they develop a slow leak. However, the financial balloons that we are talking about have been inflating over a long time, at least *20* to *40* years for many and as long as *60* to *80* years for some. They will take a lot longer to deflate as well,

---

[9] June 16, 2008 and November 14, 2008

usually between five and 10 years. The last time agricultural, commodity and farm and ranchland values declined sharply was during the 1983-1987 time period about *30* years ago. The last time a home real estate market bubble burst as severely as we are seeing now was in the 1930s, during the Great Depression. The last time the U.S. stock markets burst so vividly – the widely watched Dow Jones Industrial Averages plummeted *55%* to a March 9th, 2009 low of *6,470* from an October 9th, 2007 peak of *14,164* in about 18 months – was also in the 1930s.

Definition of easy Credit Terms, Growth of Credit and Debt and the Amount of Leverage

To see more precisely why bubbles are bursting now, it is helpful to briefly look at three of the biggest contributors to them: *easy credit terms*, excessive *growth of credit and debt* and the overuse of *leverage*. *Easy credit terms* refer to loans made on either a hope or a presumption that borrowers will repay without a strong assurance that they can or will. This includes lending without requiring borrowers to fully document their financial ability to fully repay interest and principal, loans or credit lines with little or no collateral protection against nonpayment, or *balloon notes* that feature artificially low interest rates early in the loan followed by a complete payment of principal and unpaid interest at the end. *Excessive growth of debt and credit* refers to the amount and rate of increase in the credit and debt that banks, mortgage companies, credit card companies and other lenders provide to business and consumer borrowers. *Leverage* is a ratio comparing the amount of debt a consumer or business owes to an amount that would be left over if the asset was sold and the debts repaid. But to understand how bubbles burst and what happened in 2006 and 2007 in the U.S, it is simpler and more convenient to think of *leverage* as how much or how little cash or equity borrowers need to get the credit they seek from lenders.

Looking back to 2006 and 2007, let's explore why some of these financial and asset bubbles in the U.S. reached the bursting point. The primary cause was due to several major *excesses* directly connected to easy credit terms that led to massive, excessive credit growth and excessive, unsustainable increases in leverage that led to unsustainable and excessive private debt pyramiding and growth as consumers and businesses tried *borrowing their way to prosperity*. Our economy depends heavily on the level and rate of consumer and business spending. Consumer spending, particularly since *1990*, in turn has become heavily dependent on consumers and households borrowing more and more money. By 2007-2009, consumer spending accounted for about *70%* to *71%* of the nation's total economic growth. Another *12%* to *15%* of growth in America depends on business and corporate spending and investment. In other words, these two sectors alone account for *82%* to *85%* of what drives growth and new job creation in our total economy. I emphasize this point because the bursting of the residential and other real estate, stock market and commodity market bubbles in past cycles has always led to lower and much slower than normal growth and a much higher than normal unemployment. This is the case now, as well, and will result in substantially reduced consumer, business and corporate spending, reduced profits and a lower stock market moving forward.

The Borrow, Borrow, Borrow and Spend, Spend, Spend Party is Over

Our economy, its real estate, stock and commodity markets, our overall standard of living and our productivity all soared to record high levels between 1990 and through 2007. This happened primarily because consumers went into an accelerated *borrow, borrow, borrow* mode, followed by a *spend, spend, spend* mode. The rate of spending went up and the rate of saving went down sharply. This borrow and spend party came to an end in 2008-2009. The bursting bubbles we have been talking about involve the private and the public sectors of our culture and economy, ordinary citizens, small businesses and large corporations. Recoil from the bursting will continue for at least the next five to seven years. We will experience much more stringent credit standards and requirements, significantly fewer new loan approvals, much slower growth in credit and debt, greatly reduced leverage and further write downs and write offs of private consumer, household and business debt. These trends have already resulted in a total of more than *140* commercial bank failures in 2008 and 2009 on a combined basis. *I forecast that, conservatively, at least 800 to 1,200 commercial banks will fail between 2008 and 2014*. The midpoint of that range or about *1,000* banks would represent 14% to 15% of the total *7,085* commercial banks in the U.S. in 2008[10]. That would leave about *85%* to *86%* of the banks in our country open to provide services to consumers and businesses. This reduction has tremendous implications for our economy in the next five or more years, which we will look at further in Chapter 5.

In addition to reduced spending, we will see consumers saving more of their money and demanding better values, more bargains and major discounts for practically all goods and services during the next 10 years and beyond. Consumers will become more frugal and budget conscious than in the 1990s and the early 2000s. This is an important part of what I call the *new normal* moving forward. This trend will reduce prices and costs and hold them down for at least the next five to 10 years.

Consumer, household and business spending depends heavily on the availability, use and growth of credit and debt. The level and rate of spending by

---

[10] FDIC

consumers and businesses correlates directly with how much credit, debt and leverage are available to be used and on what terms. This has been especially true since 1990. Figures 4.2 through 4.10 show how private and public outstanding sector debt, credit and leverage in the U.S. all have increased dramatically in the *51* years of 1957-2007. Federal Reserve calculations show that our combined private and public debt increased *7,776%, or 152.5%* per year between 1957 and 2007, nearly 22 times faster than the *357%*, or *7.0%* per year that our economy expanded during the same time, expressed in current dollars, i.e. not adjusted for inflation.

Our total combined private and public outstanding debt was *$643 billion* in 1957. By the end of calendar year 2007, it had risen to *$50 trillion*. Any way you look at it, the difference, shown in Figure 4.2, represents an excessive level and an unsustainable rate of debt growth.

Figure 4.2
Total Combined U.S. Private Sector and Public Sector Outstanding Debt
for the 51 Years of 1957-2007

Excessive Growth in Total Combined Debt

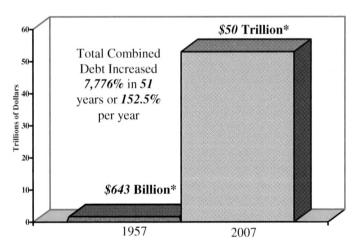

Source: Federal Reserve Board, Statistical Release Z.1, Table D.3, Washington, D.C.

*These private and public sector outstanding debt numbers have *not* been adjusted for inflation, i.e. they are expressed in current dollars.

Let me help you get your mind around the difference between a million, a billion and a trillion. For example, if one *million* seconds were subtracted from today, it would put us back *12 days*. If one **billion** seconds were subtracted from today, it would put us back about *32 years*. But, if one **trillion** seconds were subtracted from today, it would put us back to *about 29,700 B.C.* (Before Christ). *Trillions* are huge numbers.

Figure 4.3 tells us two important things about our *$50 trillion* of combined private and public debt. First, it consists of *81% private sector debt*, which encompasses all the mortgages, car loans, credit cards, business operating loans and other money that consumers and businesses borrow, *and 19% public sector debt*. Public sector debt consists of federal, state, city, county and local government debt of all kinds. Second, *80%* of the *$50 trillion* total was *added to the books* between 1990 and 2007, when borrowing shot dramatically higher. Both facts will profoundly affect our economy in the future.

Figure 4.3
The Total Combined U.S. Private and Public Sector Outstanding Debt by Year for the 51 Years of 1957-2007

Excessive Growth in *Total* Combined Debt

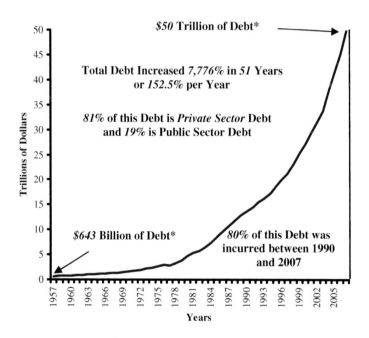

Source: Federal Reserve Board, Statistical Release Z.1, Table D.3, Washington, D.C.

*These private and public sector outstanding debt numbers have **not** been adjusted for inflation, i.e. they are expressed in current dollars.

Figure 4.4 shows the path of *private sector debt* for the *51* years of 1957-2007. From a beginning *$347 billion* in 1957, the total increased at an annual average rate of *229%* per year until it reached *$40.5 trillion* in 2007. This represents an *11,675%* total increase. However, the increase was not constant. Some *80%* of this outstanding debt was incurred after 1990.

Figure 4.4
The Total U.S. Private Sector Outstanding Debt by Year for the 51 Years of 1957-2007

Excessive Growth in *Private* Debt

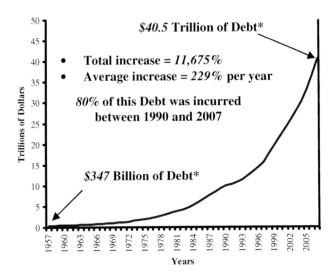

Source: Federal Reserve Board, Statistical Release Z.1, Table D.3, Washington, D.C.
*These private sector debt outstanding numbers have **not** been adjusted for inflation, i.e. they are expressed in current dollars.

Total *government debt* followed a similar path during the same 51 years, as shown in Figure 4.5. This debt was *$296 billion* in 1957, but increased at an annual rate of *63%* per year until 2007 when it reached *$9.5 trillion,* for a total increase of *3,210%*. As with private debt, about *80%* of this public debt was incurred after 1990.

Most people believe that federal, state and local government debt has been increasing faster than private debt for many years. Figures 4.4 and 4.5 indicate that just the opposite is true. Private debt grew **3.64** times faster, on average, than public debt from 1957 through 2007. One huge problem with government debt has emerged in those 51 years, however. *The size of government debt has become almost as large as the nation's total economy. For example, at the end of 2009, the size of our total U.S. economy, as measured by real GDP, was $13 trillion and our total federal government debt was $12 trillion.*

Figure 4.6 shows the dramatic increase in total U.S. Federal Government outstanding debt as a percent of real GDP from **10.4%** in 1957 to **92.3%** in 2009. This means that the federal government debt, as a percent of our real economic growth, was **890%** larger in 2009 than it was in 1957. This is clearly not sustainable. Nonetheless, the largest increases, in 2008 and 2009, will continue into 2010-2014 and beyond. This will have negative consequences for our economy moving forward. We will examine those more closely in Chapter 9.

Figure 4.5
The Total U.S. Public Sector Outstanding Debt by Year for the 51 Years of 1957-2007

Excessive Growth in Total Federal, State and Local *Government* Debt

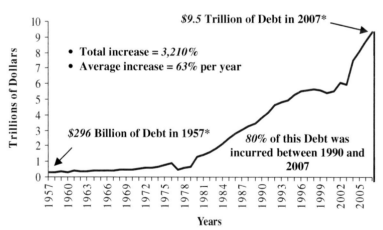

Source: TreasuryDirect.gov, Historical Debt Outstanding, and Federal Reserve Board, Statistical Release Z.1, Table D.3, Washington, D.C.

*These public sector outstanding debt numbers have **not** been adjusted for inflation, i.e. they are expressed in current dollars.

Figures 4.7 and 4.8 compare how much faster our private and public debt grew, compared to the rate of growth of our economy, in the *51 years* between 1957- 2007, and more specifically in the final 18 years of that period, 1990-2007. Debt grew about **22 times faster** than the economy since 1957 and continued to grow **four times faster** after 1990. Both rates are excessive and unsustainable.

The easy credit terms, excessive credit and debt growth and leverage party is over. Consumers and businesses will be offered much less credit in 2010-2014. They will borrow less money and use less leverage. This already has begun slowing economic growth to rates much below those that we consider normal. That slower-than-normal growth will continue.

Figure 4.6
Total U.S. Federal Government Outstanding Debt as a Percent of Real GDP for 1957-2009

This Represents Unsustainable Federal Debt Accumulation

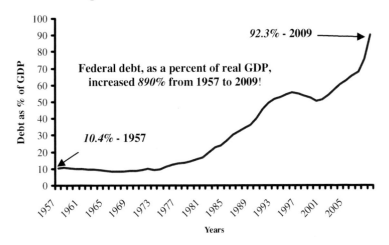

Source: TreasuryDirect.gov, Historical Debt Outstanding and the Bureau of Economic Accounts, NIPA Table 1.1.6 Real Gross Domestic Product, Chained Dollars (2005 dollars)

Recovery will be even more painful because the **$50 trillion** of combined private and public outstanding debt that we've talked about up to now does *not* include what are known as unfunded financial obligations, i.e. unfunded liabilities of many different kinds. This is money that governments or businesses have promised to pay but haven't yet allocated taxes or other revenues needed to

60

do that. For example, according to Roy Ferguson's *Tip of the Week*[11], the total *unfunded obligations* to Social Security, Medicare and private and public sector pensions totaled at least another *$60 trillion* as of mid 2009. This brings the total debt to *$110 trillion* (*$50 trillion* plus *$60 trillion*). U.S. banks and other financial institutions presently hold more than *$202 trillion* in *derivatives*, which are yet another class of unfunded financial obligations, Ferguson reports. This brings our total debt obligations, including unfunded financial obligations, to a mind-boggling *$312 trillion*. These numbers do not include the massive amounts of debt our federal and state governments incurred in 2008 and 2009, or the trillions of dollars that will be added over at least the next 10 years by the compounding effect of mounting federal government budget deficits. At the same time, federal tax revenues needed to help pay these mounting debts fell by a greater percentage in 2009 than for any year since the 1930s.

Figure 4.7
Average Annual Rate of Growth in Total Combined Private and Public Sector Outstanding Debt, Compared to the Average Annual Rate of Nominal Economic Growth (GDP) in the United States over the 51 Years of 1957-2007

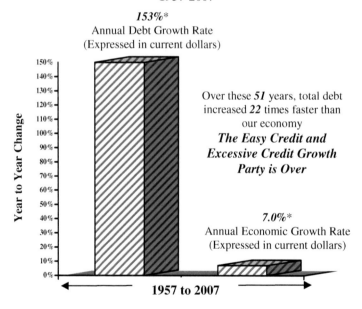

*153%**
Annual Debt Growth Rate
(Expressed in current dollars)

Over these *51* years, total debt increased *22* times faster than our economy
The Easy Credit and Excessive Credit Growth Party is Over

*7.0%**
Annual Economic Growth Rate
(Expressed in current dollars)

1957 to 2007

Source: Federal Reserve Board, Statistical Release Z.1, Table D.3, Washington, D.C.

---

[11] The Ferguson Group weekly newsletter, Tulsa, Oklahoma, dated August 10, 2009

*The rate of growth of public and private outstanding debt is based on numbers that have **not** been adjusted for inflation. Likewise, the rate of annual economic growth (GDP) also has **not** been adjusted for inflation and is expressed in current and nominal dollars. The **real** rate of growth for this *51*-year period was *3.3%* per year.

Figure 4.8
Average Annual Rate of Growth in Total Combined Private and Public Sector Outstanding Debt, Compared to the Rate of Nominal Economic Growth (GDP) in the United States for the *18* Years of 1990-2007

The Easy Credit and Excessive Credit Growth Party is Over

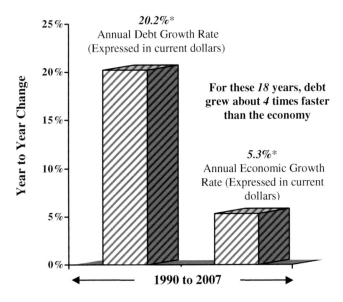

Source: Federal Reserve Board, Statistical Release Z.1, Table D.3, Washington, D.C.

*The rate of growth of private and public outstanding debt is based on numbers that have **not** been adjusted for inflation. Likewise, the rate of annual GDP growth also has **not** been adjusted for inflation and is expressed in current and nominal dollars. The real GDP growth rate for this *18*-year period was *2.89%* per year.

Bottom line, our nation has binged spectacularly on excessive debt, growth in credit, easy credit terms and leverage. The deleveraging of these bubbles began with great pain in 2008 and 2009. We will see in Chapter 5 how this will become even more painful between now and 2014.

What are Financial Derivatives?

Financial derivatives are contracts between buyers and sellers, based on the value of an underlying asset, that are traded as securities in organized markets. Most derivatives are highly leveraged and their values change, often sharply, when the value of the underlying asset changes. Stocks, bonds, commodities, currencies, interest rates and market indexes are some of the most common underlying assets on which derivatives are based. Futures contracts, forward contracts, options and swaps are the most common types of derivatives. But derivatives themselves can be used as assets on which other derivatives are based. There are even derivatives based on weather data, such as the amount of rain or the number of sunny days in a particular region.

Speculators can use derivatives to make a profit if the value of the underlying asset rises, falls or reaches a certain range in an expected way. Alternatively, hedgers can use derivatives to mitigate risk by entering into a derivative contract with values that move opposite to the changes in the value of their underlying assets and cancel all or part of the risk. The use and trading of derivatives by investors, market traders and banks can be risky. The possibilities of large financial losses are very real. I believe the odds are quite high that there will be some major problems and financial losses in 2010-2014 relating to the trillions of dollars involved with U.S. derivatives.

Home real estate prices soared to bubble peaks for many reasons in 2005-2007. Consumers and businesses were increasing spending. Eighteen years of *green light zone* economic growth and job creation beginning in 1990, plus a glut of baby boomers accelerating their investment in real estate and other markets, also pushed prices higher. Low prices for consumer goods, imported from China, Japan and other countries benefiting from a massively growing world economy, exacerbated the trends. These factors all contributed to the major home real estate and stock market bubbles that began collapsing in the second half of 2006 and continued bumping downward in the autumn of 2007 and during 2008-2009.

Inflation-adjusted annual real GDP, real personal consumption expenditures and real personal disposable income all increased *3.3%, 3.6%* and *3.4%* per year, respectively in 1957-2007, as shown in Figure 4.9. However, average annual household and consumer outstanding debt for this same *51*-year period increased *9.5%* per year or *2.9* times faster. These numbers simply show, as we saw in Figures 4.2 through 4.8, that the rate of growth in household and consumer debt finally has become unsustainable. The bubbles of easy credit terms, excessive credit and debt and leverage began bursting in 2008 and 2009. This deleveraging process will continue for at least five to 10 more years.

Figure 4.9
The Average Annual Rate of Growth in Real U.S. Gross Domestic Product (GDP), Household and Consumer Outstanding Debt, Real Disposable Personal Income (after tax income) and Real Personal Consumption Expenditures for the 51 Years of 1957-2007

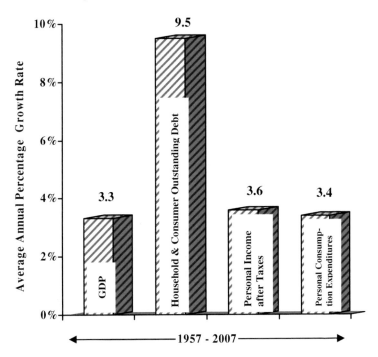

Source: The U.S. Department of Commerce, Bureau of Economic Analysis, National Income and Product Accounts, Tables 1.1.6, 2.1 and the Federal Reserve Board.

Americans became drunk on excessive debt, easy credit, excessive leverage and the acceleration in the growth of debt and leverage, particularly between 1990 and 2007. This, coupled with the impact of the *pig-in-the-python* demand anomaly created by the *78 million* baby boomers, resulted in the first bursting of home real estate and stock market bubbles in 2006 and 2007. Commercial, industrial, farm and ranch real estate bubbles and commodity bubbles followed later in 2008-2009. However, there still is enough *market hot air* left in each of these bubbles to prolong the deflation through most of 2010-2014 for many markets and perhaps even longer for a few. For example, the deflating of the housing, stock market and commodity market bubbles will likely be completed by 2012, but the commercial, industrial, farm and ranch real estate bubbles may continue to deflate even beyond 2014 (particularly for commercial, industrial, farm and ranch real estate).

Now let's talk about excess leverage. The combination of accelerated growth in the private sector debt of *11,675%* as shown in Figure 4.4 and the astounding increase and use of private debt leverage was the final force that created the real estate, stock market and commodity market bubbles that are now deflating. ***Sooner or later, all financial bubbles burst***. The bearish sellers outnumber the bullish buyers. Greed and the motivation to survive financially by borrowing and spending even more eventually turns to fear and caution, which leads to big and often painful changes. The root of evil is often attached to money. The root of bursting private debt bubbles is attached to excessive growth and use of easy credit terms, debt and leverage.

Before 1990, the normal amount of leverage or money borrowed relative to the amount of equity, in the United States, was *4 to 1* or a ratio of *$4 of debt to $1 of equity* as shown in Figure 4.10. A *$100,000* real estate purchase, for example, might be made with a combination of *$80,000* debt and *$20,000* equity or a *4 to 1* debt-to-equity ratio. Some borrowers' debt-to-equity ratios dipped as low as *3 to 1,* others borrowed as much as *5 to 1,* but few loans were made and structured outside that range.

Beginning in the early 1990s however, the ratio widened from *4 to 1* to *35 to 1* and as much as *40 to 1* for many bankers, lenders and borrowers in the U.S. and worldwide. With a debt-to-equity ratio of *35 to 1*, that same *$20,000* of equity allows individuals and businesses to borrow as much as *$700,000* instead of *$80,000*. This is what actually happened in 1990-2007. It represents *excessive* and very risky debt, leverage and easy credit any way you look at it.

Most borrowers of first lien residential, commercial, industrial, farm and ranch real estate mortgages are not aware of the *30, 35* and *40 to 1* leverage. These riskier transactions were done by mortgage lenders, investment bankers, hedge funds, Wall Street and large and medium-sized banks who in 1990-2007 *packaged* millions of first and second lien home mortgages, for example, as *mortgage-backed securities* and sold these *packaged and structured* securities to *secondary markets* and public financing investors all over the world. Similar packaging, restructuring and selling took place with commercial, industrial farm and ranch real estate, auto loans and credit cards. This private debt structure and leveraging involved trillions of dollars. Most of these *secondary markets* do not exist today and this represents a very important and major change in the financing structure for the U.S. I believe this change will continue for at least the next five to 10 years.

Figure 4.10

Illustration of Normal and Excessive Levels of Debt-to-Equity Leverage in the United States Private Sector for the 1950-2007 Time Period

The Excessive Debt Leverage Party is Over

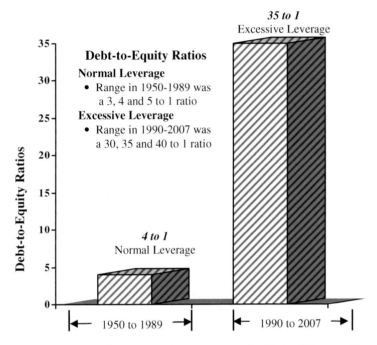

Source: Debt to equity ratios are based on data from the Federal Reserve Board, plus information from individual banks, investment banking firms, the American Bankers Association and the Mortgage Bankers Association.

Although home buyers generally didn't leverage as excessively as market traders did, many of them and their lenders injected additional risks into the transactions through a different mechanism. Many first lien home mortgages were structured in 2003-2006 as *subprime* loans. Prime mortgage loans are the ones, usually with the lowest interest rates, that lenders offer borrowers with the best credit histories and financial documents affirming they could afford the loan. Borrowers who were offered *subprime* loans were not required to document their income or demonstrate their ability to make the monthly payments or even whether they were able to afford the home or condo in the first place. Lenders simply charged higher interest rates to cover the risk. These same lenders also offered a variety of *subprime financing options* that ultimately added still more risk to these transactions. Those included (1) paying interest and principal where the home loan was fully amortized, (2) paying the interest only and no principal or (3) paying only *partial* interest and no principal each month. When homeowners chose option three, which many did, the unpaid interest was added to the principal they still owed. So, in effect, the total size of their unpaid debt was rising each month for millions of loans and home mortgages in the U.S. where the borrowers were paying only *minimum* interest. This kind of financing was not only very risky for lenders and borrowers, but could not have come at a worse time. The home real estate market bubble began to burst in the second half of 2006, shattering a core assumption on which whole lending strategies were based. Those lending and borrowing the money for new and existing home purchases and for home refinancing were fully expecting home values to continue to trend higher in the years ahead as they had been doing for the past 50 years or more. This assumption obviously did not turn out to be correct. *What goes up eventually comes down* certainly applies to residential home and condo markets and values.

Owning a home represents the largest and most important financial asset and investment for most Americans. Consequently, the home market asset class is the largest and most important of all major asset classes that economists watch, including the stock market, to monitor the economy.

When average home values were increasing, as they did for most of the years from 1957 to 2006, homeowners in general found their net worth and wealth going up. The wealth effect of this trend caused millions of individuals and families to feel good and want to increase their borrowing and spending capacity and leverage. Many took out second mortgages or created home equity lines of credit to spend more for general living expenses, vacations, home improvements or other major purchases, and for financing college educations. Others sold their homes and used home equity to buy larger, more expensive or newer homes. Still others used the money to provide *seed* or *startup capital* to begin new businesses. Home equity, in effect, became a big *piggy bank* or *ATM* card. For many years this had a very positive impact on homeowners' financial wellbeing and on the economy as a whole in the U.S.

However, in the very nature of long-term boom and bust business cycles, good times and fortunes inevitably become difficult and more challenging. Average annual home values in the U.S., measured by the Standard and Poor's/Case-Shiller Home Price Index, collectively peaked at *$22 trillion* in July, 2006.

Then, in about 36 months beginning in July, 2006, the *average* market value of homes in the U.S. declined between *32%* and *35%* (according to Standard and Poor's and Case-Shiller Home Price Indices), cutting home values and wealth for American citizens between *$7.0* and *$7.7 trillion*. This major and painful decline in borrowing and spending power represents a huge loss for many Americans who have been counting on the equity in their homes being a big part of their wealth structure. I estimate that, conservatively, home market values will continue to decline and hit the bottom by about 2012. I fully expect that average annual home values will have declined from peak to bottom by *45%* to *55%*. This will translate into a total loss of home equity and consumer wealth of about *$11 trillion* by 2012, which we will examine again in Chapter 5.

Between 2012 and 2014 at least *50%* to *60%* of all U.S. homes that have one or more mortgages will be *underwater,* meaning their owners will be unable to sell their homes for enough money to pay the debts against them. At least *35%* of all U.S. home mortgages were *underwater* at the end of 2009, according to official home mortgage data. This is an important and serious development. It has not happened anytime in the *68*-year 1940-2007 economic boom. The end result will be substantially curtailed consumer borrowing and spending for at least the next five to seven years.

The rate of homeownership in the United States will likely continue to decline over the next 10 to 20 years. The percentage of individuals and families who own homes peaked out at around *70%* in 2004 and 2005. The rate of homeownership in the United States will likely continue to decline over the next 10 to 20 years. The percentage of individuals and families who own homes peaked out around *70%* in 2004 and 2005[12]. By April-June of 2009, the percentage of homeowners declined to *67.4%*[13]. The University of Utah's Metropolitan Research Center estimates that the percentage of households that own homes will decline to about *63.5%* by 2020. *Clearly there will be more renters and less home owners in the years ahead.* The trend of more renters and fewer homeowners is being driven by:

- The home real estate market bubble bursting.
- Major declines in home market values.
- Less credit and much tighter home loan financing requirements by lenders.
- The *78 million* baby boomers spending less, saving more and downsizing.
- Changing population demographics.
- The prospect that by the years 2012-2014, close to *50%* to *60%* of all U.S. home mortgages will be *underwater.*
- The reduced cost of renting *versus* the cost of buying, maintaining and owning a home.

---

[12] U.S. Census Bureau
[13] Ibid

In the future, a home will not be looked upon as an investment to build wealth by most borrowers, but simply as a place to live and raise a family. This will be part of the *new normal* moving forward.

The growth of Hispanics and Asians as a percentage of the U.S. population by the year 2050, as discussed in Chapter 3, will alter the homeownership structure even further. Statistically, these families have tended to rent rather than buy homes. These trends will clearly result in a slow and long-term decline in the percentage of households who own homes and a similar slow increase in the percentage of households who rent homes, condos and apartments in the next 10 to 15 years and beyond. Fewer Americans will achieve the *American dream* of owning a home in the *new normal* in the years ahead.

The Easy Credit Terms, Excessive Credit and Debt Growth and Excessive Leverage Party is Over

There is no point in singling out and blaming any group in our economy's private and public sector financial system individually for the situation we find ourselves in. *All the key players were at the same party at essentially the same time. The party went on and lasted for a good many years.* The Federal Reserve contributed by implementing monetary policies that resulted in historically low interest rates and rapid increases in credit growth, debt and leverage. Past and present administrations and many members of Congress from both parties strongly encouraged both homeownership and the use of risky financing and loan standards with Fannie Mae, Freddie Mac and other mortgage lenders. Banks, mortgage lenders, Wall Street investment firms and investors became increasingly innovative in creating mortgage-backed securities and other highly leveraged and risky investments as well as easy credit loans with *flexible loan standards* for homeowners and consumers of all kinds. Home buyers also took advantage of excessively easy credit terms and increasing debt tolerance to leverage themselves ever more deeply into new or existing bigger homes. Excessive credit card and auto loan growth soon followed the same arc. These developments didn't happen overnight; they began slowly 50 or so years ago. Beginning in 1990, however, *the party took on a life of its own and blasted off like a rocket* as shown in Figures 4.2 through 4.9. Few of the partygoers recognized the financial excesses that were building. Most thought they were doing the right thing. They did not realize that their combined actions were causing major asset bubbles to grow to the bursting point. Not just one, but many bubbles were swelling at the same time – housing and stock markets, commercial, industrial, farm and ranch real estate, and the commodity markets as well.

Subprime mortgages were not the only contributors of excessively easy credit to mortgage markets. Many other kinds of exotic and creative home mortgages also became popular in the 2004-2007 lending heyday, and involved millions of homeowners who refinanced or purchased homes based on these exotic mortgages. New types of *jumbo loans* were created using the same basic subprime loan standards and guidelines in order to finance homes in the *$500,000* to *$3 million* price range. These included so-called *Alt-A* loans, offered as alternative mortgages for borrowers unable to qualify for prime quality loans and *Option ARMs* or adjustable rate mortgages. These two mortgage structures, available to borrowers of both conventional and jumbo mortgages, lured many home borrowers in with really low initial interest rates called *teaser rates* that allowed borrowers to buy or refinance homes for as low as *1%* or *2%* for two, three or five years. After that, these very low interest rates *reset* at much higher levels and monthly payments went up sharply. These *resets* resulted in a *50%* to *100% increase* in mortgage payments. *Alt-A* and *Option ARM* loans began resetting in 2009, but about *90%* will reset between 2010 and 2012. This will accelerate the number of home mortgage delinquencies and foreclosures and further drive average home values lower within at least the 2010-2012 period.

Millions of Americans, in 2003-2007 especially, also took out second mortgages, often as home equity lines of credit, which helped pump billions of dollars more into the bubble. These, too, were all structured with the use of very easy credit terms and ended up resulting in many homeowners borrowing between *100%* and *125%* of the appraised market value of their homes. At the same time, many home appraisals were set unrealistically high. These trends placed both mortgage lenders and homeowners in a risky and vulnerable financial position when home values began to decline, the economy began to slow down, and unemployment began to rise. These pressures will continue over the next three to five years as we will see in Chapter 5.

As they continue, these large numbers of second mortgages will contribute to further home mortgage delinquencies and foreclosures, declining home values, slower than normal economic growth and higher levels of unemployment moving forward. Many more bank failures will follow, along with private debt write-downs and write-offs. In a sense, the millions of second mortgages, home loans and home equity lines of credit are like consumers maxing out on three to five credit cards.

All these problems will cause home mortgage delinquencies, foreclosures and defaults to increase sharply in at least 2010-2012. More than *50%* of home mortgage *resets* will likely fail and go into default and foreclosure by the end of 2012. This will not only cause average U.S. home values to decline much further, but will also cause many more banks and home mortgage lenders either to fail or to be required to have massive amounts of new capital invested. This will result in billions and trillions of dollars of private debt being written down or written off, which will continue to contribute to deflationary pressures as discussed in Chapters 5 and 7.

The credit and leverage party was fun while it lasted and it did last for many years. But again, this is the nature of the long-term boom and bust business cycle as we saw in Chapter 2. *Now the party is over.* Bursting bubbles and the deleveraging process have created a domino effect. Consumers are holding on to more of their money. Employment is down. The stock market has dropped significantly from its October 2007 peak and is going lower in 2010-2012 as we will see in Chapters 5 and 10. Home, commercial, industrial, farm and ranch real estate values are declining. These developments will continue to negatively impact mortgage lenders and banks. Most home, commercial, industrial, farm and ranch real estate mortgage lenders have not yet marked down these loans on their balance sheets to realistic market values. *Their balance sheets do not reflect the real world. The balance sheets of many commercial banks, savings and loan institutions and of other lenders overstate the value of their loan collateral by 25% to 50% as of early 2010.* Eventually these lenders will have no choice but to face reality and *adjust* their balance sheets downward. When they do, many will become insolvent. This will result in many more bank failures in the years ahead. It is not a question of if, but when market pressures will force banks and other lenders to face the painful reality of marking down a substantial portion of the home, commercial, industrial, farm and ranch real estate loan assets on their balance sheets. The major trend for at least 2010-2014 will be price deflationary forces affecting real estate, stock market and commodity market values as discussed in Chapters 7 and 10.

Most banks and other lenders are *hoarding* capital too. They are being very cautious about making new loans and concentrating instead on refinancing or restructuring loans for *existing* consumer and business customers. Credit quality for many consumer and business borrowers became a major issue in 2008 and 2009. This issue will continue to grow in 2010-2014. Also, consumer, business and corporate loan demand is down and will remain down moving forward. U.S. and global banks and other lenders are making very limited numbers of new loans. This is contributing to much slower than normal and negative economic growth, rising unemployment, reduced consumer and business spending and investment and increased rates of consumer savings.

Businesses have had no choice but to cut costs substantially and reduce employment to survive in the new economy. This is the *new normal*. The loss of many jobs has had a negative impact on the stock market in 2008 and 2009. Toppling that domino resulted in a major reduction in wealth for Americans who were invested in the stock markets and in their homes. Many were counting on their home equity and stock market portfolios to pay for their children's college educations and their own retirements. Those plans are shattered. Unfortunately, this deflating trend will very likely get worse before it stabilizes. Remember, the odds are at least **90%** that when these asset classes finally do hit bottom in 2010-2014, they will then remain relatively flat for several years before they begin to go up slowly again. This is the nature of the **L**-shaped economic downturn and recovery we discussed in Chapter 1.

Changes over time in human behavior have a profound and important impact on our economy and vice versa. A robust economy, rising real estate values, and increasing stock market values cause consumers and businesses to borrow more and spend more, while a really poor economy and declining real estate values and stock markets cause job losses and an increase in consumers and businesses *tightening their belts*. Long-term slow changes in human behavior also significantly affect how the long-term boom and bust business cycle plays out over time. During the last half century and especially in the 18 years since 1990, America's appetite for more *stuff* and the consumption of more of almost everything grew and was satisfied in large measure by consumers borrowing more and more money, as shown in Figures 4.2 through 4.12. Rising values for our homes, the stock market profits in our 401(k) and IRA plans, and the profits from our family-owned or other businesses all gave us the confidence to borrow and spend more.

We borrowed from everyone and spent tremendous sums of money. We borrowed to buy automobiles, boats, appliances and many other things because credit was readily available for almost anything we wanted to buy and interest rates were generally low, except for credit cards. Most Americans became drunk on easy credit and from buying more goods and services and better and more expensive things. We were living way beyond our means and *borrowing our way to prosperity*. Finally this credit and leverage bubble could no longer be sustained. It began to burst in 2007-2009 and our financial and hard assets began to decline in value. American consumers and families have lost trillions of dollars of wealth since 2007 and 2008. They've lost jobs, incomes and benefits as businesses had to cut expenses, headcount and overhead in order to survive in the new economy.

When people run out of cash and cannot borrow more and when people lose their jobs or are concerned that they may lose their jobs, they naturally begin to hold on to what they have. This is what began to happen in 2008 and 2009. This is what will continue to happen in 2010-2014, as we will see in Chapter 5. It will take at least five to 10 years for Americans in general to sober up and gradually change their behavior concerning borrowing and spending. These changes in human behavior are real and predictable. *America's borrow and spend party is over.*

Health experts estimate that at least two-thirds of our total population is now obese or overweight. Growing numbers of Americans eat too much, eat or drink the wrong foods and beverages and do not exercise enough to stay healthy and keep their weight down. These behavioral trends evolve slowly over time, as are the financial excesses and aftermath we are dealing with now. They are part of the excesses we experienced over the past 50 years. Less spending, reduced consumption and rising unemployment in the changing U.S. economy may or may not have an effect on our waistbands. However, I feel much more confident about the prospects of our economy going through a *modern day* depression and a long period of painful stagnation and much slower than normal growth between now and 2014 than I do about Americans changing their dietary and exercise habits and returning to a healthier weight and lifestyle.

Finally, there are at least three other important contributing factors we need to look at that have contributed to the serious and long-lasting economic downturn and recession in 2008 and 2009.

The *first* one was the sharp rise in crude oil, gasoline and diesel fuel prices in 2008. Crude oil prices in the U.S. rose to between *$145* and *$150* per barrel in the summer of 2008, which led to *$3.50* to *$4.10* per gallon gasoline prices at the pump. The timing of these much higher fuel and energy costs seriously hurt America, causing major problems for consumers, families, businesses and government agencies in 2008. They added *insult to injury* because the bursting of the economic, financial and asset bubbles discussed in this chapter were already independently happening. Bottom line, the sharp rise in energy costs increased and accelerated the U.S. and global economic downturn and the pain already being felt. Crude oil and energy prices declined sharply after peaking in the summer of 2008 because major and very real demand destruction and deflationary forces continued through 2008 and during 2009. Demand destruction for energy will continue in 2010 and through 2014 as we will see in Chapters 5, 7 and 10.

The *second* development was that the overall global economy was also contracting and experiencing serious economic, financial and asset bubble bursting at the same time. Bank failures were rising throughout the world, particularly in Western and Eastern Europe. These developments negatively impacted our economy, our banks, financial system and our stock markets. The opposite was also true. The economic contraction happening in the United States caused and continues to cause serious problems in all other economies across the globe. This will continue to be the case. This makes sense because the U.S. economy is by far the largest and strongest economy and financial system in the world. All economies are a part of the global economic system as we saw in Chapters 1 and 2. Each one is dependent on and directly impacted by the positive or negative events happening in all the others worldwide. We truly live and compete in a global economy and this will continue to be the case for many years to come. Most other economies in the world heavily depend on the U.S. consumer buying their products. When U.S. consumers begin reducing their spending, which they have been doing beginning in 2008 and 2009, this obviously has a major and direct negative impact on all other countries and economies in the world.

The *third* development involves the Japanese economy. Japan, the second largest economy in the world as of 2009, went through a very serious and painful *modern day* depression and prolonged period of stagnation for the *15* years of 1992-2006. Its recovery since then has been very slow and remains significantly below normal. This contributed to economic woes in the U.S., in Western and Eastern Europe and in China, as well as in all other economies in the world.

Consumer spending accounted for *70%* to *71%* of our total economy in 2007-2009. In 1966, this figure was *61.9%*. The trend shown in Figure 4.11 is very clear. Increased borrowing by consumers over the years has translated into more and more spending by consumers. Our U.S. economy is heavily dependent on the level and rate of consumer spending. China, Japan, India, South Korea, Mexico, Canada and many other countries in the world also depend heavily on the rate of consumer spending and the rate of economic growth in the U.S.

Figure 4.11
The Annual Real Personal Consumer Expenditures as a Percentage of Real Gross Domestic Product (GDP) for the 53 Years of 1957-2009

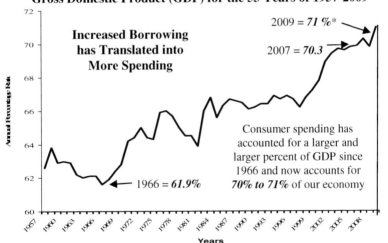

Source: Bureau of Economic Analysis, Table 1.1.6. Real GDP, Chained Dollars; revised August 17, 2009
*The year 2009 was estimated by the author.

As discussed in Chapter 10, I expect U.S. consumer spending, as a percent of GDP, to decline close to the *62%* to *64%* range within the next 10 years. At the same time, I fully expect the rate of consumer saving to increase over the next 10 years.

Consumer Spending will be Disappointing and far below Normal over the 2010-2014 period

There are many reasons why the level and rate of U.S. consumer spending will be disappointing and far below normal over at least the 2010-2014 time period. These reasons are summarized below:

1. *Rising Unemployment* – The level of monthly unemployment will reach at least the *10.5%* to *11.5%* range and will remain above *9.5%* to *10.0%* for all of the 2010-2012 time period.

2. *Major Loss of Consumer Wealth and Equity* – Consumers lost at least *$15 trillion* in wealth and equity to declining home and stock market values in 2008 and 2009. By 2014, the *additional* combined loss by consumers and households will end up being at least *$10 trillion* due to further declines in home and stock market values. This will bring the total loss of consumer wealth and equity to *$25 trillion*. These very large numbers do *not* include additional losses of wealth and equity resulting from major declines in commercial, industrial, farm and ranch real estate and commodities. Those will add at least an additional *$3 to $5 trillion* on top of the *$25 trillion*. The net result is the compromised borrowing and spending ability and capacity of consumers in the future.

3. *More Difficult Credit Terms, Reduced Credit and Debt Growth and much Reduced Leverage* – Tightening credit terms and cutting credit limits to undo years of excessive lending and leveraging will reduce and greatly slow down spending. This represents a very large and important change for at least five to 10 years and very possibly longer.

4. *Increased Savings by Consumers and Households* – The rate and level of consumer savings has been significantly increasing since 2007. This savings rate will increase further. I conservatively forecast that the U.S. annual consumer savings rate will go from *1.4%* in 2005 to *10%* to *12%* by or before 2014. Saving more means consumers will be spending less.

5. *The 78 million Baby Boomers Spending Less and Saving More* – In Chapter 3 we talked about how the whole economy is affected when a huge segment of the population changes the way they live and spend

money. Between now and 2022, this *pig in a python* will result in consumers spending significantly less, saving more and downsizing.

Figure 4.12 shows the personal average annual savings rate as a percentage of real disposable personal income for the *53* years of 1957-2009. Disposable income is the amount we as consumers, wage earners and retirees have to spend **after** we pay taxes. The savings rate is that part of the disposable income we choose to save. The total overall average savings rate for the *53* years from 1957 through 2009 was *7.0%*. But within those years, the rate was *9.0%* in the *33* years of 1957-1989 and reached an annual peak of *10.9%* in 1982. In contrast, the savings rate dropped to only *4.2%* in 1990-2009 and touched *1.4%* in 2005. My estimate for calendar year 2009 is a savings rate of *5.3%*.

The savings rate dropped sharply in the years 1990-2009 when we had a lot of easy and excessive credit, major and excessive growth in debt and credit and excessive leverage as shown in Figure 4.12. But in 2008-2009, when the credit reins began to tighten, the home market value bubble began to deflate, economic growth slowed sharply, the stock markets declined sharply and the level of unemployment began to increase sharply, the savings rate bottomed and began to go up again. I fully expect the U.S. savings rate to continue its rise and get to the *10%* to *12%* range by at least 2018 and very possibly sooner. The massive *loss* of equity, wealth, borrowing and spending power will cause consumer spending to decline and remain far below normal and the savings rate to be much higher than normal for at least the next five to 10 years.

Figure 4.12
The Annual Personal Savings Rate, as a Percent of Real Disposable Personal Income for the 53 Years of 1957-2009

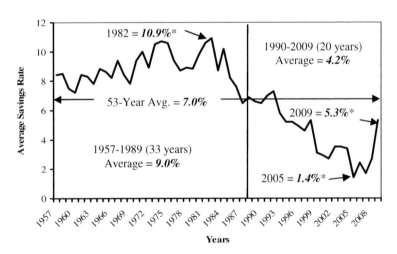

Source: Bureau of Economic Analysis; National Income and Product Accounts Table, Table 2.1, revised 8/17/09. The disposable person income numbers are in *real dollars*, i.e. they are adjusted for inflation via 2005 chained dollars.
*The average annual personal savings rate for the year 2009 is estimated by the author to be **5.3%**. The author conservatively estimates that the average annual savings rate will reach the **10%** to **12%** range by or before 2018.

Americans will become much more discerning about how they use their income moving forward. This trend will produce much slower than normal GDP growth and much higher than normal levels of unemployment. Businesses and corporations will have lower profits which will lead to new lows in the stock markets in 2010-2012. We will soon find ourselves in a *modern day* depression and in a long period of economic stagnation which will become a *new normal* within the next five years. This increased saving and reduced borrowing and spending will be positive for our economy in the longer run. But for the next 10 years, we will be deleveraging and adjusting to the *new normal*. This is a very fundamental change.

As Go the Housing and Auto Industries, so Goes the Economy

The major decline in average U.S. home values and loss of home equity since 2007 is very serious, painful and it is an important development. The bursting bubbles of easy credit terms, the excessive growth of credit and debt, and excess leverage have not only had a negative impact on the U.S. stock markets and home, commercial, industrial, farm and ranch real estate values, but also on all other sectors of our economy. Many other businesses and areas of our economy also depend heavily upon the health of the U.S. home real estate market. For example, home furniture and fixtures, carpeting, tile, glass, piping, concrete, wood cabinets, lumber, steel, electrical equipment and supplies, kitchen and bathroom appliances and fixtures, plumbing supplies, roofing, paint, brick, insulation, cleaning supplies and equipment, landscaping, wallpaper, and many other similar products and services are all negatively and directly impacted by the major downturn in the U.S. existing and new home market values. Demand for a very large number of jobs required to manufacture, market, transport, install and construct new homes and to remodel and upgrade existing homes and condos also has been severely reduced. We will see in Chapter 5 why these trends will continue in 2010-2014.

The same situation applies to the auto industry. Many businesses and sectors of our economy also depend heavily on the health of the U.S. auto industry, including new and used car sales, auto manufacturing, the manufacture, distribution and sales of auto parts, repairs and maintenance, car leasing and rentals, and the manufacturing and distribution of tires, steel, glass, plastic, leather and other auto and truck manufacturing components. This large and important industry, which also accounts for a lot of jobs, will continue to have a major impact on our economy in the years ahead. Like the single family home industry, and especially builders of larger and more costly homes, the auto industry still has very significant excess capacity today. This will continue to be a very challenging issue in the years ahead. For example, I believe it is likely that General Motors will go back into bankruptcy sometime within 2010-2014.

These two industries have been seriously wounded. They will *not* come roaring back to pre-2007 levels of growth, market values and economic activity for many more years. These important industries, which account for millions of jobs in America, will be in *intensive care* and *rehab* for much of the next 10 to 15 years and perhaps longer.

The changing demographics we have been talking about and particularly the 78 million baby boomers now beginning to think of more economical cars and smaller homes, condos and apartments, will have a tremendous impact on demand for large and expensive single-family homes and for expensive cars. Consequently, these industries will be slowly declining for the next *10* to *20* years. It will take a long time for these two industries to adjust to the *new normal.*

A Significant Portion of the U.S. Productivity Gains in 2008 and 2009 are the Result of Rising Unemployment

Ever-increasing productivity by American workers has been the biggest contributor to increases in the nation's overall standard of living since 1940. When gains in productivity occur year after year in general, employers are able to increase employee compensation over time. The facts are clear on this. Employers generally do reward their workers for being more productive. Productivity continued to increase in 2008 and 2009, which is a positive development, but why that happened also shows how a *new reality* will define much of our foreseeable future.

As discussed in Chapter 3, the U.S. is one of the most productive economies in the world and has been for many years. There are many broad reasons why and how this is so, including our freedom of choice, our capitalistic system, self accountability, the profit motive, and our American work ethic.

More specifically, however, productivity is increased when businesses, small and large, private and public, find ways to produce and market more products or services with the same number or with fewer workers than before. This often comes from the use and application of new technologies, innovations and creativity by American workers, by management and by business owners. It does *not* come from government. In many cases, small and medium-sized businesses, including the growing number of self-employed Americans, contribute most to our productivity gains.

American productivity in the *great recession* in 2008 and 2009 rose sharply for a darker reason. When employers are forced to lay off large numbers employees and to reduce corporate overhead, as they were in 2008 and 2009, most continue to produce or market large quantities of goods or provide many services, but with far fewer workers. The *net* result is a significant increase in productivity, such as we have seen in America, particularly in 2009. With unemployment rising in 2010-2012 and remaining much higher than normal for many of the next 10 years, my expectation is that we will continue to see further impressive gains in our productivity levels in 2010-2014 and beyond.

This is and will continue to be a positive development in what otherwise is now and will be a much slower than normal growth and painful economy in 2010-2014 and perhaps beyond. Higher productivity levels will make this *modern day* depression and long period of economic stagnation somewhat less serious and painful for those who have jobs. But productivity gains will not help the millions of Americans who have already lost their jobs or who will lose them in 2010-2014. They will experience serious economic, financial and emotional pain and stress. Part of the reality of the *new normal* now and moving forward will be that a much greater number of people than normal will be without jobs longer for much of the next 10 years than anytime since 1940.

Summary Sequence of Events resulting from the Home, Commercial, Industrial, Farm and Ranch Real Estate Market, Stock Market, Credit and Leverage Bubbles Bursting within 2007-2009

The years 2008-2009 represent the *beginning* of what I believe will be a *modern day* depression and prolonged economic stagnation period for the United States in the 2008-2014 time period. I believe the odds of the next *bust* period occurring within this time period are **90%**. Here is a summary of the sequence of events resulting from the bursting of credit and leverage bubbles in the home, commercial, industrial, farm and ranch real estate markets, the stock markets and the commodity markets.

These events and developments will very likely continue to play out during the 2010-2014 time period as we will see in Chapter 5:

- Home values began declining in mid 2006. By the end of 2009, the total decline in home values from their peak in 2006 was **32%** to **35%**. This translates into a very large loss of homeownership equity and family wealth of about **$7.0** to **$7.5 trillion**. This also represents a massive loss of consumer borrowing and spending capacity and net worth. Based on the Case-Shiller Real Home Price Index and a chart provided by www.biancoresearch.com[14], home values declined from a high point in about 1920 to a low point in the 1930s of close to *15%* to *20%*. Home values have already declined more in the 2006-2009 period than they did in the Great Depression. I believe home values will continue to decline significantly further in the next several years (2010-2012). The total decline from top to bottom will be in the *45%* to *55%* range within 2006-2014 as we will discuss in Chapter 5.

- Home mortgage delinquencies and foreclosures in the U.S. increased sharply in 2008 and 2009. These trends will continue and will get worse.

- A good many home mortgage lenders and banks failed and quickly became insolvent between 2007 and 2009. This situation will get much worse.

- Most banks and lenders have greatly tightened up lending standards. They are hoarding capital and making very few new loans. Many banks and other lenders have serious balance sheet problems. Theses problems will come to light and get much worse over the next five years.

- ***The excessive easy credit terms, growth of debt and credit and leverage party is over for America in this business cycle***. Banks, lenders, consumers, families and businesses all began the deleveraging process in 2008-2009. Simply stated, this means much less money being loaned, less money being borrowed and less money being spent by consumers and by businesses moving forward.

- Sharply reduced profits and major losses by corporations and businesses resulted in stock markets declining sharply in 2008 and 2009. This will be a major further issue in 2010-2012.

- Because of the above trends, consumers are spending less and saving more. The savings rate should go back up to the *10%* to *12%* range, compared to the *1.4%* level of savings in 2005.

- Reduced consumer and business borrowing, spending and the increased consumer savings have resulted in a major contraction and slowdown in the U.S. economic growth in 2008 and 2009. These developments produced serious increases in the level of unemployment. This will continue, get worse and will stay agonizingly high over the next five years. The current *recession,* which officially began in December of 2007, is the longest, deepest and most serious recession since the 1930s and has included *24* consecutive months of *major job* losses. This did not happen during any of the *11* recessions in the U.S. since 1940 relative to the length of time.

---

[14] Page 5 of the July 17, 2009 issue of the *Elliott Wave Theorist* by Robert Prechter

- During 2008-2009, we have experienced general price deflation, zero inflation or very low levels of inflation. The odds are **90%** that we will see and experience more price deflation or zero inflation and much lower than normal inflationary pressures in 2010-2020. We will explore why in Chapter 7.
- The Fed Funds interest rates will remain at historically low levels at or near zero for the years of 2010-2012. The Federal Reserve had no other realistic choice than lowering short rates to historically low levels and to increase bank, business and consumer liquidity to assist the banking and financial systems in 2008 and 2009 because of very challenging developments faced by the U.S. and global economy and banking system.
- Federal government tax revenues dropped sharply in 2008 and 2009, because of declining corporate and business profits and rising unemployment. These trends will continue. Massive federal government annual budget deficits now in the trillions of dollars will get worse. All taxes will go up, but the level and rate of increase in federal and state government spending will be forced to moderate significantly moving forward as we will see in Chapter 9.
- State and local governments all face major budget deficits and will be required by law to balance their budgets, either by reduced spending or raising taxes. This problem will become worse moving forward, adding to rising unemployment and much slower than normal economic growth in the years ahead.
- Rising taxes also will further contribute to reduced consumer and business spending, investment and much slower than normal economic growth.
- As a result of the pressure to reduce costs, businesses and corporations have had no choice but to reduce the wages and benefits for many of the employees who still have their jobs, in addition to laying off large numbers of employees. This trend will intensify over the next several years. Consumers will be demanding lower prices and more substantial discounts in the years ahead.
- Commercial, industrial, farm and ranch real estate and commodity market values will decline substantially for many of the same reasons that home real estate and stock market values declined in 2008 and 2009. When further real estate, stock market and commodity market price deflation takes place, these asset classes will not recover quickly. When these asset classes do bottom out, they will remain relatively flat and will increase in value only slowly over a period of years. This is the major difference in the **V** versus the **L** economic downturn and recovery we discussed in Chapter 1.

Chapter 5
What will Cause the U.S. Modern Day Economic Depression and Stagnation in 2010-2014?

In this chapter, we will examine key factors that will cause the U.S. economy to experience a *modern day* economic depression and prolonged stagnation period in 2010-2014. It will be much more serious and painful than most Americans have already experienced in 2008 and 2009. It is important to remember that 2008-2014 will be an **L**-shaped economic downturn and recovery lasting about seven years or longer. Many economists and U.S. citizens expect a **V**-shaped downturn and quick recovery from the 2008-2009 Great Recession because most know only the previous *11* relatively short recessions that have occurred in the U.S. since 1940. All *11* were **V**-shaped economic downturns and recoveries lasting between *six* and *16* months or *10.2* months on average.

We also will look more closely at a *new normal* for Americans that will be shaped by lost jobs and lost wealth. The next five to seven years and beyond will recast our expectations for economic growth, income, employer-provided benefits, spending, savings, employment, wealth status and standard of living. Consumers, families, businesses and federal, state and local governments will be significantly changed as a result.

Here are the forces that will plunge the U.S. economy into a prolonged *modern day* depression and period of stagnation in 2010-2014. The three years of 2010-2012 will likely be the most painful as most of the major economic and financial pressures, changes and emotional pain hits *all of us*.

The Coming Part II U.S. Bank Deleveraging, Debt and Credit Default, Write-down and Write-off Crisis

The U.S. economic, banking and financial system already has gone through a very serious and partial *meltdown* that began in the second half of 2008. *I refer to this as the U.S. banking and financial system crisis, Part I*. Quick and massive actions by the Federal Reserve, the U.S. Treasury, Congress and the Bush and Obama White Houses in 2008-2009 helped avert a complete collapse of the U.S. banking and financial system and of our economy. Many people believed in the second half of 2009 that these swift and major actions prevented the U.S. from going into an economic depression. What many do not understand, however, is that a far more serious, damaging and longer lasting storm is still headed for America in 2010-2014 as further consequences of the decades-long borrowing, leveraging and spending binge unfold. The odds of this happening are at least **90%**. Most of the impact and damage of this next storm will likely be felt in 2010-2012. There will be very little, if anything, that can be done about it. The Federal Reserve, the U.S. Treasury, Congress and the White House will be virtually powerless to stop it. *They are going to run out of bullets (money) in the 2010-2014 time period as discussed in Chapter 9.*

Federal Deposit Insurance Corporation (FDIC) data in Figure 5.1 shows there has been a great deal of consolidation in U.S. commercial banking since 1990. Total numbers of commercial banks in the U.S., for example, dropped from **12,343** in 1990 to **7,085** in 2008. This represents a decline of **5,258** banks or a total decline of about **43%** in just **19** years. Mergers and acquisitions among large, medium and smaller banks account for most of this net decline and have created banking behemoths such as Bank of America, Chase-JP Morgan, U.S. Bank, Citibank and the Wells Fargo Bank. Today, the **10** largest commercial banks account for about **50%** of all U.S. commercial bank deposits and checking accounts. This represents a major amount of consolidation in the U.S. banking system.

Figure 5.1
The Total Number of U.S. Commercial Banks for the 19 Years of 1990-2008
Major U. S. Bank Consolidation

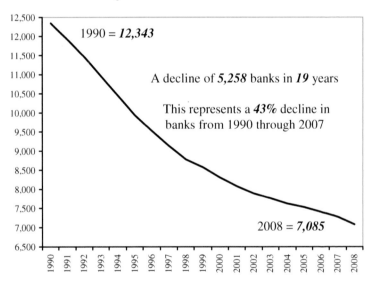

Source: Federal Deposit Insurance Corporation (FDIC)

U.S. savings and loans institutions consolidated even more quickly in those same **19** years. Their numbers, shown in Figure 5.2, dropped from **2,815** saving and loan institutions in 1990 to just *1,220* in 2008. This represents a decline of *1,595* or about *57%*. Not only were savings and loans getting larger in those nearly two decades, but Americans were saving less, as we saw in Chapter 4.

Figure 5.2
The Total Number of U.S. Saving and Loan Institutions for the 19 Years of 1990-2008
Major Saving and Loan Institution Consolidation

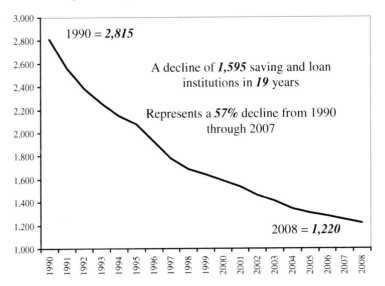

Source: Federal Deposit Insurance Corporation (FDIC)

More than five times as many banks failed in 2008 and 2009 than were closed in the preceding eight years from 2000 to 2007. As shown in Figure 5.3, the FDIC reported that there were only two, four, eleven, three, four, zero, zero and three commercial bank failures in the U.S. in 2000, 2001, 2002, 2003, 2004, 2005, 2006, 2007, respectively. However, there were *26* bank failures in 2008 and about *135* commercial bank failures in 2009. Therefore, the combined total U.S. commercial bank failures for the years 2008-2009 was about **161** according to the FDIC data. I fully expect that we will have a total of *800* to *1,200* bank failures by the time we reach 2014 for the 2008-2014 time period. This means that about *85%* of all commercial bank failures will happen within the 2010-2014 time period. This further means that at least *15%* of all the banks in the U.S. or nearly one in each six open now, will fail and become insolvent within these five years. We have not seen anything like this since the Great Depression in the 1930s.

Figure 5.3
The Total Number of U.S. Commercial Bank Failures for the Nine Years of 2000-2009

U.S. Bank Failures are Going to Increase Sharply in 2010-2014

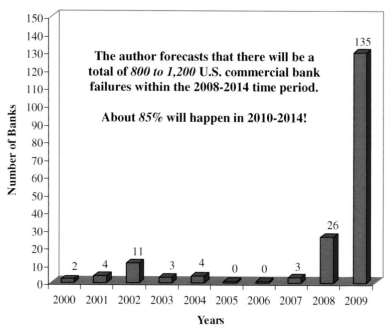

Source: Federal Deposit Insurance Corporation (FDIC)

Why Will so Many Commercial Banks Fail in 2010-2014?

As we saw in Chapter 4, everyone in the U.S. private sector got drunk on excessively easy credit terms, excessive growth in debt and credit and excessive leverage. As we also saw, the "borrow, borrow, borrow" and "spend, spend, spend" party is over. *Borrowing our way to prosperity has come to an end.* This is what always happens during the bust phase of the long-term 60- to 80-year business cycle.

This abrupt change created the beginning of a massive deleveraging process for our entire U.S. banking and financial system, including consumers and businesses. This process will take at least seven to 10 years, but much of it will occur within the years of 2010 to 2014. Our banks and the private sector borrowers will be returning to more realistic debt-to-equity ratios, such as 3, 4 or 5 to 1 for most loans. Major reductions in leverage, along with substantial

86

reductions in debt and credit growth, and much stricter credit terms will result in reduced borrowing, reduced spending and reduced investment by consumers and businesses for at least the next five to 10 years. This in turn, means much slower than normal economic growth and consumer spending and much higher than normal levels of unemployment and rates of consumer savings moving forward.

The overall reduction in leverage also will cause further very significant price and asset value deflation over the next five years. There is a *lot* more air to be let out of the home, commercial, industrial, farm and ranch real estate bubbles. There is a *lot* more air to be let out of the stock market, resulting from the bank and private sector crisis. **This is the U.S. banking and financial system crisis, Part II that will occur within the 2010-2014 time period.** The so-called **stress tests** that the U.S. Treasury Department conducted on a number of larger U.S. banks in the spring of 2009 did not even come close to revealing to the public the actual financial health and condition of the U.S. commercial banks and other lenders, particularly as it relates to their overstated balance sheets.

Profit and loss statements for most U.S. lenders currently look positive and that generally will continue. However, their balance sheets, which show the status of their assets, liabilities and equity, do **not** come anywhere close to representing reality. **Assets currently listed on many banks' balance sheets are still highly inflated and do not represent the real world.** The loan to value ratios that are used to measure institutions' equity are, in most cases, very misleading because the assets that lenders hold as collateral until loans are repaid are actually worth much less today than the amounts listed on their balance sheets in late 2009 and early 2010.

For example, with many banks, the actual price, or *real world market value,* for which they could sell homes, condominiums, apartment complexes and other residences if borrowers default on mortgages, is actually worth **25%** to **50% less** in 2009 than what many lenders show on their balance sheets. Very simply, the assets these lenders are using to gauge their own financial health are **not** reflecting the true 2009 market value, let alone what the values will likely be in 2010-2014. The same situation exists regarding all kinds of office buildings, shopping malls, factories, warehouses and other commercial and industrial real estate on which lenders have made commercial loans. These properties, much like the residential real estate market, are worth **25%** to **50%** less than the value shown on the balance sheets of most commercial banks, mortgage companies and other lenders in late 2009. This will end up also being the case for many agricultural banks and lenders relative to farm and ranchland real estate loans.

Bank owners, directors, lending officers and other executives who are watching this situation warily are hoping and expecting that the collateral they've been pledged on these loans will soon return to its former values. The bad news for these lenders, the borrowers and for our economy is that these real estate market values are going to decline significantly further over the next three to five years and will likely *not* begin to increase in value between now and 2014. This is the nature of the **L**-shaped economic downturn and recovery process that extends typically over a period of seven to 10 years, i.e. the *red light zone* discussed in Chapter 1.

Bursting bubbles of credit quality, credit default, excessive debt and credit growth and excessive leverage always result in major deflationary forces. These forces cause real estate values, stock market and commodity prices to fall, force lenders to write down or write off unrecoverable loan payments, drive consumers and businesses to bankruptcy, and produce sharp increases both in bank failure and unemployment levels. This is what we can fully expect and will very likely see during 2010-2014.

Market forces in the next five years will pressure commercial banks, mortgage companies and other lenders and investors to write down the value of their balance sheet assets by trillions of dollars. This will force the net worth of many of these lenders to go below zero and they will become insolvent. Many will be closed by the FDIC and subsequently taken over and purchased by stronger existing or new lenders. This is the basis for my forecast that by 2014 we will see at least *800* to *1,200* commercial banks and other lenders fail, wherein *85%* of these bank failures will occur within the years of 2010 and 2014. I believe this *day of reckoning* for U.S. lenders will likely hit hardest between 2010 and 2012.

As they write down assets, many lenders will not be able to secure the private equity capital required to restore their balance sheets and to remain solvent and liquid. This is why the number of commercial bank and other lender failures will be so high in 2010-2014. The last time this happened was in the 1930s. *The party is over.* Now the U.S. banking and financial system has no choice but to go through a very serious, painful and prolonged deleveraging process.

This process will also further reduce credit availability and new lending by commercial banks, mortgage lenders and other lenders in 2010-2014. This will reduce economic growth, business and corporate investment and spending, resulting in more job losses, reduced consumer spending and increased consumer savings. This deleveraging is now and will become a more ingrained part of the *new normal* that all Americans will experience for at least the next five to ten years.

Politicians, the U.S. Treasury, the Federal Reserve and the present administration naturally and predictably will attempt to solve these crises. *But the banking and financial system crisis, Part II will not be solvable by government actions.* The U.S. national debt and budget deficits are now so large that neither the money nor the political will to borrow and spend more money will be available to *bailout the banks* or *stimulate the economy.* Therefore, the policy adopted in 2008 and 2009 of *too big to fail* will be repealed and home, commercial, industrial, farm and ranch real estate asset values will keep falling until they reach realistic equilibrium levels that can be sustained by the forces of market supply and demand. The private sector deleveraging process will happen faster and will overwhelm any federal and state local government *economic stimulus* or *bailout* programs.

Farm and ranch real estate, commodities and U.S. stock market prices will continue to decline substantially during 2010-2012. The U.S. dollar will strengthen and will remain the reserve currency in the global economic and financial marketplace as discussed in Chapter 8. These developments will further compound the U.S. banking, credit default, credit quality and deleveraging crises.

Consumers, Businesses and Investors will Lose Far More Equity and Wealth in the Real Estate and Stock Markets

Consumers, businesses, investors and lenders all have lost serious and painful amounts of equity and net worth as *bursting* credit and leverage bubbles shot through the nation's residential, commercial, industrial, farm and ranch real estate markets, the stock markets, crude oil and other commodity markets. However, this financial pain and loss of equity and wealth is not over – far from it. Substantial further losses in equity and wealth will very likely occur through 2014 in America.

Figure 5.4 shows my conservative yet realistic estimates of how much equity and wealth will be lost in the markets for home real estate, stocks, commercial and industrial real estate, and farm and ranch real estate. I estimate that home real estate in the U.S. will lose 50% of its July 2006 peak value and fall to about *$11 trillion* at the low point sometime before 2014. As discussed in Chapter 4, the average decline and loss of home market equity and wealth has already been *32%* to *35%, or between $7.0* and *$7.7 trillion,* by late 2009. This has already had a major negative impact on the balance sheets of most Americans, banks and other lenders and on the economy at large. Other single family homes such as condominiums, duplexes and vacation homes also will continue to decline substantially in market value.

I also estimate that the stock market, as measured by the widely-followed Dow Jones Industrial Average (the Dow), will decline about *$13.2 trillion* resulting in a *72%* loss of wealth, from its record high of *14,164* on October 9,

2007 to a new, cyclical low between **3,500** and **4,500** sometime in the 2010-2012 time period. It is possible that the Dow will decline even further and go to the **500** to **1,500** level, the range at which it previously traded between 1956 and 1985. This will obviously hurt U.S. banks, cause U.S. consumers and businesses to spend less, borrow less and save more, and cause the growth of the U.S. economy to be much slower than normal.

Figures 5.4
What to Expect and Plan for Concerning the Major Loss of Consumer, Business and Investor Equity and Wealth in the 2008-2014 Time Period

Major Asset Classes	Years when Asset Class Values Peaked	Approximate Peak Value in each Asset Class*	Estimated Loss of Equity and Wealth**
1. Home real estate values	July, 2006	$22.0 Trillion	$11.0 Trillion
Percent decline by 2012	---	---	*50%*
2. Total combined U.S. stock market values	October, 2007	$18.5 Trillion	$13.2 Trillion
Dow High Point-	10-09-07	14,164	
Dow Low Point-	2010-2012	4,000	---
Percent decline by 2012	---	---	*72%*
3. Combined commercial and industrial real estate values	July, 2007	$6.5 Trillion	$3.3 Trillion
Percent decline by 2014	---	---	*50%*
4. Farm and ranch real estate values	July, 2008	$2.0 Trillion	$1.2 Trillion
Percent decline by 2014	---	---	*35%*
Total	---	**$49.0 Trillion**	$28.7 Trillion
Percent decline overall	---	---	*59%*

*The *Source* of these asset class values is the Federal Reserve Board, Moody's Investor Service, Standard and Poor's, Case-Shiller Home Price Indices, the New York Stock Exchange and the USDA.

** Estimated by the author.

The Dow declined to about **6,500** on March 9, 2009 and then rebounded substantially to about the **10,400** to **10,800** level in October and November, 2009. As discussed in Chapter 10, I expect the Dow to top out within about the **10,800** to **11,500** range in the February-April, 2010 time period before beginning to decline significantly for the balance of 2010 and continuing its decent into 2011. My full expectation and forecast is that the Part II U.S. banking, credit and deleveraging crises in 2010-2014, along with bursting credit, debt and real estate bubbles in the private sector, will drive the Dow down to new lows in the **3,500** to **4,500** range, or lower, sometime in 2010-2012. I expect the bulk of the U.S. stock market decline to occur during the second half of 2010 through the first half of 2012. These developments will cause unemployment to continue to go higher and stay relatively high for at least five years. Loan delinquencies and defaults will accelerate, consumer spending will moderate further and U.S. economic growth will remain much less than normal, including some quarters of negative economic growth. All of this will result in the U.S. stock markets declining further to adjust to lower business and corporate sales and profits, respectively, within the next three years.

I further expect average annual commercial and industrial real estate values to decline by at least **40%** to **60%** from the high point to the low point. This decline represents a **$3.3 trillion** loss of equity and wealth by the time we get to the year 2014. These losses could easily be more than what I am forecasting. Many commercial banks, including many smaller and medium size community banks and mortgage companies, will become insolvent as a result of the very significant declines in overall real estate values in 2010-2014. Many of these real estate loans will not be renewed. At best, they will be restructured, but lenders, borrowers and investors alike will be forced to make very painful adjustments, go through bankruptcies and lose equity and wealth in the process. Again, the deleveraging process is real and will continue to be a very painful process that will take five to seven years or longer to run its course.

I also estimate conservatively that farm and ranch real estate values will decline about **$1.2 trillion**, as I've shown in Figure 5.4. This represents a total loss of equity and wealth of **35%** from the high point in early 2008 to the low point somewhere in 2012 to 2014. Average farm and ranchland values already fell **3.2%** between January 1, 2008 and January 1, 2009, according to the U.S. Department of Agriculture. This represents the first time that average annual farm and ranchland values have declined since 1987.

As shown in Figure 5.4, I fully expect and am forecasting that the total combined loss of equity and wealth for investors in these four key real estate and stock market asset classes will be $28 trillion to $29 trillion, which represents a total decline of 59% in American wealth and net worth. No one since 1940 has seen losses this huge. Most business and financial models, plans and budgets do not account for anywhere close to this level of lost wealth and equity or the impact that such losses have on employment, investment, spending and economic growth and lost tax revenues. The same is true for consumers, families and for our federal, state and local governments. **The long-term boom and bust business cycle is alive and well. We entered the early stages of the next major *bust* portion of this business cycle in 2008 and 2009.** But the most painful portion of this *bust* phase relative to major asset and price deflationary forces has yet to come. The *Part II banking and financial crisis is still ahead of us in 2010-2014*.

The Wealthiest Americans will be the Hardest Hit in 2008-2014

Wealthy Americans will suffer the largest losses of wealth and equity during the 2008-2014 bust. According to the IRS, the top *10%* of all U.S. income earners accounted for about *50%* of all personal income and paid about *72%* of all federal personal and individual income taxes in 2008. In contrast, the bottom *50%* of all U.S. income earners in 2008 accounted for about *13.5%* of Americans' personal income and paid *2.9%* of all federal personal and individual income taxes collected. The financial health, income, net worth and wealth of the top *10%* income earners in America has had and will continue to have a major impact on our economy during the next five to ten years. These top income earners have been the big spenders, major investors and major employers for the past *30* years. That is now changing in a big way. These are the same people who have generally been seriously hurt by the major decline in the asset values shown in Figure 5.4. Consequently, they will be investing significantly less, employing fewer persons, and spending much less than they did before 2008. These changes will have a profound impact on our economy and will contribute heavily to much higher than normal unemployment in the U.S. in 2010-2014.

In the fiscal year ended September 30, 2008, the U.S. federal government collected *$2.524 trillion* in total tax receipts, according to the Congressional Budget Office (CBO). That number dropped in fiscal 2009 by *17%*, or *$418 billion*, to *$2.106 trillion*, CBO calculated in a preliminary estimate. At the same time, the federal government *budget deficit* for fiscal 2009 increased to *$1.409 trillion*. This represents the biggest absolute and percentage year-to-year decline in federal government income tax receipts and by far the largest annual one-year budget deficit ever. Driving those numbers are: (1) the sharply rising number of Americans who have lost their jobs and the millions who are underemployed, (2) the substantial decline in the wealth, net worth and incomes of the top *10%* income earners in the United States and whose tax payments account for *72%* of all federal personal and individual income taxes collected, (3) the significant decrease in consumer spending and the significant increase in the rate of consumer saving and (4) the much slower than normal rate of U.S. economic growth in 2008 and 2009. I expect these same forces will continue negatively impacting the U.S. economy during 2010-2014.

CBO also estimates that the U.S. federal budget deficit more than tripled in fiscal 2009, soaring to *$1.409 trillion* from *$459 billion* a year earlier. These annual budget deficits of over *one trillion dollars* are *not* sustainable. That means either federal government spending will need to be reduced substantially, federal government taxes will have to be increased significantly, or some combination of the two will occur. This has important implications that we will explore in Chapter 9.

The U.S. experienced *11* recessions during the 68-year boom from 1940 to 2007. Each of these recessions followed a **V**-shaped downturn and recovery path that lasted an average of only *10.2* months. Home real estate, commercial, industrial, farm and ranch real estate and stock market values suffered relatively modest and temporary losses in equity and wealth during those downturns. Average annual farm and ranchland real estate values dropped sharply in the mid 1980s and are a major exception to the pattern of otherwise modest and short-lived economic setbacks since 1940.

All this changed beginning in 2008. U.S. home, commercial and industrial real estate markets and stock markets fell farther and across more of the nation than at any time since the 1930s. Decline, deflation and the loss of equity and wealth will deepen even further in 2010-2014. I believe most of this decline will happen in the three years of 2010-2012. The collapse of multiple credit, debt and leverage bubbles that started the downturn will continue through at least 2010-2012 and perhaps longer. Bottom line, my estimated total loss of equity and wealth of about *$28.7 trillion* by or before 2014 will disproportionately impact the wealthy. Hence the *top 10%* of the U.S. income earners will suffer greater losses than the rest of the American population. Therefore, there will be less investment, less hiring of employees, reduced spending, slower than normal U.S. economic growth and major reductions in federal income taxes collected over the next five to 10 years. These top 10% income earners represent the major capitalists in America today. This is well covered in Chapter 9.

Major losses of equity, wealth and income among the top 10% of the nation's income earners also will result in continued major declines in federal tax collections during at least the next five years, because more than *70%* of the collected money comes from those highest income earners relative to individual and personal income taxes paid. Budget deficits will in turn become much larger than the members of Congress, the current administration, the U.S. Treasury, the Federal Reserve and the American people are now expecting or planning for. This will force the federal government and Congress to begin reducing spending substantially, which will be a good thing. Americans will come to realize and understand better than they ever have before that the financial load in terms of federal government income tax revenue collections depend heavily on the financial health and well-being of the wealthy in America. When this locomotive engine weakens, the entire U.S. economy is broadly and seriously affected, including collection of the tax revenues needed to fund federal spending programs that millions of Americans depend on. We will discuss this further in Chapter 9.

In addition, the *78 million* baby boomers will be spending less, saving more and downsizing over the next 10 to 20 years. This process began in 2008-2009, but will intensify between 2010-2022. This will have a significant impact.

U.S. Unemployment Rates will Reach Heights Not Seen Since 1940 and Will Remain Much Higher Than Normal

The bursting of the many credit, debt and leverage bubbles that began in 2008, along with the prolonged *Part II* banking and financial crisis of the next five or more years, will continue to push American unemployment to agonizingly high levels through at least 2012. Figure 5.5 shows how the average annual number of people unemployed in the U.S. has fluctuated in the **72** years from 1942 to 2012. In 1961, the number of Americans that were unemployed was *4.7 million*. The average annual unemployment rate was *6.7%*. In 1983, the number of Americans that were unemployed was *10.7 million* with an average annual unemployment rate of *9.7%*. I conservatively estimate that in January-March, 2010, the number of unemployed Americans will reach at least the *10.5* to *10.8 million* level with an unemployment rate of *10.2%* or higher.

Figures 5.5
Average Annual Number of People Unemployed
in the U.S. for the 72-years from 1942-2012
Within the Year 2012, about 18,600,000 people will have lost their jobs via a standard unemployment rate of about 12.2%

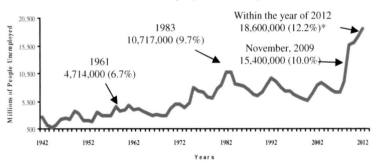

Source: U.S. Department of Labor
*Forecasted by the author.

94

I estimate that the number of Americans that will be unemployed will be close to *18.6 million* with an unemployment rate near *12.2%* within the year of 2012. These levels of unemployment in America are highly likely and will result in a lot of financial and emotional pain for millions of Americans, for businesses and for our U.S. economy, banks and other lenders and for federal, state and local governments. Bottom line, the major economic, banking and financial problems resulting from the rising unemployment in 2008 and 2009 will continue and will get significantly worse in 2010-2012.

Figure 5.6
The *Real* and Effective Rate of U.S. Unemployment is much Higher than the *Standard* Reported Unemployment Numbers (Both Numbers are Published by the U.S. Department of Labor)

Key Unemployment Categories	Actual Figures for November, 2009	Estimated Figures for within the Year of 2012*
1. The *standard* U.S. unemployment numbers published by the Bureau of Labor Statistics, U.S. Department of Labor	15,400,000 10.0%	18,600,000 12.2%
2. The *real and effective* U.S. unemployment numbers also published by the Bureau of Labor Statistics, U.S. Department of Labor**	26,600,000 17.3%	32,200,000 20.0%

*Estimated by the author.

**Includes total unemployed persons, plus all marginally attached workers who currently are neither working nor looking for work, but are persons who want and are available for a job and have looked for work sometime in the recent past, plus discouraged job seekers who would like to have a job, plus the underemployed (people working part-time or for much less income and reduced benefits than they want or need).

Figure 5.6 shows a more *realistic* unemployment picture. The Bureau of Labor statistics[15] each month publishes *both standard* and *real* estimates of the number of people in America that are unemployed and a corresponding

---

[15] U.S. Department of Labor

unemployment rate for both estimates. *Standard* estimates generally measure jobless workers actively seeking new jobs. *Real* estimates count those workers, plus millions more who are underemployed or have given up active job searches. In November, 2009, for example, the *standard* number of Americans out of work was *15.4 million*, with an unemployment rate of *10.0%*. The *real* number of Americans out of work that month was actually *26.6 million*, with an unemployment rate of *17.3%*. This *11.2 million* represents an increase in unemployed people above the *standard* number of *15.4 million* published for November, 2009. The difference between the *standard* and the higher *real* or effective unemployment number is *typically* between *72%* and *74%*. This is very significant.

Atlanta Federal Reserve Bank president Dennis Lockhart said on August 26, 2009 in a speech he gave to the Chattanooga (Tenn.) Area Chamber of Commerce, "If one considers the people who would like a job but have stopped looking—so-called discouraged workers—and those who are working fewer hours than they want, the unemployment rate would move from the official 9.4% to 16%." What I believe Dennis Lockhart is saying is that the difference between the *9.4%* and the *16%* unemployment rate numbers is *71%*. In other words, the *16%* unemployment rate number is *71%* higher than the *9.4%* number. As of July, 2009, the *9.4%* number represents the *standard* unemployment rate and the *16%* number represents the *real or effective* rate as reported by the U.S. Department of Labor. In addition, the real and effective unemployment numbers also account for the millions of men and women in the U.S. who are underemployed on a monthly basis.

How does the U.S. Department of Labor calculate and define the *real* level and effective rate of unemployment each month? The *real* number includes the total number of unemployed Americans, plus all marginally attached workers who currently are neither working nor looking for work, but are persons who want and are available for a job and have looked for work sometime in the recent past, plus discouraged job seekers who would like to have a job, plus the underemployed (people working part-time or for much less income than they want or need).

Millions of American men and women today are substantially under-employed. These are Americans, young and old, who want and need jobs, but are forced by slow economic growth and the bursting of economic bubbles to work for much less income, fewer hours and with fewer job benefits than they enjoyed between 1990 and 2007. This is very significant because a growing number of the *90%* of Americans who did have jobs in late 2009 will be facing reduced incomes and benefits in 2010-2014. These trends will contribute to the

2010-2014 time period being a *modern day* depression and prolonged period of economic stagnation in the U.S.

As shown in Figure 5.6, I conservatively estimate that the U.S. Department of Labor **standard** number for within the year of 2012 will be about **18.6 million** Americans out of work, pushing the unemployment rate to near **12.2%**. This will be by far the highest and most painful rate of unemployment that Americans will have experienced since the Great Depression years of 1930-1939. I also estimate that the **real** unemployment numbers for America will be about **32.2 million** with a **real** and effective unemployment rate of about **20%** within the year of 2012. **Standard** and **real** unemployment levels in America in 2010-2012 will result in a lot of financial and emotional pain for all Americans, for businesses and for our federal, state and local governments. These trends will become an important part of the *new normal* in America moving forward.

Bottom line, consumers will be spending less and saving more in 2010-2014. This is a major and very important change. Our U.S. economy and its growth are heavily dependent on the level and on the rate of consumer spending. Consumer spending in the past several years accounted for **70%** to **71%** of GDP. As consumer spending moderates and stays lower than normal, which it will over at least the next five to seven years, the rate of unemployment will stay at much higher than normal levels for at least those same five to seven years.

Four Key Developments in 1980-2006 Delayed the Inevitable

The U.S. and global economy is large and complex. As we saw in Chapter 2, history is clear that there typically are *60 to 80* years in the *boom* phase of the long-term business cycle and usually *seven to 10* years in the *bust* phase. The key financial excesses that build up over time, as we saw in Chapter 4 and in this chapter, eventually result in major real estate and financial asset bubbles bursting. Major losses of wealth and net worth follow the bursting, along with general price deflation, zero inflation or much less than normal rates of inflation. Sometimes, however, economic, financial or political developments, trends and policies cause the *boom* phase to last longer than normal.

I believe the 1940-2007 or *68-year boom* phase of our long-term business cycle would likely have been somewhat shorter *if* the following four key economic and financial trends had not happened:

- Major growth in global trade, financing and economic interdependence from the 1980s through 2006 was very positive for the U.S. economy. It resulted, for example, in improved economic GDP growth, job creation and incomes, increased real estate and stock market asset values, higher standards of living, increased profits and greater tax revenues for federal, state and local governments. This growth across so broad a spectrum lengthened the time for the 1940-2007 U.S. economic *boom* beyond what it likely would otherwise have been.

- The **78 million** baby boomers reached the peak spending and investment stages of their lives during 1980-2006, which also was a major contributor prolonging the *boom*.

- The rapid development and growth of new technologies throughout the U.S. economy had a very important impact on the positive GDP growth in our economy during 1980-2006. New jobs were created and we had improved productivity gains and better wages and a higher standard of living in the U.S. because of the development and use of these many new technologies throughout America such as the internet and the highly advanced computers and software packages. Without them, the 1940-2007 *boom* would likely have ended sooner than it did.

- The rapid growth of easy and excessive credit terms, the excessive growth of private sector credit and debt and the excessive growth of leverage also clearly increased the length of the 1940-2007 *boom*, particularly from 1990 to 2006.

The Bottom Line...

The average annual rate of real GDP economic growth in the U.S. will be much slower than normal in 2008-2014. The *1.5%* to *2.0%* average annual rate of economic growth which I am forecasting for this period will result in our economy being classified by the National Bureau of Economic Research as a depression or at least a prolonged period of serious economic stagnation for a period of about seven years. Consumer spending will be much slower than normal in these years. Unemployment and consumer savings will be much higher than normal. Growing numbers of Americans will experience a reduced standard of living. These developments and trends will result in a *new normal* for Americans for at least the next five to ten years.

With general and persistent price and asset CPI deflation over most of the 2009-2020 time period as discussed in Chapter 7, businesses will have essentially no pricing power relative to being able to raise prices of the goods and services they sell moving forward. Most businesses will find that they will have no choice but to reduce prices in order to get consumers to buy. This will negatively impact profits. This will also, therefore, cause most businesses to reduce costs and overhead expenses further. This means that many U.S. businesses will reduce labor costs more by laying off additional people and/or reducing salaries, hourly wages and benefits, particularly within the 2010-2014 time period and beyond. One of the key results of general price deflation is rising and persistently high and painful unemployment levels in the U.S. over at least the next three to five years. You should plan accordingly.

Chapter 6
How will the 2010-2014 U.S. Modern Day Economic Depression and Stagnation Impact You?

Businesses, banks and governments are not the only forces shaping the economy. What we do as individuals counts too. Now let us examine steps that each of us can take in the next five to seven years both to mitigate some of the pain of the 2010-2014 U.S. *modern day* depression and to realize some of the opportunities that also will be part of the *new normal economy*.

Specifically, this chapter addresses (1) private and public sector workers, (2) privately and publicly owned businesses, organizations and institutions, (3) retirees and (4) the elected officials and policymakers in federal, state and local governments in the United States. The goal herein is to better understand, prepare for and take advantage of *new normal* economic and financial conditions that all Americans will be dealing with during the second decade of the 21st century.

Plan and Prepare for the Unexpected

It is human nature and normal to plan for the future based on past experience. In our nation, that experience economically has been forged primarily by *11 V-shaped* recessions since 1940, mere bumps in the road that have lasted for an average of *10.2 months* with only modest and short-lived slower economic growth and higher unemployment. We all have a journey in life. That journey consists of hopes, dreams, visions and expectations. Based on past experiences and expectations for the future, Americans generally are *not* planning to encounter a *modern day* depression or prolonged stagnation in our economy. If this occurs between now and 2014, as I fully expect it to, *I strongly recommend that you plan and prepare now for an unexpected new normal that may last for the next five to 10 years.* This is why I have written this book.

Prepare for much slower than normal economic growth, reduced consumer spending and much higher than normal unemployment in 2010-2014. Plan for the major economic and financial forces discussed in Chapters 4 and 5 to reduce the average annual rate of U.S. economic growth to within the *1.5%* and *2.0%* range between 2008 and 2014. Expect the level of standard unemployment to rise to within *10%* and *12%* between 2010 and 2012 and for the rate of real and effective unemployment to be within the *17%* and *20%* range for the same three-year time period.

Most Americans alive today have *not* experienced a five- to seven-year period of such protracted slow growth or high unemployment. The last time this happened was during the 1930s in the 10-year Great Depression. Beginning in 2008-2009 and continuing during the five years of 2010-2014, economic and financial conditions will be significantly different and much more challenging than most Americans alive today have ever experienced. I recommend that you plan now to prepare for what it really means to experience a *new normal* through an **L**-shaped downturn and recovery. Below are the things I recommend that you prepare for and seriously consider:

A. *For private and government employees, families and retirees:*

- Do everything you can to keep your job. Work extra hard, show up early and leave late. Be more productive and work smarter than you ever have before. Help your employer survive and succeed through these difficult economic times that will last for years. *Make a concerted effort to become and remain a **necessity** in the eyes of your employer.*

- Be prepared for the distinct possibility that you may lose your job with very little warning. This applies to almost all sectors of the U.S. economy.

- Consider the very real possibility that you or other members of your family might become one of the millions of *underemployed workers* within these years. You might have a fulltime or part-time job, but your income will be considerably less than what it was two to five years ago and perhaps much less than what you and your family may need to cover your living expenses. You may be dealing with the painful reality of loan delinquencies, late payment fees, high interest rates and possible foreclosure on a home or auto loan.

- Prepare for the possibility that your wages may be reduced by *10%* to *25%* and your bonus may be eliminated, reduced or postponed. Prepare for your children having more difficulty finding jobs upon graduation from high school and college during the next five years. Plan on your children, out of economic necessity, needing to stay and live at home longer than they and you had originally planned for.

- Be prepared for the possibility that your employee benefits might be reduced, postponed or even eliminated. Prepare for the possibility of paying more or all the cost of your own healthcare premiums.

- When employees pay for all or at least half of their health insurance premiums, they will have a major incentive to find ways to increase competition and lower costs. Prepare for both employees and employers to orchestrate a competitive bidding process for buying health insurance. This will encourage more competition and lower healthcare insurance premium costs in the future.

- Expect unemployment to remain much higher and for longer than it has been since 1940. Plan on few U.S. companies hiring new employees or rehiring previous employees. This will be in sharp contrast to what most Americans experienced during and following the 11 short recessions in the U.S. since 1940.
- Prepare for standards of living to decline for growing numbers of Americans. Economic and financial conditions in the U.S. and around the world will force most consumers and businesses to become more frugal. There will be some positive things resulting from this trend, but for the most part, these adjustments will be difficult and painful. It will take five to 10 years for Americans to adjust to reduced standards of living. Many will be surprised how long it will take for the U.S. and global economy to stabilize. Significant *belt tightening* will be the norm for the next five years and quite possibly longer.
- Plan for discretionary spending to decline sharply over the next five years. Consumers are consciously reevaluating their purchases of what they considered as *necessities* just a few years ago. Persistently high unemployment, vanishing income and benefits and falling home values and retirement savings will result in some of the following outcomes:

1. Auto purchases and leases will decline as drivers keep their current automobiles longer.

2. Fewer homes will be purchased, less furniture will be bought, and increased demand will make apartments harder to find.

3. Food sales will suffer as consumers choose less expensive food items in the grocery store and dine out less often.

4. Spending on medical care will be reduced or postponed, especially for elective surgical procedures such as dental work and annual physicals. Insurance costs will rise as more people postpone treatment.

5. Air travel and hotel bookings will decline as fewer people take vacations.

6. Fewer students will attend private colleges or out-of-state colleges. More will choose two-year junior and local colleges and more teenagers will try to find jobs to help out at home or with college expenses.

7. Charitable giving and donations will be reduced.

8. Recreational spending on entertainment such as plays, musicals, movies, sports games and golf will decline, along with spending on

clothes, jewelry, home furnishings, arts and crafts and country clubs.

9. Businesses will be forced to reduce costs by more than they have had to for many years. Doing so will mean the difference between surviving and not surviving in the future for many businesses. They will reduce borrowing, cut more and higher paying jobs, do less hiring and cut advertising, travel and other budgets to reduce overhead expenses.

- Plan to spend and borrow less. Demand lower prices. Take advantage of major discounts, including those on *big ticket items* such as homes, apartment rentals and cars. Reduce your debt and save as much as possible.
- Be prepared to postpone retirement and work longer. Do *not* count on receiving a company pension and do not count on Social Security payments satisfying your retirement income needs in the years ahead. Do not count on Social Security even being available when you retire. Plan to fund your own retirement.
- Prepare to pay significantly higher federal, state and local government taxes in the years ahead.
- Prepare to provide more collateral relative to any money that you may want to borrow in the future. Lenders will be loaning less money and requiring larger down payments and more equity in the years ahead, compared to the past *20* years.
- Plan to live much more frugally and to save significantly more money on a regular basis. This is basic to the *new normal* in 2010-2014 and likely for much longer.
- Expect the U.S. average annual home market values in the U.S. to decline **45%** to **55%** from their July, 2006 peaks by 2012. The actual declines will vary region to region, but all homeowners will experience substantial reductions in wealth, net worth and borrowing capacity. Do not plan on the value of your home increasing much or perhaps at all during the next 10 years. Prepare for your home being worth less than what you currently owe on it, if that has not already happened. Plan for your home being the place where you live and raise a family, not as an investment as many people have been doing over the past 25 years.
- Be prepared for the U.S. stock market to fall to new lows within the 2010-2012 time period. I estimate that the Dow will decline to **3,500** to **4,500** and may even go as low as **500** to **1,500** by 2012.
- Brace for longer lasting lows in stock market prices than many investors are prepared for now. Lost jobs, declining home values and tighter credit all will cause consumers to spend much less and save

more in the years ahead. Investors and traders are counting on spending resuming quickly and producing a **V**-shaped downturn and recovery. That will not happen and the U.S. economy will experience an **L**-shaped downturn and recovery instead. As discussed in Chapter 1, prepare for and plan on the *red light zone*.

- I recommend that anyone still in the U.S. stock market seriously consider getting completely out no later than February-April, 2010. This includes selling any stock held in your 401(k) or other retirement plans. Prepare to begin investing in U.S. stocks again when the Dow gets down to the *3,500* to *4,500* range. At that time, consult with your stockbroker or financial advisor for appropriate stocks and other diversified investment advice as discussed in Chapter 10.

- *Plan to place a high priority on protecting the return of your available cash and investment capital.* I recommend that you seriously consider putting your available investment capital into cash investments, such as FDIC-insured bank Certificates of Deposit (CDs), 30-year U.S. Government Treasury Bonds, Treasury Notes, Treasury Bills, high quality and carefully selected investment grade corporate bonds and very carefully selected insurance company fixed rate annuities. The financial return on your cash and investment capital should *not* be a top priority until we get past the 2010-2014 time period and at minimum until we get past the 2010-2012 time period.

- Plan for interest rates on savings accounts, bank CDs, U.S. Treasury securities and other cash investments to be very low. This will be a painful reality for most retirees on fixed incomes in 2010-2014. The good news for these same people will be general price deflation, zero inflation or much lower than normal rates of inflation during the next five to seven years, as we will examine in Chapter 7. This means that the cost of living and of doing business will be lower than usual. This will also help retirees and others on fixed incomes.

- Be very patient in buying a home and all other real estate. Most home and condo prices will likely decline further between now and 2012. Rental rates for houses, condos, duplexes and apartments will also decline during this period. It will be a *buyers' and renters' market.* Plan accordingly. Be patient and negotiate for lower prices. Take time in 2010-2014 to look for good deals on new and used homes, autos, furniture and home furnishings, appliances, clothing, food, medical services and for many other things you might want to buy. General price deflationary forces will be your friend during these *years and will represent a new normal.*

- Seek variable interest rates rather than fixed rates when you borrow money for *big ticket* items such as homes, cars, remodeling or appliances between now and 2014. Do *not* fix interest rates and pay a substantial premium. Find a monthly variable and floating interest rate tied to the New York prime rate. Pay off all your credit card balances as soon as you possibly can. Cash will be king for you and your family in 2010-2014.

- Improve your credit score and provide more cash or other equity for down payments on *big ticket* purchases. The days of easy credit terms are over. Getting a new loan will be much more difficult over the next five years than it has been in the last 20 years.

- Expect crude oil, gasoline and energy prices to stay relatively low between now and 2014. The typical trading range for crude oil prices will likely be within the *$30* to *$80* per barrel range. This translates into *$1.50* to *$2.70* per gallon for unleaded gasoline in the United States central Midwest. It is possible that crude oil prices will reach the *$5* to *$15* per barrel range for a short time within 2010-2014. It also is possible they will reach *$90* to *$110* per barrel for a short time within those same five years.

- Prepare for significant increases in crime, civil unrest and riots, largely stemming from years-long abnormally high unemployment levels. Plan for more home and car break-ins and theft. If you have not already done so, invest in a home security and alarm system. Keep in mind that *35%* of Americans lived on farms in the 1930s Great Depression. Today only, *2%* to *3%* of all Americans live on farms. This represents a large difference.

B. *For private sector businesses, banks, other lenders, their owners, managers, and executives, plus all other organizations and institutions in general:*

- Maintain a very *high* priority on increased productivity throughout your company. Remain more focused on reducing labor, payroll, employee and other overhead costs in the months and years ahead. This includes all trade organizations, colleges and universities, churches, hospitals and all other organizations and institutions.

- Plan to shift all or a major portion of your healthcare insurance premium costs to your employees to encourage competition and to reduce your overhead expenses. Work closely with your employees in obtaining competitive bids from eight to 10 health insurers to increase competition and to reduce costs.

- Prepare for the rate of economic growth and consumer spending to be much slower than normal. *Do not count on the level of American consumer spending to bail out the U.S. economy or your business. This will not happen.* Plan for annual sales to be lower or increase much more slowly over the next five years, compared to the last 20 years.

- Expect U.S. consumers to respond to lower prices, major discounts and what they perceive as *bargains* on *big and little ticket* items. Assume your company will have very little or no power to pass higher prices and costs on to consumers. American consumers will spend less, save more and will generally be much more frugal than they have been in the past 25 years.

- Plan for general price deflation, zero inflation or much lower than normal inflation over the next five years and beyond. The *new normal* economic environment for businesses in these years will be focused on maintaining margins and improving profits by reducing costs and improving productivity. *Do not plan on escalating inflation to bail out your company or the U.S. economy. This will not happen.* Plan on year-to-year declines in actual price deflation over most of the next 10 years as discussed in Chapter 7.

- Expect an overall downward shift in consumer demand on many fronts as U.S. consumers watch pennies more closely than at any time since at least 1981-1983. For example, Americans love beef. But to save money, they will purchase even more ground beef and less steak than in the past to satisfy their desire for good quality and nutritious protein. Similarly, they will choose to rent rather than own, drive rather than fly and in general opt for the more budget-conscious choice on most decisions they make. The impact will be very disappointing retail sales and generally reduced margins and net operating profits across the board in the United States over the next five years.

- Do not expect consumer spending to return to 1990-2007 levels anytime in the next 10 years. As discussed in Chapters 4 and 5, **the consumer and business "borrow, borrow, borrow and spend, spend, spend" party is over**. The excessively easy credit terms, excessive growth of credit and debt and the excessive leverage that fueled the party is also over.

- Plan on needing much more cash and equity moving forward. Lenders will be loaning less money in the next five to 10 years than in the last 20. Lending standards and requirements will become much tighter. Expect difficulty and be prepared for less credit and less leverage in the next 10 years. Plan on the major deleveraging process for both borrower and lender to continue for the next 10 years. As a reminder, deleveraging simply means that the borrower is required to put up significantly more cash or equity moving forward than was the case between 1990 and 2007. For example, for most businesses who want to make a real estate purchase or a major capital improvement moving forward, it is going to require 20% down as opposed to only 5%, 10% or less before.

- Expect lenders to be much more focused during the next 10 years on (1) your cash flow, (2) your true monthly and annual profit and loss statements and (3) on your balance sheet. Banks and other lenders especially will be challenging the true value of the assets shown on their customers' balance sheets in the deflationary environment now at work. For example, all lenders will be carefully comparing the real estate and inventory values reported by borrowers against current actual marketplace values for those assets. In the *new normal* economy of the near future, expect many lenders to discount these asset market values by **25%** to **50%** when extending credit or making new loans. Almost all banks and lenders are aware that their own balance sheets are *overstated* significantly because of the declining asset values of the collateral pledged by their borrowers as discussed in Chapter 5.

- Expect lender appraisals moving forward to be much more realistic and consequently much lower than during the last 20 years. Also plan on the loan-to-value ratios approved by lenders to be far narrower and conservative than before. This will be part of the overall deleveraging process banks, businesses and consumers are going through.

- Prepare for the further significant decline of home, commercial, industrial, farm and ranch real estate values. The same is true for commodity, stock market and inventory values. These developments will *significantly* further reduce the net worth of most private businesses. This will make it much more difficult for those businesses to maintain or to increase existing borrowing, let alone add to it. Business and corporate spending and investment will continue to slow as a result. *Easy credit terms are a thing of the past.* All private sector businesses, organizations and institutions should prepare accordingly for at least the next seven to 10 years.

- I strongly recommend that you *not* plan on higher rates of inflation within the 2010-2014 time period. This is not likely to happen. Prepare for significant price and asset deflation for at least the next five years, as discussed in Chapter 7.

- Give top priority through the first quarter of 2010 to *nailing down* any business loans and operating credit lines that you need as soon as possible. I strongly believe that during the second half of 2010 and beyond, it will become increasingly much more difficult to get this done successfully.

- Plan for the strong possibility that one or more of your existing banks or other lenders will fail in the next five years. As discussed in Chapter

5, I expect that *800* to *1,200* commercial banks will fail in the U.S. by the year 2014.

- Be very patient when buying or leasing anything during the next five to seven years. Those years will see *buyers'* and *renters'* markets for most *big ticket* items as well as for office space, equipment, machinery and other major leased material. *You will be handsomely rewarded for your patience.* You can expect general price deflation, zero inflation or much lower than normal rates of inflation over the next five to seven years. Plan for further significant declines in many major asset classes that will create the opportunity for good value purchases and leases for businesses. Sharpen your negotiating skills.

- Plan for an **L**-shaped not a **V**-shaped economic downturn and recovery period. I believe the likelihood of this happening is *90%* and just the opposite of what most people and most business owners and managers are thinking and planning for in 2010 and beyond.

- Plan on crude oil, gasoline and energy prices to stay relatively low between now and 2014. The typical trading range for crude oil prices will likely be within the *$30* to *$80* per barrel range. This translates into *$1.50* to *$2.70* per gallon for unleaded gasoline in the central Midwest region of the United States. It is possible that crude oil prices will reach the *$5* to *$15* per barrel range for a short period in 2010-2014. It is also possible that we will briefly see *$90* to *$110* per barrel as well.

- Place a much higher priority on security of various kinds and protect your banks, property, equipment, machinery, autos, trucks and inventory more than you have in the past. Prepare for theft attempts because of much higher than normal levels of unemployment and underemployment, plus all the other difficult economic conditions that I have outlined in this book.

- Expect even more federal, state and local government regulations, larger and more expensive government, much higher taxes on many fronts and more government socialistic policies that will make doing business more difficult and expensive. Plan for this resulting by itself in slower than normal economic growth. Our federal government likely will be saying to us *we can do it better* or *we know best*. This, of course, is not true, but it will make owning and running any business more difficult, challenging and risky. This important matter is extensively discussed in Chapter 9.

The Growing Dependency in America on Federal, State and Local Government Services and Financial Assistance is a Major Issue

Since 1940, Americans have demanded increasingly more services and financial assistance from our federal, state and local governments. Government has become much larger and more expensive and laws and regulations of many kinds have multiplied as a result. Our taxes on all levels have increased as well.

As we saw in Chapter 1 and as further discussed in Chapter 9, the percent of our national income consumed by the public sector (all of our governments combined) soared from *12%* in 1930 to *43%* in 2007[16]. That reduces the share left to the rest of us, the private sector, from *88%* in 1930 to *57%* in 2007. The trend continues and I estimate that by 2014, our public sector governments will be consuming at least *50%* of our national income. Therefore, the other *50%* of our national income will be consumed in the private sector. This is obviously not a positive trend.

Many issues arise from this growing dependency on government regarding the economy. These include the competing interests of capitalism and socialism in America, which we will examine in Chapter 9. More immediately, however, the same slow growth, reduced consumer spending and higher unemployment that puts consumers and businesses in a bind will severely reduce tax revenues too. Government officials and their constituents both face some difficult, slow and painful changes.

For federal, state and local and county government politicians, elected officials, policymakers and appointed government staff in 2010-2014:

- Prepare for income, sales and other government tax revenues to fall far below the levels of 1990-2007. This began in 2008, increased in 2009, and will very likely continue for the next five to seven years.
- These ongoing major reductions in government tax revenues are the direct result of the substantial slowdown in U.S. economic growth, the major increase in both *standard unemployment* and *real unemployment*, coupled with the slowdown in consumer spending and the increase in the rate of savings that began in 2008 and continued through 2009. These same basic trends will continue through 2014.
- Expect the overall economy to experience an **L**-shaped downturn and recovery, *not* a **V**-shaped recovery, in these years. In an **L**-*shaped* economic scenario, *all* governments in the U.S. will face massive and clearly unsustainable *budget deficits*. Federal deficits will be much worse than state or local deficits because nearly *95%* of our federal government tax revenues come from personal and business income and FICA payroll taxes. Most state and local government taxes come from sales, real estate, fees and various excise and special taxes, which don't fall as precipitously as income taxes when the economy falters.

---

[16] Bureau of Economic Analysis and U.S. Department of Commerce

- Look for more state and local government employees to lose jobs, for construction projects to be delayed and maintenance to be postponed. Most state and local county governments are required to balance their budgets every year. When tax revenues fall, these governments have no choice but to reduce spending, raise taxes or try some combination of the two. State and local governments throughout America already began reducing spending in 2008 and 2009. All state and local government officials, agencies and departments should plan for more major cost reductions in 2010-2014 because total tax revenues will fall far short of actual and budgeted expenses.
- State and local government workers and agencies that survive those spending cuts or who provide vital services such as highway and street maintenance, police and fire protection and trash removal all need to plan and prepare to substantially increase productivity, restructure and make reduced tax revenues go much further than they did in the last 20 years.
- All government officials need to balance their budgets without raising taxes. In theory, increasing taxes paid by consumers, families, property owners, businesses and others would help state and local governments find revenue to meet rising costs. But with much higher than normal unemployment levels, slower than normal economic growth, declining real estate and other asset values, and reduced consumer spending and profits by businesses, raising taxes in the *new normal* economy will simply make things much worse. Government officials and departments should plan to (1) greatly increase efficiencies and productivity, (2) substantially reduce costs and services, (3) not raise taxes and (4) begin reducing taxes now for consumers, families and businesses.
- Elected and appointed government officials need to seriously consider redefining their roles in the *new normal* economy. Specifically, they should prioritize all government functions and services to reduce costs, eliminate, restructure or downsize unneeded agencies and services, and outsource those operations and services that private businesses can provide more cost effectively.
- The federal government needs to plan for all the implications I have been stressing regarding the **L**-shaped downturn and recovery process in the next five to 10 years.
- Representatives of the federal government should prepare for substantially lower federal tax revenues and dramatically larger annual budget deficits than they are currently projecting for the next five to 10 years. Our debts are *metastasizing*. As shown in Figure 6.1, it took the U.S. *233* years to accumulate a *$12 trillion* national debt as of late 2009. It can conservatively be estimated now that our federal

government debt will double to the **$24 trillion** level by the year 2020 or in only **11** more years! The increase in our government debt is out of control and is *not* sustainable.

- Now is the time for our government officials to make a commitment to reduce federal government spending and programs, to balancing our budget within at least five to seven years and to keep it balanced in future years. This will realistically require major and ongoing reductions in total federal spending, including spending less for Social Security, Medicare and Medicaid. Taxes should *not* be raised to balance the budget. This would be a serious mistake as discussed in Chapters 5 and 9. The reason for this is that the top **10%** of U.S. income earners, who currently account for about **72%** of all federal government personal and individual income tax revenues and would be taxed the most, also have been hurt the most by losses in the real estate and stock markets. Reducing their net worth, wealth, income, profits and taxpaying power even more would further limit their ability to reinvest in jobs, growth and the economy.

- All members of the present and future administrations and members of Congress between now and 2014 will be faced with slower than normal economic growth and consumer spending, declining stock markets, much *higher than normal* unemployment and major increases in commercial bank failures.

- Do not plan to implement any further *bailout* or *economic stimulus* programs. Be prepared for the federal government to *run out of stimulus bullets* in 2010-2014. All members of the present and future administrations and members of Congress between now and 2014 will be faced with slower than normal economic growth and consumer spending, declining stock markets, much *higher than normal* unemployment and major increases in commercial bank failures. The political will to increase federal spending and deepen budget deficits and the national debt will *not* be present as more Americans demand that all facets of the federal government do what the private sector is now doing. Citizens, families, businesses and organizations in the private sector have no choice but to live much more within their means and face increased unemployment and underemployment, while making many painful and difficult financial and human decisions.

- Governments at all levels need to prepare and plan for increases in serious riots, civil unrest, theft and crime throughout America, particularly in urban centers. The negative developments I have been discussing in this book will be the driving force behind this unrest.

Figure 6.1
Total U.S. Federal Government Gross Outstanding Debt for Calendar 2009 Versus 2020

The increase in our Federal Government debt is out of control and is *not* sustainable

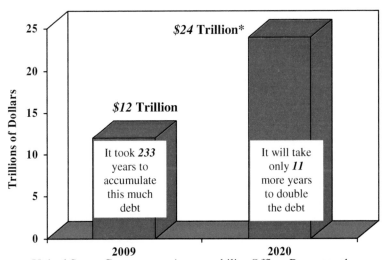

Source: United States Government Accountability Office, Report to the Secretary of the Treasury (Financial Audit, November 2008); TreasuryDirect (Historical Debt Outstanding as of 9-30-08)

*Forecasted conservatively by author.

Summing Up

Figure 6.2 summarizes the key factors that I believe will represent the increased risks and greatest challenges, plus some of the major opportunities and positive developments that will occur during the next few years for consumers, businesses and our governments. This is a good *roadmap* for the *new normal* economy.

These guidelines apply to everyone and every sector of the U.S. private and public economy. I believe you will find them thought provoking and a good discussion outline.

Figure 6.2
Summary of the Key Factors that Represent Major Risks, Pain, Problems and Challenges for the Private and Public Sectors of our U.S. Economy, Compared to the Major Opportunities and Positive Developments and Trends during the 2010-2014 Time Period

Major Risks, Pain, Problems and Challenges for the Private and Public Sectors	Major Opportunities, Positive Developments and Trends for the Private and Public Sectors
1. U.S. economy will experience an *L-shaped, not a V-shaped* economic downturn and recovery resulting in average annual growth of 1.5% to 2.0% for 2008-2014 and an average annual unemployment rate of 9.5% to 12% in 2010-2014.	1. An overall reduced cost of living and cost of doing business because of general price deflationary forces, including lower energy and food costs.
2. Much slower than normal economic growth and consumer spending, i.e. many more purchases will become discretionary by consumers.	2. Substantially reduced cost of buying a home and reduced home and apartment rental rates, i.e. improved affordability.
3. Much higher than normal levels of standard and real unemployment and consumer savings, plus reduced consumer confidence and increased concerns about the economy.	3. Substantially reduced cost of buying commercial, industrial, farm and ranch real estate and property, including cheaper prices for autos, trucks and *big ticket* equipment and machinery.
4. Increased risk of job/benefits loss or reduced wages, benefits and bonuses.	4. Record low interest rates for borrowing money on a monthly variable and floating interest rate basis.
5. Substantial further declines in home, condo, commercial, industrial, farm and ranch real estate market values and in U.S. stock market values resulting in a major loss of equity and wealth. The Dow will very likely reach the *3,500 to 4,500* range.	5. Get completely out of the stock market by February-April of 2010.
6. Bank and other lenders' standards and requirements will become much stricter, i.e. less credit available, major deleveraging and much more cash and equity required to maintain an existing or obtain a new loan or credit line.	6. Begin buying selected U.S. stocks again when the Dow gets down to the *3,500 to 4,500* level even though the stock market may go lower than these numbers.
7. Reduced and lower than normal bank and other lenders' standards and requirements will become much stricter, i.e. less credit available, major deleveraging and much more cash and	7. Businesses will have the opportunity to hire talented and well qualified employees from a much larger labor pool for reduced wage and benefit costs.
	8. Businesses will be able to significantly improve labor force productivity gains.
	9. Increased opportunities for men and women to own businesses and

equity required to maintain an existing or obtain a new loan or credit line.

8. Reduced and lower than normal business and corporate profits and investment in *big ticket* new plant, equipment and machinery.

9. General price deflation, zero inflation or much lower than normal rate of inflation, i.e. consumers and businesses will *not* be able to depend on inflation to bail them out. Plan on general price deflation over much of the next 10 years.

10. Much lower government tax revenues and higher taxes for all citizens and businesses.

11. Increased civil unrest, riots and escalating theft and crime resulting from persistently high levels of unemployment.

12. The decline in the standard of living in America for a growing number of citizens moving forward.

13. The growing dependency in America on government services and financial assistance by consumers, families and businesses is resulting in more socialism and government regulations and less reliance on capitalism, which is negative for the U.S. economy moving forward.

work out of their homes, including those who have lost jobs or who are significantly underemployed.

10. Consumers, families, businesses and other private sector organizations and institutions implementing new ideas, production methods and technologies to improve sales and profits in the *new normal* economic environment.

11. Consumers, wage earners and families will save more and depend more on themselves and depend less on their employer or government to fund their retirement, plus they will reduce personal debt and borrow less money moving forward.

12. The American people will be taking back their country and saying *No* to socialism and to the sharply rising national debt and runaway government spending in the 2010 and 2014 elections. They will be demanding a balanced budget primarily by reducing spending in the years ahead.

Source: This summary was created by the author.

Chapter 7
Inflation vs. Deflation in 2008-2014 and Beyond
Prepare for Deflation

Many people believe that massive increases in federal debt, government spending and a potential decade of annual trillion dollar budget deficits that began in 2008 will cause inflation to soar in 2010-2014. I disagree. *I believe that the surprise for many will be that deflating prices very likely will dominate our economy and financial landscape during the next five to 10 years.*

In this chapter, we will look at why some combination of price deflation, zero inflation or very modest and much lower than normal inflation rates will occur between now and at least 2014 and likely longer and how you can plan to deal with those changes.

First, let's take a close look at the history of the Consumer Price Index, or CPI, in the United States. The average annual rate of change in the CPI, reported each month by the Bureau of Labor Statistics, is the nation's most widely followed statistical gauge of general retail-level price trends for virtually everything consumers buy.

The CPI specifically consists of *more than 65* items that are used by our federal government as indicators of the prices consumers and businesses pay for whole groups of goods and services at the retail level. Some examples are food purchases and consumption at home and away from home, housing expenses of many different kinds, clothing, medical care and services, transportation expenses, recreation and education expenses, and a wide variety of other purchases. In short, the CPI inflation and deflation numbers published by the Bureau of Labor Statistics give us a good estimate of the cost of living.

The impact of these inflationary or deflationary forces on all consumers and businesses, and on real estate values, commodity prices, interest rates, stock markets, Federal Reserve monetary policy, the U.S. dollar and governments at all levels, is very important. This is why I have devoted a separate chapter to this subject.

The U.S. economy is going to experience a *new normal* relative to general price deflationary pressures in 2009-2014 and also very likely during the 2015-2020 time period that will be in direct contrast to the persistent general price inflationary forces that it experienced during the *69* years from 1940 through 2008.

During the **10 years of the Great Depression,** the U.S. economy experienced an average annual CPI deflation rate of about *-2%*. This means that altogether; the total combined net CPI rate of inflation and cost of living *declined 20%* between 1930 and 1939. This is what normally occurs in the economic *bust* phase of the long-term business cycle. But the drop was not an unbroken one, as you can see in Figure 7.1. Consumer living costs generally rose, or *inflated,* in *four* of those 10 years (1934, 1935, 1936 and 1937) and fell or *deflated*, in the other six years. This is very typical of what happens during **L**-shaped economic downturns and recoveries in the course of seven to 10 years. Prices in an economic depression or prolonged stagnation characteristically either fall, remain unchanged or rise much less quickly than normal for at least five to seven years. At the same time, GDP growth slows to much below normal rates, usually *1%* to *2%,* and unemployment remains high. This is what happened during the 10-year Great Depression in the 1930s. This is also what happened in Japan during the *15* years of 1992-2006. Japan still has not recovered from that prolonged economic stagnation and continues to struggle with its own version of a *modern day* depression.

Figure 7.1
The Consumer Price Index (CPI) Average Annual Rate of Change for the 10-Year Great Depression Period of 1930-1939

The Great Depression experienced an average annual CPI deflation rate of -2% for these 10 years or a total reduction in the cost of living of *20%*

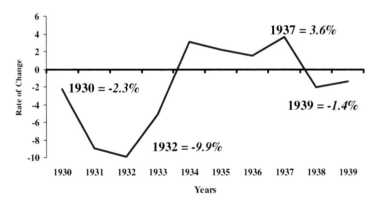

Source: Bureau of Labor Statistics

In the U.S., the *69* years from 1940-2008 show a relatively long stretch of general CPI *price inflation*. The average annual CPI rate of inflation for those *69* years was about *4%* with very little or no general price deflation, which is consistent with the *boom* portion of the long-term business cycle. Overall, the total combined net CPI rate of inflation and cost of living **increased 276%** between 1940 and 2008 in the U.S.

But like the falling living costs of the 1930s that preceded this boom, living costs in 1940-2008 did not rise on an unbroken path, as shown in Figure 7.2. During parts of and following World War II, the average annual rate of CPI price inflation was much higher than normal. It reached a peak of **14.4%** in the year 1947 and another peak in the year 1980 of **13.5%**. In other years, the average annual CPI dropped to **-1.2%** in 1949 and bumped around an annual average **3.1%** rate for the 24 years in 1985-2008. It popped to **3.8%** in 2008, largely as a result of the sharply higher crude oil prices that peaked that June and July in the **$145** to **$150** per barrel range.

Figure 7.2
The Consumer Price Index (CPI) Average Annual Rate of Change
for the 69 Years of 1940-2008

For these 69 years, the average annual CPI *rate of inflation* was 4% or a total increase in the cost of living of 276%

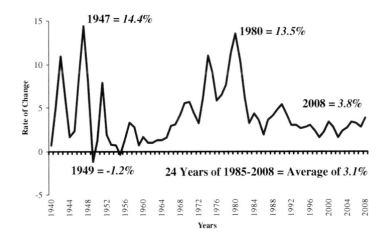

Source: Bureau of Labor Statistics

Figure 7.3 provides a good perspective of the significant ups and downs in the average annual rate of inflation in the U.S. for the **47** years from 1962 through 2008. For example, the average annual rate of consumer price inflation (CPI) was **4.33%** per year for these 47 years. The CPI averaged **3.1%** per year for the **24** years from 1985-2008. The annual low point for the CPI was in 1962 at *1.2%*. The annual high point for the CPI was *13.5%* in 1980. The average annual CPI for the first 11 months of 2009, as discussed below, compared to the first 11 months of 2008, was down over six tenths of one percent or -0.63% as shown in Figure 7.4.

Figure 7.3
The Consumer Price Index (CPI) Average Annual Rate of Change
for the 47 Years of 1962-2008
For these 47 years, the average annual CPI *rate of inflation was 4.33%*

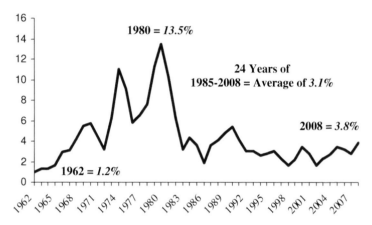

Source for Figures 7.3 and 7.4: Bureau of Labor Statistics

Figure 7.4
The Consumer Price Index (CPI) Average Monthly Rate of Change for the
First 11 Months of 2009, Compared to the First 11 Months of 2008

The average monthly *rate of CPI deflation* for January through November of 2009, compared to the same 11 months in 2008, was *-0.63%*

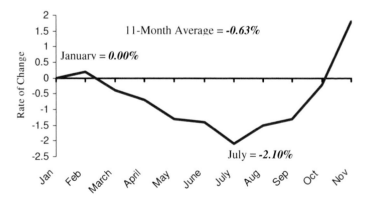

There also were *11* economic recessions that interrupted this general inflationary trend during the 1940-2008 time period. These 11 *V-shaped* economic downturns and recoveries lasted only *10.2* months on average. Thus, while CPI inflation rates went up and down, most Americans became very accustomed to inflation being a *way of life* for a long time. Consumers today do not expect prolonged general CPI price *deflation*, zero inflation or much lower than normal rates of inflation coming in 2010-2014 and very likely for a longer period of time. Most people expect just the opposite, so the change will come as a real surprise to consumers, the Federal Reserve, bankers, the stock markets, investors and many others.

The monthly CPI numbers published by the Bureau of Labor Statistics for 2008 and 2009 clearly show that the early stages of general price deflation at the consumer and retail level have already begun. For example, Figure 7.4 shows the average monthly rate of CPI deflation for January through November of 2009 has dropped about *-0.63%* below the levels for the same 11 months a year earlier. This is very significant because while the CPI *often* fell below year-earlier levels in the 1930s, as shown in Figure 7.1, that has happened *only twice, very briefly* in 1949 and 1955 since then, as shown in Figure 7.2. The U.S. economy very simply has *not* experienced CPI general price deflation prior to 2009 for *67* years except for the years 1949 and 1955, which, again, is normal in the long-term *boom* portion of the business cycle.

As shown in Figure 7.5, I fully expect that the six-year average rate of CPI price inflation/deflation for 2009-2014 to be within the *+1.0%* to *-3.0%* range. The six years of 2009-2014 will likely experience an average annual CPI price inflation and deflation rate similar to the rate of price inflation and deflation of close to *1.0%* to *-3.0%,* which hasn't happened since the Great Depression.

Figure 7.5
The Author's Forecast for the Average Annual U.S. Consumer Price Index (CPI) Rate of Inflation and Deflation for the Six Years of 2009-2014

1. The six-year average annual rate of CPI price inflation and deflation for the 2009-2014 time period is estimated by the author to be within the *+1.0%* to a *-3.0%* range. This represents a part of the *new normal* moving forward and what can be expected in the *bust* phase of the long-term business cycle.

2. The six years of 2009-2014 will likely experience an average annual CPI price deflation rate similar to the rate of deflation which occurred in the Great Depression years of between a *-1.0%* to a *-2.0%*.

When the rate of average annual CPI price inflation increases sharply, as it did in the late 1970s and early 1980s (see Figure 7.2), interest rates rise sharply.

We experienced this in 1980 when the average annual CPI rate of inflation in the U.S. reached *13.5%* and the prime interest rate reached *17%* to *21%* in the same year. Conversely, when the CPI rate of inflation declines sharply or when we experience CPI general price deflation, interest rates decline sharply and stay down. We saw this in late 2008 and throughout 2009 when what is known as the federal funds rate, a linchpin of banking system liquidity, dropped to zero and the prime rates banks theoretically charge their most credit worthy customers fell to about *3.0%* to *3.25%*. These represent historically low interest rates last touched in the early 1940s.

Because I fully expect the average annual rate of CPI price inflation to be very low and range between *+1.0%* and *-3.0%* per year through at least 2014 and likely for a longer period of time, I believe the fed funds and U.S. banking prime rate will remain at or very close to historically low levels for these same six years. When the rate of CPI price inflation is much lower than normal or when our economy is experiencing general CPI price deflation, short and long interest rates will remain very low.

Inflation accelerates when demand outstrips supply. Here are the major reasons *why* I believe that will not happen for many years and *why* the U.S. economy will experience price deflation, zero inflation or much lower than normal inflation for at least the six years of 2009-2014 and likely to about the year 2020:

- Growth in our economy and in consumer spending will be much slower than normal for the next five to seven years. I believe it will fall into the *red light zone* described in Chapter 1, as average annual GDP growth rates fall to between *1.5%* and *2.0%* per year. With these trends, escalating inflation will *not* happen.
- Persistently high unemployment will play a key role in keeping inflation down. I fully expect the rate of unemployment to be at least within the *10%* to *12%* range for standard and *16%* to *20%* range for real and effective unemployment numbers between now and 2014.
- The escalating write-down and write-off of billions of dollars of private sector debt by banks and other lenders, plus increasing numbers of commercial bank failures during this period, will prove to keep the rate of inflation down. Write-downs and write-offs of private sector debt are always deflationary. This has historically been the case in the U.S., Japan and Europe. The write-downs will include home, commercial, industrial, farm and ranch real estate, credit card, automobile and student loan debt, corporate and business operating line, machinery, equipment and commodity inventory debt, etc.

- The trillions of dollars of lost equity and wealth that have already occurred since 2008 and the likelihood of further substantial loss and declines in the next few years will also fuel deflationary forces.
- Substantially lower amounts of borrowing and substantially reduced lending will contribute to lower inflation rates. These trends will continue to keep inflation down as they have always done historically.
- The prospect of high inflation will diminish as consumers spend less and save more. If the U.S. consumer saving rate goes to the *10%* to *12%* range, as I fully expect it to, escalating inflation in the United States cannot happen.
- Average wages, incomes and employee benefits are declining. For the first time since the 1930s, the wages and benefits of many working Americans are being cut. These developments and trends reduce consumer and household spending and will continue to cause the price of goods and services to decline.
- There will continue to be general commodity price deflation over at least the next five to 10 years. Bottom line, the U.S. and global supply of most commodities exceeds demand today and this will continue to be the case over at least most of the next 10 years. In order for U.S. and global producers of commodities to sell more goods and commodities to U.S. consumers, they will have to lower the prices in order to get these goods and commodities sold and moved out of inventory. These trends are now and will continue to contribute to general price deflation over the next 10 or more years.
- The dominant trends of excessive private sector easy credit terms, the private sector excessive growth of credit and debt and the private sector excessive leverage from the early 1980s to about 2007 are now reversing course. There will be much stricter credit standards, significantly reduced debt and credit available and major deleveraging underway over the next 10 or more years within the private sector. These trends are now and will continue to contribute to reduced consumer spending and borrowing capacity and to general CPI price deflation over the next 10 years.
- There will be additional major excessive credit and credit default bubbles bursting in the 2010-2012 time period for the U.S. and globally. In the U.S., these further credit default bubbles, on top of those we have already seen in 2008-2009, will include home, commercial, industrial, farm and ranch real estate, plus further credit default bubbles bursting for credit cards, banks, other lenders, auto loans, insurance companies, consumers and large and small businesses. There are also going to be major credit default bubbles bursting globally in 2010-2012 in China, Japan, other Asian countries, Europe

and in South America. These developments will be price and asset deflationary in the U.S. and will be generally bullish on the U.S. dollar in 2010-2014. *Remember, economic and financial credit default bubbles are the result of excessive easy credit terms, excessive growth of debt and credit and excessive leverage relative to the ratio of debt to equity over time.*

- Our industrial output is hitting historic lows. For 2009, the level of the total annual U.S. industry and industrial capacity utilization fell to *69.5%,* the lowest figure recorded since this data series began in 1960. This degree of excess capacity fosters price deflationary forces. As shown in Figure 7.6, the last 50-year average annual total capacity utilization was *81.4% or 18%* higher than the *69.5%* number. This is highly significant. The all time record high level of U.S. industry and industrial capacity utilization in the U.S. was *92.1%* in the year *1967*.

- Supplies of goods and services both in the U.S. and globally are sharply higher and *increasing significantly* while *demand is declining* for these same goods and services. The very significant increase through the use of new technology in the U.S. results in greater productivity gains. The production of more goods and services with fewer people required to produce them, plus more efficient and cost effective inputs of labor and capital is by definition *price deflationary*. The agriculture industry provides a number of examples of the impact of new technology:

  1. Substantially increased corn yields and production per acre.
  2. More beef, pork and poultry production per cow, sow and chicken.
  3. Increased milk production per dairy cow.

  This and countless other examples of new technology are clearly price deflationary or at minimum, they will keep CPI rates of inflation at zero or at much less than normal levels moving forward.

- More products are manufactured outside of the U.S. with much lower labor and overhead costs, then shipped to the U.S. and purchased by Americans at lower prices. These lower prices hold down CPI inflation in the U.S. Also American consumers, who choose to spend less and save more, force overseas exporters to lower prices even further to encourage Americans to buy their products. These trends are price deflationary and will likely continue to be in the years ahead.

- Consumers and businesses are responding to major discounts and perceived bargains and will continue to be even more frugal moving forward. They are now and will continue to demand lower prices and costs as they become increasingly more price conscious. Given this trend, escalating inflation will *not* happen anytime soon. *Producers and businesses throughout America, large and small, public and private, will have very little, if any, pricing power relative to passing on increased costs to consumers over the next 10 years.*

Figure 7.6
Average Annual Rate of U.S. Industry Capacity Utilization
for the 50 Years of 1960-2009
U.S. capacity utilization declined to an all time low of *69.5%* in 2009
for these 50 years

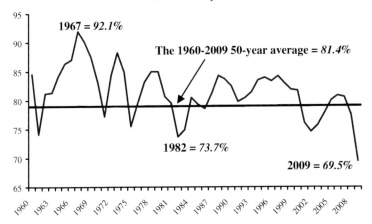

Source: Federal Reserve Statistical Release G.17, August 14, 2009

- The impact of the **78 million** baby boomers spending and investing less, saving more and downsizing and changing their lifestyles over the next 10 to 20 years will contribute considerably toward price deflation or zero to minimal inflation until at least 2014 and likely to the year 2020.

- Key inflation bellwethers are pointing lower. Both the market-driven average annual interest rates for 10-year U.S. Government Treasury Bonds and broader bond market rates are important and very helpful indicators of future inflation rates. Billions of dollars are traded daily in the U.S. Government Treasury Bond market. In Figure 7.7 you will see that the average interest rate for the **47** years of 1962-2008 hit an all-time **low of 3.66%** in 2008. Rates for these 10-year U.S. Government Treasury Bonds will be even lower in 2009 and for the years 2010-2012. As shown in Figure 7.8, for the first 11 months of 2009, compared to the same 11 months of 2008, the average monthly interest rate was **3.78%** in 2008 and **3.14%** in 2009 for 10-year U.S. Government Treasury Bonds. This represents a decline of 64 basis points or **17%** in the average monthly interest rate in 2009, compared to the same 11-month period for 2008. This is very significant, as these heavily traded bonds are good proxies of lower than normal rates of inflation, zero inflation or general price CPI deflation for at least the next five to seven years.

Figure 7.7
The 10-year U.S. Government Treasury Bond Average Annual Interest Rate for the 47 Years of 1962-2008
For these 47 years, the average annual interest rate was *6.97%*

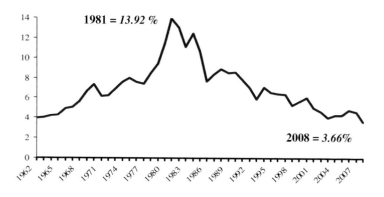

Source: Federal Reserve Statistical Release H.15

- Two important Federal Reserve indicators of future inflation rates also indicate slower future growth. Both the *velocity of money*, which clocks how quickly money is spent and the growth in *consumer credit* have been growing more slowly in 2008 and 2009 than a year earlier. These are meaningful indicators of zero rates of general CPI price inflation and price deflationary forces in the future.

- According to Robert Prechter and his *Elliott Wave Theorist* newsletter, dated December 18, 2009, the Federal Reserve has swapped over a trillion dollars of new money for old debt in 2008 and 2009 and banks are typically not lending new money. He points out that *"the money multiplier is back in negative territory and reached new lows in late 2009, which means that there is more debt being re-tiered than there is new money being created. **In other words, deflation is winning.**"*

- Another very important factor that I strongly believe will contribute to general U.S. price and asset deflation during the next 10 years is the degree and scope of further major federal government regulations impacting literally all aspects of the U.S. banking and financial system. Regulatory efforts to curb past excesses will result in *substantial reductions* in credit instruments, credit extensions, plus innovative and creative financing, which in turn will slow the amount and rate of lending and borrowing throughout the entire private and public sectors of our U.S. economy. Bottom line, reduced credit inflation will significantly contribute to credit, price and asset deflation over the next 10 years. You can and should plan accordingly. These increased financial, banking and other lender regulations will include increased regulations and guidelines for real estate and other appraisers, bond and financial rating companies. This will also contribute to longer-term asset and price deflation in the United States over the next 10 years.

- Since 1749, the U.S. has had six major time periods where there was general year-to-year wholesale price deflation[17]. These periods were peacetime periods of 1749-1755, 1764-1774, 1784-1811, 1816-1845, 1866-1916 and 1919-1940, which lasted 6, 11, 28, 30, 51 and 22 years, respectively. The average length of time was *20* years of price deflation. The next period will very likely be from about 2008 to 2025.

- Assuming the U.S. does not get into a major and prolonged war, then the odds of the U.S. experiencing general CPI price deflation over at least the next five to seven years is at least *90%*. Should the U.S. become involved in a major war which lasts several years or more, this could potentially result in some general wholesale and CPI price inflation.

Figure 7.8
The 10-year U.S. Treasury Bond Annual Interest Rate
for the 11 Months of January-November, 2008
Compared to January-November, 2009

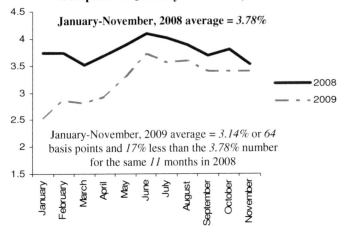

Source: Federal Reserve Statistical Release H.15

---

[17] A. Gary Shillings *Insight* newsletter, Chart 2, November, 2009 (page 2)

How Changing CPI Inflation Rates Affect Investment Results

Declining rates of CPI inflation also change the effective bottom line for many consumers, which is what their money really earns. Ten-year U.S. Government Treasury bonds, which are a market bellwether, provide us with an example of how. Figure 7.7 shows that the average annual interest rate on 10-year Treasuries was about *6.97%* for investors who bought the bonds during the *47* years 1962-2008. But the purchasing power of those returns would be diminished by inflation, which as we saw in Figure 7.3, was *4.33%* during those same 47 years. That drops the real rate of return (the interest income of *6.97%*, less the rate of inflation of *4.33%*) to *2.64%* per year for a very low risk investment.

For the first 11 months of 2009, the average interest income on the same 10-year government bonds was *3.14%* as shown in Figure 7.8 and lower than the average annual CPI inflation rate of *4.33%* during the 47 years 1962 to 2008 as shown in Figure 7.3. For the first 11 months of 2009, the average rate of CPI inflation was *-0.63%* as shown in Figure 7.4. That increases the real rate of return, adjusted for inflation, to *3.77%* for a very low risk investment. This illustrates only one of the many reasons why the rate of inflation or deflation is so very important to many aspects of our economy, including investors, consumers who want to put money into various savings programs and to business owners, managers, banks and others.

Chapter 8
The U.S. Dollar in 2010-2014 and Beyond
I am Bullish on the Dollar

At any given moment in the world's markets, the U.S. dollar is either stronger or weaker compared to other countries' currencies than it was just one transaction before. Such changes are normal. This is supply and demand at work.

But when trends develop, and the dollar is persistently stronger or weaker, there also are important implications to consider for our banking system, the currency exchange markets, capital flows, import and export trade, global economic competitiveness, and government policies, U.S. and global stock markets, interest rates and many other aspects of the U.S. economy. Because trade with a multitude of countries is so important to both the U.S. and the global economies, we will now look at some of the ways that the foreign exchange value of the dollar will help shape our economic future in the years immediately ahead.

The objective of this chapter is to provide a better understanding of the U.S. dollar relative to:

- Its fluctuating foreign exchange value over time
- What entity determines the U.S. trade-weighted dollar index
- What countries are included in the dollar index
- Important economic and financial implications associated with a weak vs. a strong dollar
- The factors that have historically caused the dollar to weaken
- The factors that have historically caused the dollar to strengthen and why I am *bullish* on the dollar for most of 2010-2014
- Why the dollar will remain the reserve currency of the world in the years ahead

Comparing the value of the U.S. dollar against the currency of each of the world's approximately 195 countries individually would become an analytical quagmire. As an alternative to such a cumbersome analysis, the Federal Reserve's *U.S. dollar index* has served as a reliable summary measurement for determining foreign exchange values and movements of the dollar. Recent revisions that acknowledge significant changes in the worldwide economy ensure that the dollar index will continue to be a dependable tool moving forward.

The *Major Currencies Dollar Index*, as it is formally named, is a theoretical basket of seven currencies – the euro shared as a common currency among 11 European countries, plus the currencies of Australia, Canada, Japan, Sweden, Switzerland and the United Kingdom. The 11 countries sharing the euro are Austria, Belgium, Finland, France, Germany, Ireland, Italy, Luxemburg, the Netherlands, Portugal and Spain.

This major seven currency index not only compares the competitiveness of U.S. goods and services relative to goods produced and services provided by the other major industrial countries, it also serves as a gauge of upward and downward financial pressures on the dollar over time, such as the ones shown in Figures 8.1 and 8.2.

Figure 8.1
Price Adjusted, Major Currencies Dollar Index for the 37 Years of 1973-2009*

The average annual dollar index for these 37 years was *94.70*
The author fully expects the U.S. dollar to strengthen for most of 2010-2014

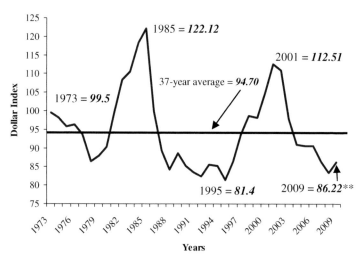

Years

Source: Federal Reserve Board

*The *price adjusted,* major currencies annual dollar index is adjusted for inflation by the Federal Reserve Board for all 37 years.

**The *price adjusted,* major currencies annual dollar index is based on actual numbers for January through December, 2009.

One benefit of this major currency group, which consists of the currencies used in the world's deepest, most liquid and highly developed financial markets, is that it excludes currencies of trading partners with a history of high inflation rates relative to the United States, such as Mexico and Argentina. This provides a useful gauge of the dollar's day-to-day and long-term foreign exchange values in both inflation-adjusted and unadjusted terms. Including inflation-prone currencies in index baskets is difficult because the large depreciations of those currencies tend to dominate the index and mask the contributions of movements in the dollar's nominal value against other currencies[18].

Figure 8.2
Price Adjusted, Major Currencies Dollar Index for the 36 Months from January, 2007 through December, 2009*

The average monthly dollar index for these 36 months was *85.35*
The author fully expects the U.S. dollar to strengthen for most of 2010-2014

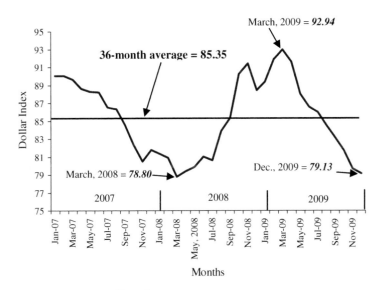

Source: Federal Reserve Board

*The *price adjusted*, major currencies annual dollar index is adjusted for inflation by the Federal Reserve Board for all *36* months.

The seven-currency index also uses a *weighting system* that compares the value of the dollar against other currencies based on how competitive U.S. goods are compared to other countries' goods. Changes in the value of any given foreign currency are weighted, or given more importance, according to that

---

[18] Information provided by The Federal Reserve Bank

country's share of trade with the U.S. The index counts that share as equivalent to the degree of competition from that country.

Competition in foreign markets is counted in two ways. A weight equal to a country's share in U.S. exports is used to measure the extent to which U.S. goods compete directly with a foreign country's goods in that country's home market. A second type of weight is used to measure the extent to which the U.S. and a competing nation's goods compete in third-country markets, as when U.S. goods compete with German goods in Japan. This type of competition is measured by multiplying Germany's share in Japan's imports by the share of U.S. exports going to Japan. This calculation produces higher combined export rates for countries that figure prominently as direct destinations for U.S. exports or are major exporters to other countries that take a large share of U.S. exports. The simple average of the two calculations becomes the weight used to calculate the seven-currency index according to The Federal Reserve Bank.

Why the Strength of the U.S. Dollar Matters

Generally speaking, when the U.S. dollar weakens against the *basket of currencies* we've described, U.S. produced goods and services become less expensive to most foreign buyers. U.S. exports generally *increase* as a result and the U.S. trade deficit decreases. Selling more goods and services to other countries typically increases our country's rate of economic growth as measured by GDP. However, a *persistently weak* U.S. dollar also has very *negative consequences* for the economy, including significantly increased rates of price inflation, much higher interest rates, reduced purchasing power and a lower standard of living for most Americans.

In contrast, when the dollar strengthens against other currencies, U.S. produced goods and services become more expensive to most foreign buyers. U.S. exports generally *decrease* as a result and our trade deficit becomes larger. Lower exports of goods and services are typically negative for our country's economic growth, but there are *positive consequences* as well. Inflation rates and interest rates fall or remain low while purchasing power and standards of living rise.

Bottom line, a stronger U.S. dollar significantly increases the prospect of building wealth for Americans and greatly encourages investment and savings. A stronger dollar makes it much easier to finance our federal government and national debt. A stronger dollar makes traveling to many other parts of the world, for example, more affordable.

The relative strength or weakness of the U.S. dollar has a direct and indirect impact on Americans' wellbeing. The dollar broadly determines the level of competitiveness of our economy and the overall stature, strength and power of the U.S. Therefore, there is a great deal at stake regarding the future direction of the U.S. dollar. A stable and relatively strong dollar is clearly the best for America.

I strongly believe the U.S. dollar will strengthen in the next three to five years, even though it was relatively weak in the May-November period of 2009. If the dollar does not strengthen for most of 2010-2014, the future will not be as bright as many Americans expect.

Let's now look at some informative history of the U.S. dollar. Figure 8.1 shows the long-term price-adjusted major currencies dollar index for the *37 years* of 1973-2009[19], when the dollar generally was stronger than many currencies. The average value of the index in those 37 years was *94.70*, ranging between a low *81.4* in 1995 and two high points of *122.12* and *112.51* in 1985 and 2001, respectively. The figure also shows the current, relatively weak, dollar index rose slightly in 2009 from its 2008 level.

Figure 8.2 provides a closer look at the shorter term, recently weaker price adjusted, major currencies dollar index for the *36 months* from January, 2007 through December, 2009. The average monthly dollar index for these *36* months was *85.35*. It touched a low *78.80* in March, 2008 and a high *92.94* in March, 2009. The dollar index was *79.13* in December, 2009.

Both Figures 8.1 and 8.2 show the rather extensive volatility in the U.S. dollar index that is typical. I believe the dollar will strengthen for most of the 2010-2012 time period, compared to 2008 and 2009 levels, particularly after we get past the February-April period of 2010. Although I am bullish on the dollar for the years of 2010 through 2014, I am in the minority on this point.

What are the Major Factors that Cause the U.S. Dollar to Weaken in the Global Marketplace over Time?
Why Did the Dollar Decline in 2007, 2008 and 2009?

- The U.S. today is far and away the largest debtor nation in the world relative to our federal debt. It took America *233* years to accumulate a *$12 trillion* national debt as of late 2009. As we saw in Figure 6.1, it is very likely that this number will double to *$24 trillion* in only *11* more years, or by 2020. This pace is an important contributor to the weakness in the U.S. dollar in 2007, 2008 and 2009. Massive federal budget deficits and federal government spending typically are *bearish* on the dollar, which we saw in 2008 and 2009.
- Total U.S. federal outstanding debt, calculated as a percent of real economic output, increased dramatically in the *53* years 1957 through 2009. As we

---

[19] Federal Reserve Board

saw in Figure 4.6, our U.S. national debt soared from *10.4%* of GDP in 1957 to *92.3%* of GDP in 2009. *This represents an **890%** increase or an average annual rate of increase of **16.8%** per year. Our national debt increased nearly **five times faster** than our economy grew during these same **53** years.*

- Relatively low U.S. interest rates, and specifically the fed funds rate which is set and controlled by the Federal Reserve Board, are typically associated with a weaker dollar. In November, 2008, in response to much slower than normal economic growth, a financially fragile banking system and rising unemployment, the Fed reduced the fed funds rate to a historically low *0.0%* to *0.25%*. These historically low fed fund rates continued through 2009. I expect them to remain at or very close to these very low levels for most of 2010-2012. Federal Reserve interest rate policy decisions contributed significantly to the U.S. dollar's weakness in 2008 and 2009 and will continue to do so for at least the early part of 2010.

- Generally speaking, low U.S. interest rates are associated with a contracting and struggling economy that is experiencing a recession or depression, reduced consumer spending and rising unemployment. These same conditions also are typically associated with a weaker dollar, as was the case in 2008 and 2009.

- The U.S. Treasury borrowed record amounts of money in 2008 and 2009, crowding out other consumer and business lending and producing a dramatic increase in the Federal Reserve balance sheet. A sharp increase in the balance sheet of the Federal Reserve Board or a substantial increase in the velocity of money typically will result in a weaker U.S. dollar. The velocity of money, or turnover of dollars in the economy, however, did not increase and in fact declined in part of 2008 and during all of 2009. These trends have actually contributed to CPI price deflation in 2009 of *-0.65%* for the first 11 months of 2009, compared to the first 11 months of 2008.

- Typically, the dollar also weakens when U.S. federal budget deficits increase sharply from year to year. This is what happened in 2008 and 2009. For example, the U.S Federal Government budget deficit soared from *$163 billion* for fiscal year ended September 30, 2007 to *$455 billion* and *$1.4 trillion* in fiscal 2008 and 2009, respectively. The fiscal 2009 ending deficit was *8.6 times larger* than the deficit for fiscal 2007.

- Widespread expectations that inflation will escalate or that U.S. *bailout, economic stimulus* and deficit spending will generally result in a declining dollar. Both of these things happened in 2008 and 2009, resulting in massive government intervention in private business that also helped depress the dollar.

- Negative GDP growth, rising unemployment and reduced consumer spending generally result in a declining U.S. dollar. These clearly happened in 2008 and 2009.

What Major Factors Cause the U.S. Dollar to *Increase* Significantly in Value? Why do I Believe the Dollar will Generally Strengthen During the 2010-2014 Time Period?

- Deflating prices, zero inflation or a much lower than normal rate of CPI inflation will increase the value of the dollar over time. As discussed in Chapter 7, these are the conditions I fully expect for most of 2009-2014. I am in the minority. Most people currently believe that the U.S. will experience substantial rising inflation in 2010-2014.

- Rising U.S. interest rates are generally *bullish* on the American dollar. I believe that interest rates via the fed funds rate will stay low and will increase very little in 2010-2012 due to below normal economic growth and much higher than normal levels of unemployment. I fully expect the average annual rate of GDP growth to be within the *1.5%* to *2.0%* range, far below the average annual *3.82%* rate in the *68* years of 1940-2007. Fed funds interest rates were essentially zero in 2009 and will remain at or very close to zero for most of 2010-2012. The next move for short-term U.S. interest rates over time, however, is *up*. This will generally be positive for the U.S. dollar longer term.

- The Federal Reserve in 2008 and 2009 made unprecedented monetary policy decisions in an effort to be accommodating and add liquidity to the U.S. financial system. This is typically *bearish* for the dollar as was the case in 2008 and 2009. For most of 2010-2014, though, the Federal Reserve Board will gradually decrease its balance sheet and take away the *monetary punchbowl*. This will be *bullish* for the dollar.

- The dollar will strengthen when the federal government's massive budget deficits begin declining and when serious commitments are made by Congress to balance the budget. This is what I expect to happen during 2010-2014 and beyond as discussed in Chapter 9. This will be positive for the U.S. dollar.

- The level and rate of productivity gains in the U.S. has a profound and major impact on the relative value of the dollar. As discussed in Chapters 2 and 7, the U.S. is among the top two economies in the world relative to productivity gains. So long as we remain in the number one or two spot in the world relative to year-to-year productivity gains, the U.S. dollar will remain relatively strong on a longer-term basis. The rate of U.S. productivity gains have been at a record level and pace in 2009. I fully expect this general trend to continue to be the case for at least the 2010-

2014 time period. Bottom line, the buck will remain king in part because of the gains in productivity now and in the years ahead.

- When sound-minded people within the U.S. and the *17* other countries that make up the major currency index search for a better alternative to the U.S. dollar, at least *95%* are going to conclude that the dollar represents the best and lowest risk option moving forward. This will be positive for the U.S. dollar moving forward.

Why the U.S. Dollar will Remain the World's Dominant Currency in the Years Ahead

During George W. Bush's second term and during the Barak Obama administration so far, there has been no firm U.S. commitment to a strong U.S. dollar. Both administrations have allowed the dollar to weaken. We've already noted that a weaker dollar often leads to increased exports. Some observers believe that these increased exports now will be needed to make up for the lower rates of U.S. business and consumer spending that many people, including those in government, now realize will not match previous years. I believe those expecting these increases will be surprised that they will *not* be realized. As we saw in Chapter 4, consumer spending today accounts for *70%* to *71%* of GDP growth, and business investment and spending account for another *12%* to *15%*. Together, these two key categories account for *82%* to *86%* of GDP in the U.S. Exports of U.S. goods and services, at most, account for *7%* to *10%* of GDP. Thus, even though I project modest improvements in exports during the next five years, those exports will not offset the combination of less-than-normal business and corporate spending and investment, higher unemployment and significantly higher consumer saving between now and 2014. In addition, I believe that consumer spending, as a percent of GDP, I believe will be declining from the *70%* to *71%* level in 2008-2009 to the *62%* to *64%* level within the next 10 years.

Consumer spending and economic growth in Europe and Japan will be generally even slower during 2010-2014 than in the United States. Both major economies have aging and declining populations, as we discussed in Chapter 3. As a result, even the lower-than-normal increases in U.S. consumer spending and consumption will exceed European and Japanese consumer spending growth and this by itself will gradually become positive for a strengthening U.S. dollar.

China, the United States' biggest creditor, desires and needs a stronger U.S. dollar. When the U.S. dollar weakens, this has a substantial negative financial impact on China. However, a weaker U.S. dollar significantly improves the prospects for increased U.S. exports. Although China has been the world's largest buyer and owner of U.S. Government securities for 25 years and will continue to be for at least five more, China needs the U.S. far more than the U.S.

needs China. China depends heavily on exports and U.S. consumers are by far its largest customers. It needs the strongest dollar manageable to sustain U.S. demand for Chinese products. Now, the odds are very high that the American consumer will continue to spend less on products made in China for at least the next five to seven years.

China cannot realistically make up the difference in reduced exports to the U.S. and elsewhere with increased spending by its own consumers during 2010-2014. Consumers generally in China have relatively low incomes, so their spending power is limited.

Nor can China stop or sharply reduce its purchase of U.S. debt or begin selling its large holdings of U.S. dollars. This would send the global economy into a prolonged depression, resulting in massive unemployment and serious banking and financial market dislocations worldwide. China would be the big loser of such a decision. The Chinese communist government would likely lose control of its *1.3 billion* people and the potential for serious rioting and civil unrest in China would increase.

Even though China likely will become the world's second largest economy, replacing Japan, within the next three years, both the Japanese and Chinese economies *individually* will still be only *36%* to *38%* the size of our economy. Thus, I am *bullish* on America, on the American people, on the U.S. dollar and on the prospects of the dollar remaining the reserve currency of the world over the five years of 2010-2014 and beyond.

Meantime, the rate of reckless and excessive U.S. federal debt accumulation and deficit spending is clearly out of control and *cannot be sustained*. For many reasons, I believe the rate of federal government spending will begin moderating and, unlikely as it may seem in late 2009 and early 2010, a serious commitment will be made to work towards a balanced budget in the next five to seven years and beyond.

Simply stated, when the American people begin to realize that the average annual rate of growth of our economy is much less than normal (*1.5% to 2.0%*) and the rate of unemployment remains painfully high (*10% to 12%*), they will demand that the federal government begin *seriously* reducing government spending. They are going to demand that our government start living within its means in the same way as American consumers and businesses are now forced to do.

I believe that a majority of Americans today are *right of center* where finances and budgets are concerned. Most Americans do *not* like the massive federal government deficit spending and the sharply rising U.S. national debt. Most Americans know that the irresponsible spending and borrowing by our federal government is negative for them, their families, U.S. businesses and for our overall economy. Most Americans do not want to pay higher taxes and to receive less take-home pay. Most Americans do not want our nation to go bankrupt, to lose its *Triple-A credit rating* or to be unable to pay our federal government bills and service our national debt. Seriously addressing these key factors will be *bullish* on the U.S. dollar during the next several years.

Chapter 9
Capitalism vs. Socialism in America
Capitalism Works
Socialism Does Not Work

There are many reasons why governments cannot cope successfully with the *new normal* economic changes that are now unfolding. We've looked in the last several chapters at some of them, such as changing population and demographic trends and the power of long-term boom and bust business cycles. But there is a philosophical issue that must be considered also.

Periods such as the one we have now entered often escalate the debate between those who believe that some form of broadly socialistic and collectively organized decision making better serves the public interest, compared to those who believe that individual initiative, free market competition, capitalism and limited governmental involvement provide better solutions.

The primary purpose of this chapter is to help you better understand the following:

(1) **Why** socialism does not work. I define socialism as much larger, rapidly growing and more expensive government and bureaucracy, including much higher taxes.

(2) **Why** federal government bailouts and stimulus programs have not worked historically in the U.S., Europe or Japan and why they are not working now as advertised and expected.

(3) **Why** freedom of choice, limited government, competition and capitalism have worked historically and will continue to work in the U.S. in the years ahead to increase and sustain positive economic growth, new job creation, wealth creation, rising standards of living, incomes and productivity gains for most Americans.

(4) **How** Americans can take back their country and say no to socialism. There is an important role for government in the U.S. However, that role must be limited for the long-term success of our country. We will soon examine how the role and size of government has been anything but limited, particularly from 2001 to late 2009 and why this trend is very negative for our economy.

Important as the government's role may be, however, there is a much more important role for the privately and publicly owned businesses and their employees in the U.S. private sector. The private sector begins new businesses or expands existing ones, hires more employees, makes capital investments, increases compensation and other incentives, and generates huge contributions to federal, state and local tax bases. Businesses pay federal, state and local taxes. Their employees pay federal state and local taxes. And so do the federal, state and local government employees whose jobs are funded by taxes paid by the private sector. These things do *not* come from the government. Without these capitalists in the private sector, the U.S. economy and the financial wellbeing of Americans will be seriously hurt. Some *71%* to *72%* of the more than *$1.1 trillion* of the total personal and individual federal income tax revenues collected, as shown in Figure 9.12, come from just the *top 10%* of all U.S taxpayers, according to IRS statistics. These are the capitalists in America and in 2007 they had adjusted gross incomes above *$113,018*. For the year 2008, total personal and individual income taxes accounted for over *45%* of the *$2.5 trillion* of total federal government tax revenues collected as shown in Figure 9.11. Almost all of these higher income tax payers are in the *private sector* and are single or partial business owners. Wage earners pay taxes too, of course. But many of them, in both the private and public sectors of our economy, are among the *bottom 50%* of all U.S. taxpayers and income earners who pay only *2.9%* of all annual federal government personal and individual income taxes, according to the IRS data.

Except for borrowed funds, all of the money spent by governments at all levels come from taxes and fees paid by businesses, institutions, for-profit and non-profit organizations, private and public sector employees, consumers and tourists. At the federal government level, at least *93.2%* of all taxes collected, which totaled *$2.524* trillion[20] in 2008, were personal, corporate and business income and FICA payroll taxes as you will see later in this chapter in Figure 9.11. Federal income taxes include taxes paid on personal income and wages, capital gains, dividends, interest and rental income, and corporate and business profits. The Federal Insurance Contributions Act, or FICA, are payroll taxes collected to pay for Social Security and Medicare. These taxes are split 50-50 between workers and their employers who each pay a *7.65%* rate, or half the total. Self-employed small business owners pay both halves of the tax, or the full *15.3%* rate. These FICA payroll taxes in 2007 and 2008 counted for about *35%* to *36%* of the grand total taxes collected by the federal government.

Well capitalized lenders with strong balance sheets are vital to the private sector. However, we currently have many lenders in America that do *not* have

---

[20] www.taxpolicycenter.org

strong balance sheets and are *not* making many new loans to consumers and businesses. This was the case in 2008 and 2009 and I believe it will continue to be the case in 2010-2014. For reasons that I outlined in Chapter 5, I am confident that many U.S. banks have serious balance sheet problems and I conservatively estimate that *800* to *1,200* commercial banks will fail between 2010 and 2014. Such reduced credit and lending capacity prevents the private sector free enterprise system from working as well as it normally does. This is part of the normal and cyclical economic and financial cycle. Unfortunately, when the federal government gets involved extensively through bailout programs, economic stimulus policies and investing our taxpayer dollars in U.S. banks and in other private sector companies as they have done in 2008 and 2009, this actually makes an already bad situation much worse. We will see later in this chapter how that happened in Japan over the 15 years of 1992-2006.

It is important to understand that *governments do **not** create jobs.* Yes, governments do employ millions of workers and the number of workers employed by all governments in the U.S. has increased substantially over the years.

However, men and women employed by our various governments are paid with tax dollars. Most of those tax dollars come from the private sector where businesses and organizations create jobs by expanding and hiring more employees, making profits, making good investments, taking risks, making positive productivity gains, and using new and better technologies. The use of taxes to transfer wealth and income from the private sector to governments at all levels is what makes it possible for governments to expand and to hire more employees.

When the U.S. economy contracts and growth slows down to a less than normal pace and falls into the *yellow light* or *red light* economic zones we discussed in Chapter 1, government tax revenues decline sharply. For example, U.S. Federal Government total tax receipts for calendar 2009, compared to calendar 2008, were down about *20%*[21]. I expect this to continue to be a very important issue in 2010-2014. This economic slowdown results in sharp increases in government budget deficits and forces state, city, local and county governments to reduce costs, lay off workers and to reduce and/or eliminate some government services and construction projects in order to balance their budgets. These governments are required to balance their budgets by law. Unfortunately, such laws and balanced budget requirements do *not* exist today at the federal government level. I believe this is going to change as discussed later

---

[21] Congressional Budget Office

in this chapter. *At the end of 2009, 48 out of the 50 states had serious annual budget deficits.*

America has become increasingly dependent on government for more services and more income assistance

Since the 1980s, the growth and size of government at all levels has increased substantially in the United States. This has been particularly true since about 1990, and even truer since 2001. Americans have demanded and received more services and financial assistance over the past 30 years, particularly from federal and state governments. These trends are well illustrated in Figures 9.1 through 9.4.

Figure 9.1

United States Federal Government Annual Spending for the 53 Years of 1957-2009
The average annual year-to-year percentage change in total Federal Government Spending for these 53 years was *8.0%* per year

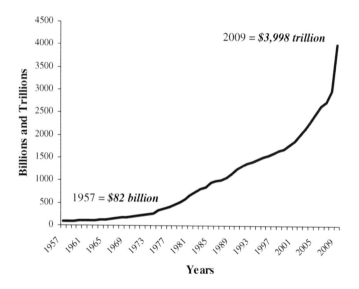

Source: USGovernmentSpending.com

Figure 9.1 shows the path of an average annual 8% growth rate in federal government between 1957 and 2009. In 1957, total federal government spending was *$82 billion*. In the year 2009 or *53* years later, that figure had risen to *$3.998 trillion*. The rate of federal government spending started significantly increasing in the early 1980s and has been dramatically increasing each year since 2001. *Total* government spending by all levels of government combined followed a similar path during those same 53 years, as shown in Figure 9.2.

Figure 9.2
United States Total Government Annual Spending for the 53 Years of 1957-2009
The average annual year-to-year percentage change in the *Total* Combined Federal, State and Local Government Spending for these 53 years was *8.1%* per year

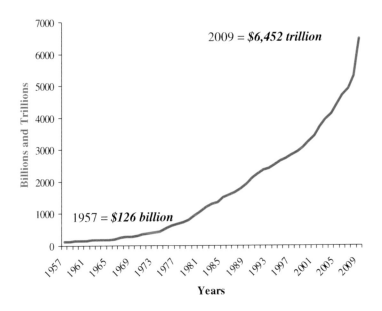

Source: USGovernmentSpending.com

Figure 9.3 shows one measure of increasingly unsustainable growth in the national debt. Growing at an annual average *4.3%* rate, federal debt has risen from being about one-tenth the size of the U.S. economy, at *10.4%* of GDP in 1957, to more than nine-tenths or a whopping *92.3%* of GDP in 2009. Figure 9.4 illustrates that unsustainable growth from another viewpoint. It shows that it took the U.S. *233 years* to run up the *$12 trillion* national debt that seems so shocking in 2009. But I estimate that at current rates of growth, it will take only *11 years* or until 2020, to double that national debt to *$24 trillion*.

Notice too how the size and growth of government in America has accelerated over the last *30* years. The American people have indeed become increasingly more dependent on all levels of government to provide services and financial assistance. *We have become a nation based on dangerous levels of dependency, i.e. the obvious evolution of a culture of dependency in America.*

Figure 9.3
Total U.S. Federal Government Outstanding Debt as a Percent of Real GDP for the 53 Years of 1957-2009

This Represents Unsustainable Federal Debt Accumulation

The average annual year-to-year percentage change in Federal Debt, as a percent of Real GDP, for these 53 years was *4.3%* per year

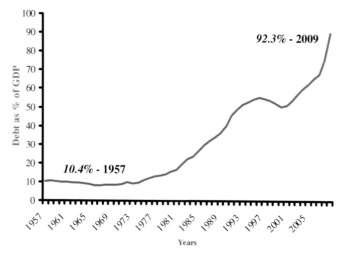

Source: TreasuryDirect.gov, Historical Debt Outstanding and the Bureau of Economic Accounts, NIPA Table 1.1.6 Real Gross Domestic Product, Chained Dollars (2005 dollars)

Bigger and rapidly expanding government translates into more taxes which must be paid. Increased bureaucracy is very expensive and very inefficient. The money fueling our citizens' increasing dependency on government help, and the growing bureaucracies organized to provide that help, comes *100%* from the taxes and fees paid by employees and business owners. At the federal level, this growth also translates into large and irresponsible budget deficits, significant borrowing of money we do not have and much higher taxes. At the federal level, this dependency also results in ever larger shares of the money we borrow coming from overseas sources such as China, Japan and the United Kingdom. Foreign countries, or more specifically, their central banks, owned about *$3.5 trillion* of the U.S. federal debt in late 2009, or some *29%* of the *$12 trillion* total, the U.S. Treasury and Federal Reserve calculated in October. The three largest holders of U.S. debt are China, Japan and the United Kingdom. Those countries collectively hold about *$1.8 trillion* of U.S. debt or *15.2%* of the total and roughly equal to the combined holdings of U.S. depository institutions, insurance companies, government and private pension plans, mutual fund companies and Wall Street investors.

Figure 9.4
Total U.S. Federal Government Gross Outstanding Debt for Calendar 2009 Versus 2020

The increase in our Federal Government debt is out of control and is *not* sustainable

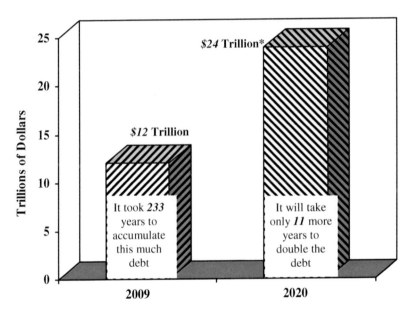

Source: United States Government Accountability Office, Report to the Secretary of the Treasury (Financial Audit, November 2008); TreasuryDirect (Historical Debt Outstanding as of 9-30-08)

*Forecasted conservatively by author.

If our U.S. Federal Government debt does increase from the *$12 trillion* level in late 2009 to close to *$24 trillion* by the year 2020, as I expect it will, it is very likely that the U.S. will become more dependent on foreign governments, banks and individual investors to finance our substantial annual budget deficits. It is positive, however, that as of late 2009, of the *$12 trillion* of the total U.S.

Federal Government debt, including approximately half of this amount that is held by the Federal Reserve, *71%* owned by Americans. *Most Americans want to see this percentage stabilize and then increase over the next 10 years. Similarly, the majority of Americans want to see our federal government annual budget get balanced and stay balanced without raising taxes.*

Government Spending and Federal Debt are growing Faster than our Population, our Economy, the Rate of Inflation and the Already Unsustainable Growth in Federal Debt as a Percentage of GDP

Spending and debt accumulation are increasing approximately two to five times faster than other economic forces that keep them in balance. Government influence over our economic lives becomes distorted as a result. But the imbalance also sets up federal, state and local governments for some painful contractions like those businesses and consumers are now going through. A series of charts in this chapter outline the severity of this situation.

Figure 9.5 shows the average annual population growth for the *53* years of 1957-2009. The numbers of people born in the U.S., plus those who have immigrated both legally and illegally in that timeframe, have increased our nation's population an average of *1.47%* per year in each of these 53 years. Although that is a low rate and, as we saw in Chapter 3, below the *2.1%* average annual increase required to sustain both the population and economic growth, it has lifted the U.S. population from *172 million* in 1957 to *306 million* in 2009. Figure 9.6 shows the average annual rate of growth of real GDP for this same 53-year period, which averaged *3.2%* per year despite some wider fluctuations, including a number of recessions. Consumer prices rose a bit faster, by an average of *4.0%* annually, even though some year-to-year changes varied more widely.

Figure 9.7 shows the average annual year-to-year percentage change in the rate of CPI inflation for the *53* years of 1957-2009. As you can see, the *53*-year average annual rate of CPI inflation was *4.0%*, ranging from a high of *13.5%* for the year 1980 and a *-0.65%* for the year 2009.

Figure 9.8 shows that government spending, represented by the two bars on the right of the graph, increased at least twice as fast as the other key economic indicators shown in this graph.

For example, in the *53* years of 1957-2009, our total combined federal, state and local governments spending increased *5.5* times faster than our population, *2.53* times faster than our economy, *2.03* times faster than CPI inflation growth and *1.9%* times faster than federal debt as a percent of GDP growth. This is obviously why the percentage of our U.S. national income consisting of wages earned in the public sector increased from *12%* in 1930 to *43%* in the year 2007.

Any way you look at these numbers, they clearly represent excessive and unsustainable growth in government spending and debt accumulation at all levels during the last *53* years. Figures 9.1 and 9.2 also show that government spending was far greater in 2008-2009 than for the entire 53-year average. This increasing level of spending seems very likely to continue unless something happens to slow the pace very significantly. But for reasons we will soon explore, I believe the odds of just such a slowdown are quite high. I believe that Americans will begin to replace members of Congress with men and women who commit to reduce spending and balancing the budget as soon as practical without raising taxes.

Figure 9.5

United States Annual Population Growth for the 53 Years of 1957-2009

The average annual year-to-year percentage change in the U.S. population for these 53 years was *only 1.47%* per year

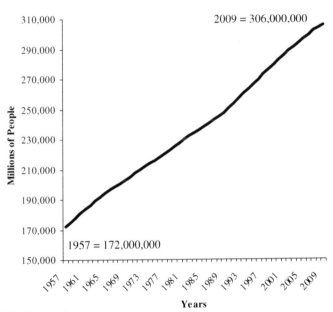

Source: U.S. Census Bureau

The problems directly associated with this extreme and unsustainable government debt and spending are very similar to those we examined in the private sector in Chapters 4, 5 and 6. Just as businesses and households in the private sector are going through a major deleveraging process because of these trends, governments in the U.S. will also soon be going through the same process and will end up being forced to take serious steps to reduce spending and balance their budgets.

Between now and 2014, the rate and level of federal government spending, the size and growth of budget deficits and the growth of our federal debt must and will begin to be seriously addressed. Firm commitments must be made toward balancing all these government budgets in the years ahead. Tax revenues will continue to be significantly less than what most of the present members of Congress and others are now planning on, just as unemployment will be higher than normal and the average annual rate of economic growth will be slower. These trends will bring about some long overdue and necessary changes in Washington, D.C. The public sector will have to face the reality of beginning to live within its means, just as voters and taxpayers are now having to do in the private sector. The financial, market and economic forces at work now will serve as a major *wakeup call* to U.S. voters and to elected officials who must change their ways at all levels of government in the years ahead. The catalysts for this coming change will be much slower-than-normal economic growth, reduced consumer spending, rising and persistently higher levels of unemployment and continued major losses of wealth resulting from further *declines* in real estate values, commodity prices, stock market values, plus reduced profits, incomes and employee benefits and persistently low tax revenues, particularly for the federal government.

Figure 9.6
The Average Annual Year-to-Year Percent Change in the U.S. Real Gross Domestic Product (GDP) for the 53 Years of 1957-2009
The 53-year average annual year-to-year percent change in Real GDP was 3.2% per year

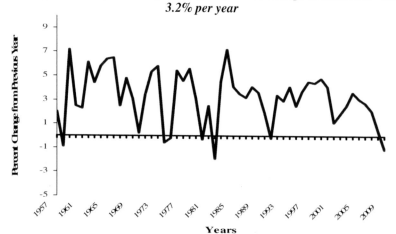

Source: U.S. Department of Commerce, Bureau of Economic Analysis (NIPA Table 1.1.1

146

Figure 9.7
The Average Annual Year-to-Year Percent Change in the U.S. Consumer Price Index (CPI) for the 53 Years of 1957-2009

The 53-year average annual year-to-year percent change in the CPI was 4.0% per year

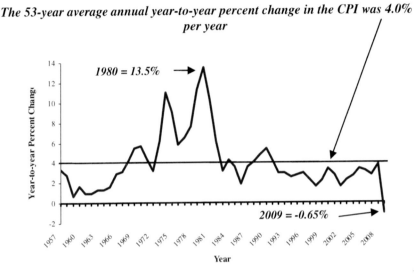

Source: Bureau of Labor Statistics

The substantial growth of the public sector as a percentage of our total economy along with a corresponding significant shrinkage of the private sector means that the U.S. has become significantly more socialistic and less capitalistic since the early 1980s. This has become particularly true since 2001.

Why Increased Socialism is Negative for America

Most people agree that if they want something done well, fast and cost effectively, they would *not* ask the government to do it for them. There are many reasons for this. One major reason is that in the private sector, meeting profit, debt and other financial requirements and timing metrics is essential. This causes most private sector businesses and employees to reduce costs, improve productivity levels, work harder and smarter, build wealth and net worth, improve employee income and benefits, invest in new technologies, expand the company and make other improvements. Most of these incentives do not exist in the public sector.

Because government is supported by tax revenues, fees and borrowed funds, the practical function of the public sector at the federal and state levels is to redistribute wealth, income and profits created in the private sector by using that money to assist lower income Americans and to fund the U.S. broad-based military operations. The larger and more expensive government becomes, the higher the level of dependency on government becomes and the more America moves toward a socialistic country. Bottom line, politicians and government workers typically know how to grow and expand government, but they typically do not understand or really know how to successfully expand and grow the private sector on a long-term and sustainable basis.

Figure 9.8
Comparative Average Annual Year-to-Year Percentage Change in U.S. Population, Real GDP, CPI Inflation, Federal Debt as a Percent of Real GDP, Federal Government Spending and Total Combined Federal, State, Local and County Government Spending for the 53 Years of 1957-2009

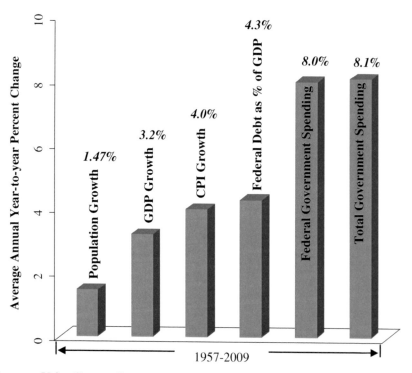

Source: U.S. Census Bureau; U.S. Department of Commerce, Bureau of Economic Analysis (NIPA Table 1.1.1); Bureau of Labor Statistics;

TreasuryDirect.gov, Historical Debt Outstanding and the Bureau of Economic Accounts, NIPA Table 1.1.6 Real Gross Domestic Product, Chained Dollars (2005 dollars); USGovernmentSpending.com

There are many examples where serious financial mismanagement by our federal government consistently takes place. Representative examples are:

- **Social Security** will be broke and insolvent within 10 years, following its current path. The system's total annual payments far exceed tax revenues collected. Social Security unfunded liabilities, or future obligations it cannot pay with the assets it has now, reached about *$17.5 trillion*[22] in January, 2009, according to the Social Security Administration. The Social Security average annual shortfall is in the billions of dollars.

- **Medicare** similarly will be broke and insolvent within *five* to *seven* years. Medicare total annual payments far exceed the Medicare total annual tax revenues. Medicare unfunded liabilities hit about *$89.3 trillion*[23] in January, 2009, according to the Medicare Administration. The average annual Medicare shortfall is in the billions of dollars.

- The combined *$107 trillion* unfunded liability for Social Security and for Medicare will require the U.S. Congress to begin making some major changes by significantly reducing costs and services.

- **Medicaid,** the joint federal and state funded companion plan to Medicare, is also badly underfunded and will soon become insolvent and go broke without some major changes. The average annual Medicaid shortfall is also in the billions of dollars.

- The **U.S. Postal** system loses large amounts of money each year.

- The U.S. Government **Amtrak** railroad system also loses large amounts of money each year.

- The federally chartered mortgage giants **Freddie Mac, Fannie Mae** and **FHA**, which were created to help raise money on Wall Street to finance home mortgages, are billions of dollars in the red and have required large amounts of our tax dollars and federal government-borrowed funds in 2009 and early 2010 to remain solvent. Together, in May, 2009, Freddie Mac and Fannie Mae accounted for at least *70%* of all U.S. home mortgage financing. In late 2009 and early 2010, FHA was as a practical matter the sole home mortgage entity making loans for existing and new homes. Over the next three to five years, FHA and all the other home mortgage lenders will be experiencing very serious financial problems relative to mortgage delinquencies, foreclosures and

---

[22] National Center for Policy Analysis, No. 662 (June 11, 2009)
[23] Ibid

further declines in home values, plus *massive credit defaults*, write-downs and write-offs of bad home mortgage debt.

- The U.S. Federal Government has run up annual budget deficits every year since fiscal 2002. Its total *combined* deficit in the first seven of those years, 2002-2008, was about *$2 trillion* not adjusted for inflation, according to federal budget statistics. This amounts to an average annual U.S. Federal Government budget deficit for these seven years of *$286 billion* per year. More ominously, the deficit shot to about *$1.450 trillion* in just the next year, fiscal 2009, and escalated the total since 2002 to a staggering *$3.45 trillion* or an average annual *$432 billion* per year. *These financial trends are not sustainable. Our U.S. Federal government rate of spending, the rate of deficit spending and the sharply rising national debt are obviously out of control. The majority of the American people are keenly aware of this.* The realistic prospect of our national debt doubling from *$12 trillion* in late 2009 to *$24 trillion* in only *10* to *12* years is very frightening.

Our federal government's track record regarding managing money and major government programs is terrible – I would give them a grade of "**F.**" There is no commitment or accountability toward a balanced budget or reduced spending, and the problem is getting much worse instead of better.

There are some things that our federal government has spent money on, our tax dollars, which were very positive and that have resulted in a great boost to our economy, to America, to businesses, to consumers and to families. All of these positive expenditures, however, took place many years ago. Some examples are listed below:

- *The TVA Project* – The Tennessee Valley Authority (TVA) following the Great Depression in the 1930s made a very positive contribution to making electrical power available to many key parts of rural America.
- *The GI Bill* – This legislation and expenditure following World War II helped to make it possible for many surviving members of the U.S. Armed Services to go to college, get better educations and to become more valuable and productive wage earners and business owners.
- *The Moon Shot* – The many new technologies that were associated with the successful U.S. spaceship launch to the moon in 1969 resulted in the creation of many new businesses, private sector jobs and ways to conduct business.
- *The U.S. Interstate Highway System* – The design and construction of our very extensive U.S. interstate and intrastate highway system has had many very positive economic and financial benefits for our overall

U.S. and state economies. The U.S. interstate highway system was begun during President Eisenhower's administration.

In the context in which I am discussing socialism, the words *socialism, communism, Marxism and progressivism* all have one major thing in common: none of these four ideologies represent freedom. All four ideologies are based on one very important and common principle, which is that a central authority of government should govern the means of production (labor and capital) and control decisions regarding incomes and benefits, irrespective of the level of productivity of the workers involved. They generally believe that all employees should make a livable wage and that businesses should not be allowed to fail. They believe governments can *manage* economies better than free and competitive markets can do on their own. They believe in every worker and business being winners and that there should be no losers. They generally believe in class warfare and taking from the rich and giving to the poor to achieve a redistribution of income and wealth. They do *not* understand the critical importance of entrepreneurship and a capitalistic system. Unfortunately, the above described principles of socialism are also embraced by many members and leaders of U.S. labor unions in America today.

Total union membership in the United States has declined substantially since 1983, which is the first year for which comparable and official government labor union data is available. In 2008, Union workers in the U.S. accounted for *12.4%* of all wage and salary workers in the public and private sector in 2008 on a combined basis, compared to *20.1%* in 1983. Therefore, over the past *26* years (1983-2008), labor union workers in America have declined *39%*[24]. But the changes have not been uniform:

- Labor union membership for *public sector* workers, employed by federal, state and local governments, accounted for *36.8%* of all public sector employees in 2008. Government workers are about *five* times more likely to belong to a labor union than in the private sector.
- Within the public sector of our economy, city, local and county government workers had the highest union membership rate of *42.2%* in 2008. These workers are, for example, teachers, police officers and fire fighters.
- Labor union membership for the *private sector* was only *7.6%* in 2008. Even though *less than 8%* of the total private sector labor workforce is unionized, union membership is relatively high in specific industries such as transportation, utilities, telecommunications, airport security, construction and U.S. auto manufacturing.

---

[24] U.S. Bureau of Economic Statistics, News Release dated January 28, 2009

Union membership since the early 1980s has declined more sharply in the private sector, but has actually been increasing in the public sector, which should not be at all surprising. This is part of the ongoing trend of increased dependency on the public sector in America, which is a negative trend for our country.

It is positive for our economy that labor union membership is now running under *8%* of the total private sector labor force and has declined significantly over the past *26* years. It is not positive that public sector labor union membership is growing and is now close to *37%*. The average hourly wage and benefit costs for labor union workers are significantly higher than for hourly workers who are nonunion. Hourly union workers are *not* more productive than hourly nonunion workers. Almost all U.S. private sector employers feel strongly that nonunion employees are significantly more productive and cost effective than union employees.

Union membership, as a percentage of the total labor force in both the public and private sectors in Western and Eastern Europe and in Japan, is much higher than in the U.S. This is a major reason why employee productivity levels are so much lower in those countries and why their labor costs, including employee benefits, are much higher than in the U.S. The more socialistic and dependent a country becomes on the public sector and on labor unions to raise hourly wages and benefits, the less productive such countries and economies become. This is one reason why the standard of living is significantly higher in the U.S. than in Europe, Japan and in many other countries.

Many people in America today have very little appreciation for the potential loss to our economy if we did not have individual capitalists such as entrepreneurs and business owners. Sadly, many people want to eliminate or at least sharply curtail the number and role of capitalists. Most of these capitalists are men and women who own, operate and manage relatively small businesses, and who have created at least *75%* to *80%* of all new jobs in America for the last 30 years. *Capitalism requires both winners and losers to produce its many positive benefits. Not everyone can be equal in the level of income earned, wealth generated and in the standard of living achieved.* Those who believe in the principles of socialism do not agree with or understand this.

The billions and trillions of dollars of *bailout* and *economic stimulus* spending by Congress and the executive branch in just *24* months in 2008 and 2009 represents very excessive, dangerous and irresponsible government growth and interference with our U.S. competitive free markets and capitalistic system. This has pushed the federal deficit to a record *$1.45 trillion* for fiscal 2009 and has put our national debt on course to double from *$12 trillion* in 2009 to nearly *$24 trillion* by the year 2020.

Adding a federally run public option to proposed healthcare reform or something close to it and passing the proposed cap and trade legislation – both of which Congress and the administration were discussing in December, 2009 – would be very negative for the U.S. economy for many years to come. These two major programs would significantly increase unemployment and would sharply increase our already out-of-control federal government spending and national debt for the next *10* years with nothing to show for it other than a struggling economy, a lot of red ink and far higher taxes. The idea of our federal government attempting to *manage* and control our U.S. healthcare system that currently represents *17%* of our total U.S. economy is truly absurd.

Figures 9.9 and 9.10 sketch out in more detail many of the *major negative aspects of public sector socialism and increased dependency on government compared to the major positive aspects of private sector capitalism, more limited government and increased self reliance. I encourage you to take time to review these two figures carefully.* There are badly misinformed and misguided people in America who desire more socialism and more dependency on government. There also are, unfortunately, a number of politicians who want more people to become increasingly dependent upon government and particularly the federal government, so they can have more control of peoples' lives to win more votes and longer terms in office.

Figure 9.9
The Major Negative Aspects of Socialism in the Public Sector with Increased Dependency on Government vs. the Major Positive Aspects of Capitalism in the Private Sector with More Limited Government

The Major Negative Aspects of Socialism with Increased Dependency on Government	The Major Positive Aspects of Capitalism with More Limited Government
1. Typically has not and will not improve the incomes, wealth and the standard of living of Americans in the private sector.	1. Has and will continue to significantly improve incomes and the standard of living for Americans.
2. Has typically not created any new wealth for Americans or for business owners and this will continue to be the case in the future.	2. Has been historically and will continue to be the sole factor that has created new wealth for Americans and for business owners in the years ahead.
3. Results in reduced incomes, wealth creation, reduced standard of living and	3. Results in creating many more and ever changing opportunities for more and more Americans to

significantly reduced opportunities for Americans to achieve the American dream.

4. Reduces gains in productivity by employees and will cause America to lose its leading role and dominance in productivity gains in the world.

5. Has not been and will never be responsible for creating new jobs on a sustainable and long-term basis in the private sector.

6. Reduces risk taking, investment, entrepreneurship, new business startups, bank lending and results in fewer new jobs and capitalists.

7. Significantly reduces the average annual economic growth rate on a longer-term and sustainable basis.

8. Increases substantially the role, influence, dominance and interference of government in the daily lives of Americans and for businesses.

9. Substantially reduces the freedoms, the freedom of choice and the liberty for all Americans and businesses.

10. Greatly increases the dependency of Americans on government and greatly expands the power, bureaucracy, control and influence of government on the lives of all Americans.

achieve the American dream and climb the economic ladder within their lifetimes.

4. Increases significantly the prospects for further gains in productivity by employees in America on a sustainable and long-term basis and to maintain its global dominance in productivity gains.

5. Has historically and will continue to be the major catalyst for creating many more new jobs on a sustainable and long-term basis.

6. Significantly increases risk taking, investment, entrepreneurship, new capitalists, new business formation, business expansion and bank lending.

7. Significantly increases the average annual rate of economic growth on a longer-term and sustainable basis.

8. Reduces the role, dominance and interference of government in the daily lives of Americans and for businesses. It rewards the *goose that lays the golden egg*, i.e. the capitalist.

9. Substantially increases the freedoms, the freedom of choice and the liberty for all Americans and businesses.

10. Greatly reduces the dependency of Americans on government. Fosters more limited government and encourages Americans to depend more on themselves, on businesses and on their employers.

11. Greatly increases government regulations, plus results in substantially higher cost of living, cost of doing business and taxes for most Americans and for all businesses.

12. Results in reducing the economic strength and power of America and reduces the value and purchasing power of the U.S. dollar.

13. Results in excessive growth in government, wasteful government spending, excessive government employment and irresponsible and damaging federal government budget deficits and national debt accumulation.

14. Results in very negative *too big to fail* policies, government *bailouts* and *economic stimulus* programs that have not worked historically, are not now working as advertised and will not work in the future.

15. Socialism and increased dependency on government results in the policy that say *"there shall be no losers, i.e. there will only be winners."* This policy always fails and will end up *reducing* incomes and the standard of living of most Americans.

16. Results in reducing the national security and safety of America and of Americans because of a weaker economy that is

11. Helps to moderate government regulations, plus results substantially lower cost of living, cost of doing business and taxes for most Americans and businesses. Broadens the tax base.

12. Results in increasing the economic strength and power of America and increases the value and purchasing power of the U.S. dollar.

13. Results in more limited government, reduced growth in government, reduced government spending, reduced government employment and reduced federal government budget deficits and works toward a balanced budget.

14. Results in the positive aspects of (a) banks and businesses in the private sector being allowed to fail and (b) no massive government *bailouts* and *economic stimulus* programs. This results in saving U.S. taxpayers billions and trillions of dollars and also results in lower rates of inflation and interest rates.

15. Capitalism and increased dependency on self, the private sector and on businesses results in *both* winners and losers. This clearly *improves* the incomes and the standard of living of most Americans over time.

16. Results in improving the national security and safety of America because of a stronger economy and an increased dependency on the

excessively dependent on government.

17. Results in substantially reducing the number of high income and high net worth individuals and business owner capitalists by taxing and regulating them excessively. This ends up being very negative for average Americans because of reduced incomes, fewer employment opportunities and a lower standard of living. The proponents of socialism want to discourage and reduce the number of millionaires and billionaires in America by redistributing their income and wealth.

18. The proponents of socialism and increased dependency on government believe that the wealthy Americans and capitalists are typically the *bad guys*. They want to take from the rich and give to the poor. They are committed to the principle of redistributing income and wealth, without realizing that a *declining tide lowers all boats* and therefore incomes and the standard of living for all Americans generally goes down. They believe more government and more regulations will *fix* the United States economy and result in a better life for most Americans.

private sector and on our capitalistic system.

17. Results in encouraging and increasing the number of high income and high net worth individuals and business owner capitalists by taxing and regulating them less. This ends up being very positive for average Americans by increasing incomes, creating more employment opportunities and improving the standard of living for most Americans. The proponents of capitalism want to encourage and increase the number of millionaires and billionaires in America, plus they want to greatly increase the prospects of individuals achieving the American dream.

18. The proponents of capitalism and of more limited government believe and know that the wealthy Americans and capitalists are typically the *good guys*. They want the rich and wealthy to do well and to become more plentiful because they know these are the people and families that are largely responsible for making most new investments, improving incomes, creating new jobs, expanding existing businesses and starting new ones, for positive economic growth and for paying _72%_ of all the federal government individual income taxes each year. They understand that a *rising tide raises all boats* and, thus the standard of living for most Americans goes up.

Source: This table was created by the author.

Figure 9.10
Illustration of Capitalism, Limited Government and the Private Sector at Work in Our U.S. Economy vs. Socialism, Bigger Government and the Public Sector at Work

Businesses, wage earners and consumers paying trillions of dollars in taxes

The public sector base, bigger government and the foundation of socialism at work

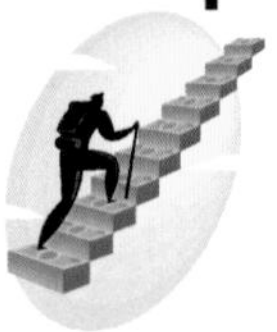

The redistribution of wealth and income from the private sector

Americans climbing the economic ladder, limited and reduced dependency on government and increased reliance on self and individual effort

Government employing millions of people and spending trillions of tax dollars (generally more than what the tax receipts are)

Improved standard of living, improved productivity and higher incomes

The public sector creates no new wealth and no new jobs and contributes very little to economic growth

Economic growth and new job creation

Increased dependency on government for income and financial assistance, much bigger and more expensive government and much less reliance on self and individual effort

Private sector investing, wealth creation, profits and new business formation

Government spending trillions of our tax dollars

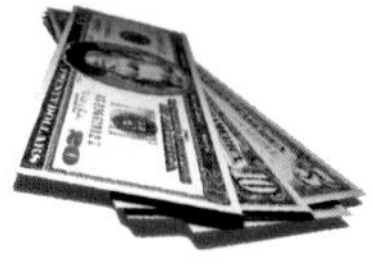

The private sector base, limited government and the foundation of capitalism at work

Illustration created by author

Those who believe that the creation of new wealth, better incomes, new jobs and an improved standard of living come from government, not from the private sector, are seriously misinformed. Unfortunately many people in America today do think this way and depend on more government for a better life. Such misinformed thinking is even more widespread and broader based in Western and Eastern Europe, Japan, Eastern Canada, Mexico, South America and Russia.

Socialism, by its very nature, has the following flaws:

- Much larger and more expensive government, including significantly higher taxes and much more bureaucracy, reduced efficiency and lower productivity levels.
- A greater number of people working for government, a greater percentage of our total national income coming from government spending, and government becoming a substantially larger percentage of our total economy over time.
- No real incentives or requirements, particularly at the federal level, to reduce costs, improve productivity, improve efficiencies, balance the various departmental and overall budgets or reduce regulations of many different kinds.
- Redistribution of incomes and wealth created in the private sector.
- Increased and expanded regulations that often make the private sector economy less effective and less productive, while increasing the cost of doing business and the cost of living.
- Investments of very large amounts of money into banks and other lending institutions, insurance companies, automobile companies, mortgage companies such as Fannie Mae, Freddie Mac and others. This often leads to taking on actual ownership positions and effectively controlling these companies and injecting political considerations on issues such as executive compensation.

Our government's policy in 2008 and 2009 of *too big to fail* is seriously flawed and clearly socialistic by its nature. When any lending institution or other business becomes insolvent, it should be allowed to fail and start over again under new ownership, with new *private capital* and with new management. Massive federal interference, control, involvement, investment and *management* in the private sector has historically and will again make the situation worse in years ahead. This is what happened in Japan during its *modern day depression* from 1992 to 2006 and in Western and Eastern Europe during the last 80 years.

Why increased Capitalism, more Limited Government and Less Socialism is Positive for America

Americans who believe in our U.S. capitalistic system know that capitalism is not perfect – it never has been and never will be. However, those who believe in freedom of choice, free market competition, limited government and the entrepreneurial use of private capital investment to create jobs and wealth also truly understand that this is by far the best system in the world for building a strong economy and achieving a better standard of living for most Americans. Many people know that these key and positive factors do *not* come from government.

Capitalism, as used and defined in this book, depends upon the private sector, *not* the government sector, to create and sustain economic growth, new jobs, new wealth, better incomes for workers, improved productivity levels and an improved standard of living for Americans. The success and dependability of capitalism moving forward will depend heavily on maintaining a relatively strong U.S. dollar, low inflation, relatively low interest rates, relatively low employee and business taxes and the willingness and financial ability of banks and other lenders to realistically loan more money. In addition, the federal government must make a serious commitment to work towards a balanced budget within the next five to seven years, mostly by significantly reducing government spending.

Capitalism and the Business Cycle go Hand in Hand Relative to the Ups and Downs in the U.S. Economy

The U.S. capitalistic system today and historically is based on the long-term 60- to 80-year boom and bust business cycle and on the periodic recession cycle.

The U.S. economy, the stock markets, energy costs, interest rates, commodity prices, real estate market values and airfares go up and down over time. So also do the debt and income of consumers, families and businesses. Even the health conditions of most Americans go through ups and downs, much as weather conditions change seasonally and over time. The very nature of capitalism is reflected in cycles of ups and downs. The ups typically last years longer and far overshadow the downs, which usually last for no more than several months. However, when the U.S. economy is going through the longer-term *bust* phase of the business cycle of a *modern day* depression, as is happening now, the financial pain of a *down* period typically can be expected to last for a period of seven to 10 *years*. This is much longer than a normal recession *down* period and much longer than **95%** of the American people and elected politicians are expecting.

159

Banks and other lenders typically are not making many new loans under these conditions, while unemployment levels are much higher than normal. With significant losses of asset wealth, reduced consumer spending and slower-than-normal U.S. economic growth, the call for the federal government to *help* is predictable, including a call for more government regulations. The point I am making, however, is that *now is not the time* to blame the U.S. capitalistic system for our current economic and financial problems. The truth is that getting our federal government more involved to fix the problems is a very big mistake and will clearly make things worse as has been the case historically in the U.S, Japan and Europe.

The *boom* phase of the long-term business cycle typically lasts many years. The last U.S. economic *boom*, for example, lasted 68 years, from 1940 to 2007 as discussed in Chapters 1 and 2. The last *bust* phase, before that boom, occurred during the 10 years from 1930 to 1939. There also were *11* recessions during the 1940-2007 boom, each lasting ***10.2 months*** on average, but the most recent *bust* phase of our long-term business cycle began in 2008-2009 and will likely continue at least through 2014 and possibly longer. Because recessions are short lived, the economic setback and relatively quick recovery often look like a letter **V** when charted on a graph. Longer term *busts* such as I believe we are in now last for years, during which smaller and slower economic growth and higher than normal unemployment form something more like a letter **L** when its path is charted.

The *bust* phase of the long-term business cycle typically lasts for a period of five, seven or 10 years and always is associated with one or more major financial excesses and bubbles. Examples of these bubbles would be residential housing, commercial and industrial real estate, farm and ranch real estate, commodity markets and the stock markets. These bubbles eventually start bursting as we saw in Chapters 4 through 6. When these bubbles burst, major wealth is lost, our borrowing and spending capacity is diminished and the economy grows much more slowly than normal. This leads to substantially higher-than-normal levels of unemployment, large numbers of bank failures, major price and asset deflation, increased consumer savings and major credit defaults and private debt write-downs and write-offs.

Most people in America today believe the U.S. was in a serious recession in 2008 and 2009. These same people believe our economy will get back to normal and *sustained* positive and normal economic growth (within the *3%* to *4%* range per year) beginning in 2010 and beyond. Most people in late 2009 believe the U.S. recession is over. I do not agree.

Capitalism and the business cycle go hand in hand. The very nature of capitalism is that there are periodic recessions and about once in a lifetime, there is an economic depression. This will happen for the next 200 years as it has been happening for the past 234 years. It is a major mistake for Americans and for government policymakers to allow government to get as involved as it has become in 2008 and 2009. Economic ups and downs come with the figurative territory in a country founded on the principles of capitalism, freedom, limited government and competitive free markets. America's longer-term economic growth, new job and wealth creation, productivity and increasing standards of living historically have fared well under this structure. For this to continue, the socialistic trends of bigger and more expensive government, reduced freedoms, more regulations and higher taxes must be turned around. Smaller and more limited government and lower taxes, along with reduced government spending will be positive for Americans and for our U.S. economy in the years ahead.

Capitalism protects our freedoms and our competitive free market system. Our capitalistic system has made the U.S. economy the largest and strongest in the world. Our *$13 trillion* economy is *2.7 times* bigger than the world's second largest economy, Japan. Japan has a *$4.8 trillion* economy. However, the biggest threat to America, our economy and capitalism is the loss of more of our freedoms to a much bigger, more expensive and more socialistic and controlling federal government that has been evolving since the early 1980s, accelerating from 2001 to 2007, and has become completely out of control in 2008-2010.

Capitalism is not perfect. From time to time there are abuses and fraud by individuals, banks and other lenders and by individual companies in the private sector of our economy. The same thing, however, can be said about government at all levels within the public sector. Neither the private nor the public sectors are perfect. This has been true historically and will continue to be true for centuries to come.

Government controlled and centrally planned economies do *not* work and have *not* ever worked anywhere in the world when you compare income levels, wealth creation, productivity levels, and general standards of living to Americans'. The incomes, wealth, productivity levels and standard of living of Americans are unequalled anywhere else in the world. No other country in the world even comes close, except for Canada. This is because capitalism works and socialism and centrally planned economies like China and Russia do *not*. The income and standard of living levels, for example, in countries like China, Russia, Mexico and South America are dramatically *lower than in* America. I believe America is at a real crossroads in its relatively young history. I do, however, have faith in the American people and in their ability to take their country back and to say *no* to more dependency on higher taxes and to bigger government and *no* to socialism moving forward.

Capitalism is the Primary Engine in our Economy and it is Being Seriously Threatened

Capitalism and, more specifically, the increase in the number of American capitalists, millionaires and billionaires represent the proverbial *goose that lays the golden eggs* for America. These are the individuals, families and business owners that have made it possible for America to become the largest and strongest economy in the world in a relatively short *234* years compared to all other countries in the world. How and why did this happen? The key factors that have made this possible are (1) our freedom, (2) limited government and (3) the desire of individual investors, consumers, capitalists, wage earners and entrepreneurs to achieve the American dream. American capitalism is based on the principle of both winners and losers and periodic economic and financial ups and downs. *Capitalists are the good guys, not the bad guys.*

I worry that a record number of these capitalists will be financially wiped out in 2010-2014. The reason is the sharp decline of equity and wealth resulting from the major declines in real estate values, commodity values and stock market values in that time. It will take many years for a new set of capitalists to emerge and replace those who have lost all or a major portion of their wealth by the time we get to 2014. Few people in the private sector and in government today appear to be thinking about this or to have a real concept of how serious this problem will be for America in the next *10* years and beyond.

Between the seven years of 2008 and 2014, America will likely lose *70%* to *80%* of its capitalists. At minimum, most of our capitalists will experience a sharp decline in the market value of their assets and a sharp reduction in wealth, net worth and income. These are the *10%* of all U.S. taxpayers with incomes above *$113,000* who pay *71%* to *72%* of all federal government personal and individual income taxes.

Losing these capitalists and their income tax payments means that federal, state and local government tax revenues will continue to decline significantly and will remain much lower than what most government officials and politicians are planning on. The federal level of government will experience the most serious pinch because it is more dependent than state or local governments on income taxes. This will put more pressure on Congress and the present administration to quickly start reducing federal government spending and seriously working towards a balanced budget. It also means that economic and private sector growth and investment will remain much slower than normal and that unemployment levels will go much higher and stay much higher than normal for at least five years. These are some of the serious consequences that will result from the *wounded* capitalists.

One irony is that the very nature of our capitalistic system is creating this problem. Our economy is now going through the *bust* phase of our long-term business cycle or *modern day* depression. This natural and inevitable part of the cycle will continue to strike a serious blow to America's individual capitalists because they are among those with the most financial strength, wealth and income to lose. It took many years for a new generation of capitalists to emerge following the Great Depression of the 1930s, when America last experienced such a major loss of its capitalists within a generally price and asset deflationary period.

Another irony is that the current administration and the current Democratic-controlled Congress are determined to eliminate or substantially reduce our U.S. capitalists through much higher taxes, more regulations and a serious loss of freedom. Many of the American capitalists will start moving what capital they have left out of the U.S. over the next several years because of the much higher taxes and increased regulation in government bureaucracy that are forthcoming. Bottom line, most politicians have no real appreciation for how critically important our American capitalists are to our economy or to our future, and they have no real appreciation of where America is today in terms of our long-term business cycle bust. Thus many are now trying to eliminate the capitalistic *geese that lay the golden eggs* needed to end the crisis.

Dr. Adrian Rogers (1931-2005), one of the most respected Christian leaders of our time, eloquently summed up the dilemma in a widely quoted plea for the recognition of the value of hard work in our society:

"You cannot legislate the poor into freedom by legislating the wealthy out of freedom. What one person receives without working for, another person must work for without receiving. The government cannot give to anybody anything that the government does not first take from somebody else. When half of the people get the idea that they do not have to work because the other half is going to take care of them, and when the other half gets the idea that it does no good to work because somebody else is going to get what they work for, that my dear friend, is about the end of any nation. You cannot multiply wealth by dividing it."

The Creation of New Net Wealth in the United States Depends Heavily on Manufacturing, Mining, Energy, Agriculture and Construction of Products and Tangible Goods Over Time

I have said and written for many years that *new net wealth creation* within the U.S. economy depends heavily upon improving productivity gains, which generally improves America's standard of living over time, and upon manufacturing, mining, agriculture, growing or building many different kinds of tangible structures, goods and products.

U.S. manufacturers create wealth by producing many different types of *big ticket* and *small ticket* products that Americans and overseas customers buy and use on an ongoing basis. Mining, energy and natural resources companies create wealth by producing all kinds of metals, such as iron ore, gold, silver, copper, platinum and many other types of minerals, plus many types of natural resources such as crude oil, coal, water, natural gas and lumber. Farmers, ranchers and the U.S. agricultural and food industry are a key source of new net wealth creation in our country. For example, the American people spend *$75 billion* annually on beef alone, which represents by far the largest single segment of the total U.S. agriculture and food industry. Builders create wealth when they erect new homes, apartment buildings, new office buildings, shopping centers, malls, hospitals, warehouses, factories and industrial construction projects of many different kinds in the U.S.

Consider the words of Professor Tom Eagar at MIT, which were in *Manufacturing and Technology News*, dated July 3, 2003:

"The U.S. economy is dependent on manufacturing, mining, agriculture and construction as being the only sectors that create wealth. All other sectors, including finance, healthcare, services and government either consume wealth or redistribute it. 'Over half the jobs in the country are in the service sector and they are created by a strong manufacturing base,' says Eagar. 'If we don't have a strong manufacturing base, we'll lose service sector jobs and we'll see unemployment at the French level.'

The key to our U.S. success 'is to create new jobs faster than the jobs we're losing,' he adds. 'You can't fight what is inevitable. Transitions are difficult. We're going to continue to have them in each industry as they become global. But the investment in manufacturing builds productivity, technology, education and a better standard of living.'

The long-term decline in U.S. manufacturing employment can be tied directly to steady improvement in productivity over the past 50 years, he adds. Manufacturing productivity has increased at an annual average rate of 2.78%, meaning U.S. workers are producing 400% more today than they were in 1953. Yet per capita consumption has not increased by a similar amount. Without substantially increasing exports 'we're going to lose direct labor,' says Eagar. 'What's your choice? Quit improving productivity?' Jobs associated with trade have grown faster than any other sector of the economy over the last half century, with 12 million jobs now dependent on exports, he says.

The growth of manufacturing in China and India represents 'a ticking time bomb' for the United States economy, says Eagar. The constraints that have limited China's growth as an industrial powerhouse are quickly fading. The cost of transporting products to overseas markets is low. Communication bottlenecks have been eliminated. A highly skilled technical workforce is being trained and employed. And there is plenty of low-cost capital available – something that didn't exist until recently.

'We're not even paying attention to the fact that they have the technology, the people and the capital,' says Eagar. China is graduating 300,000 engineers per year as compared to about 30,000 graduating from U.S. universities. 'Japan hit us in the 80s, but China will knock our socks off in the 2020s and it will be a much bigger blow because it will hit us when all the baby boomers are looking at their pensions.'"

The prospect of our U.S. economy going through a very serious and painful further slowdown and loss of growth, loss of wealth, loss of jobs, loss of incomes, loss of private sector investment and a decline in America's standard of living over at least the next five to seven years is very high and very real. I believe 2010-2014 will be particularly painful. The biggest mistake that U.S. politicians and Americans generally can make is to blame capitalism or the capitalists. The best thing politicians and Americans can do is to let our capitalistic system work and elect members of Congress and a new president who are firmly committed to a much more limited and less expensive government and to balancing our federal government budget without raising taxes. In fact, taxes need to be reduced in the future.

There is *one* simple and very important truth regarding how and why in 2008 and 2009 the U.S. private and public sectors have experienced the most serious economic and financial problems since the Great Depression. *We have clearly lived far beyond our means. We have tried hard to borrow our way to prosperity by building up massive amounts of debt and leverage within both the private and public sectors of our economy.* Many bubbles have already burst as a result in the residential, commercial, industrial, farm, ranch, commodity, stock and credit markets. The private sector is painfully dealing with this reality by going through a major deleveraging process that will last for at least 10 years. The public sector will have no choice but to begin following the same path by seriously reducing spending, balancing government budgets, lowering taxes and deleveraging the public sectors of our economy. All sectors must begin to live much more within their means by borrowing and spending less money. The bust phase of our long-term business cycle will end up making this happen in *both* sectors. *Our U.S. economy will experience a modern day depression within the 2008-2014 time period.*

There is a good correlation over time between total taxes paid by individuals and businesses, the health, growth and size of any major economy and the degree of capitalism or socialism that exists. Based on information from the National Tax Foundation in Washington, D.C., total annual federal, state and local tax revenues in 2008, as a percent of GDP, were about *40%*, *27%* and *27%*, respectively, for Europe, Japan and the United States. The second largest economy in the world, as of 2009, is Japan, yet the Japanese economy is only *36% to 38%* the size of the U.S. economy. Western and Eastern European economies are significantly more socialistic than the U.S. economy and have experienced less growth, lower incomes, less wealth creation and a lower standard of living than the U.S. for the last *50* years. Western and Eastern Europe and Japan also have aging populations which will continue to cause declining consumption and economic growth in these countries over the next 30 to 60 years as discussed in Chapter 3.

Total tax revenues as a percent of GDP were *48%* higher in Europe than they were in the U.S. and Japan in 2008. More capitalists, more limited government, less regulations and lower taxes in the U.S. are key reasons why our economy has performed relatively better than the economies in Europe. These are also why the U.S. must reduce the size and growth of government and start living within its means. Doing so will result in keeping the U.S. economy number one in the world in all key categories.

Corporate and business *tax rates* in America are far too high and need to be significantly reduced. As of 2009, the corporate and business top tax rate was *39.5%* in Japan, *39.1%* in the United States and *26.3%* in Europe. Lowering U.S. corporate and business tax rates would significantly improve private sector investment, job creation, economic growth and the competitive position of the U.S. Raising taxes on U.S. corporations, businesses and capitalists will produce just the opposite results. Unfortunately, this is what the current administration and the Democratic-controlled Congress want to do. Higher taxes are *not* a cure. Higher taxes will be the final blow to the struggling U.S. economy and capitalists, especially during the next *10* years.

Federal budget statistics for fiscal year 2008 for seven major categories of federal taxes, shown in Figure 9.11, show that *93.2%* or *$2.351 trillion* of the federal government's tax receipts that year came from *income taxes*. These include personal income taxes, FICA payroll taxes and corporate income taxes, which accounted for *45.4%*, *35.7%* and *12.1%*, respectively, of all federal tax receipts that year. The remaining *6.8%* or *$173 billion* of federal tax collections came from excise taxes, customs duties, estate and gift taxes and all other federal government taxes.

Figure 9.12 shows that the top *1%* and *5%* income earners in the U.S. for the year 2007, which are the latest statistics available from the Internal Revenue Service (IRS), paid *40.4%* and *60%*, respectively, of the total federal individual income taxes collected. These were Americans and families who numbered *1.4 million* and *7.1 million* and who had adjusted gross incomes of more than *$410,096* and *$160,041*, respectively. The effective individual income tax rates for these American taxpayers were *22.5%* and *20.5%*, respectively, for 2007.

Figure 9.11

The U.S. Federal Government Budget and Actual Tax Revenues (Receipts) for Fiscal Years 2007 and 2008 for the Seven Major Tax Receipt Categories

Major Federal Government Tax Revenue and Receipt Categories	Billions of Dollars for 2007	Percent of Total	Billions of Dollars for 2008	Percent of Total
1. Personal and individual income taxes	1.100	43.9	1.146	45.4
2. FICA payroll taxes (Social Security, Medicare and other retirement taxes)	.870	34.7	.901	35.7
3. Corporate income taxes	.370	14.8	.304	12.1
Subtotal	2.340	93.4	2.351	93.2
4. Excise taxes	.065	2.6	.066	2.6
5. Customs duties	.026	1.0	.028	1.2
6. Estate and gift taxes	.026	1.0	.028	1.0
7. All other federal government taxes	.047	2.0	.051	2.0
Grand Total Tax Revenues	2.504*	100	2.524*	100

*These two numbers are *$2.504 trillion* for fiscal year 2007 and *$2.524 trillion* for fiscal year 2008.

Source: President's Budget, Office of Management and Budget, Summary Table S-3 (published February 26, 2009)

Figure 9.12

Individual Federal Government Income Taxes Paid by the Top 1%, 5% and 10% Income Earners versus the Bottom 50% Income Earners for the Year 2007
(Based on a total of 141,071,000 Taxpayers)

Major Taxpayer Categories	The *Top 1%* Income Earners in 2007	The *Top 5%* Income Earners in 2007	The *Top 10%* Income Earners in 2007	The *Bottom 50%* Income Earners in 2007
1. Number of tax returns with a positive adjusted gross income (AGI)	1,410,710 (**1%** of total)	7,053,549 (**5%** of total)	14,108,000 (**10%** of total)	70,535,000 (**50%** of total)
2. Percentage share of the total individual income taxes paid	40.4%	60.6%	71.2%	2.9%
3. Income (AGI) split point	An AGI of *above $410,096*	An AGI of *above $160,041*	An AGI of *above $113,018*	An AGI of *below $32,879*
4. Average tax rate	22.5%	20.5%	18.8%	3.0%

Source: The Internal Revenue Service and the Tax Foundation

IRS data in Figure 9.12 also shows the *top 10%* income earners in the U.S. for the year 2007 accounted for *71.2%* of the total federal individual income taxes paid. These were Americans and families who numbered *14.1 million* and who had adjusted gross incomes of *more* than *$113,018*. Their average effective individual income tax rate in 2007 was *18.8%*. In contrast, *70.5 million* income earners in the *bottom 50%* of the taxpaying public, with incomes below *$32,879*, paid only *2.9%* of the total federal individual income taxes collected. Their average effective income tax rate was *3.0%* in 2007. These numbers show a very progressive federal government tax system, wherein relatively few (the top *10%* of the income earners) of all U.S. taxpayers pay between *71%* and *72%* of all federal government individual income taxes. This percentage was at a historically high level in 2007 based on the latest data from the IRS. The above numbers *exclude* FICA payroll taxes or Social Security, Medicare and Medicaid and corporate income taxes.

For the year 2007, total federal government tax revenues from individual income taxes paid was *$1.100 trillion.* Data from the IRS and the Tax Foundation, as shown in Figure 9.13, illustrates that the **top** *1%, 5%* and *10%* of all U.S. income earners in 2007 paid total federal government individual income taxes of *$444 billion, $666 billion* and *$783 billion*, respectively. Their individual tax payments on average were *$314,735, $94,421* and *$55,000*, respectively. In contrast, the **bottom** *50%* of all wage earners paid, on an average annual basis, individual federal income taxes per tax return of only *$454* in 2007 and paid a total on a collective basis of only *$32 billion* in total taxes for the year 2007, which represented only *2.9%* of the total individual income taxes paid in that year. In other words, the *14.1 million* U.S. taxpayers who made up the top *10%* of the U.S. income earners in 2007 paid *71.2%* of the total federal personal and individual income taxes, while the *70.5 million* U.S. taxpayers who made up the bottom *50%* of the U.S. income earners in 2007 paid only *2.9%* of the total federal personal and individual income taxes paid that year.

Figure 9.13
The Relatively Few Americans who Pay Most of the Federal Government Individual Incomes Taxes
($1.100 Trillion Tax Receipts Collected in 2007)

Major Taxpayer Categories	Top 1% Income Earners	Top 5% Income Earners	Top 10% Income Earners	Bottom 50% Income Earners
1. Number of tax returns with a positive AGI	1,410,710	7,053,549	14,108,000	70,535,000
2. Percentage share of the total individual income taxes paid	40.4%	60.6%	71.2%	2.9%
3. Combined grand total individual income taxes paid in 2007	$444 billion	$666 billion	$783 billion	$32 billion
4. Average annual individual income taxes paid per tax return in 2007	$314,735	$94,421	$55,500	$454

Source: The Internal Revenue Service and the Tax Foundation

Federal Spending Must also be Controlled

Federal government spending and the massive annual budget deficits, particularly for the years 2008, 2009 and 2010, are increasing sharply and are truly out of control. Federal Office of Management and Budget numbers for fiscal 2008 shown in Figure 9.14, for example, show that *62.5%* of the total *$2.983 trillion* that the U.S. spent that year were what are called *mandatory* expenses. That means they cannot be negotiated between the President and Congress. The money, *$1.863 trillion*, primarily went to Social Security, Medicare and Medicaid and similar programs and to pay interest on the federal debt. Other expenses, which are counted as *discretionary* because the amounts are negotiable, are considered essential. Defense spending is one example. It accounts for *$592 billion*, or *19.8%* of the federal total. Adding defense spending to mandatory spending leaves only *17.7%* percent of the federal total, or *$528 billion,* from which to cut money needed to reduce a *$1.45 trillion* budget deficit.

Figure 9.14

The U.S. Federal Government Budget and Actual Spending for Fiscal Year 2008 for the Six Major Combined Mandatory and Discretionary Spending Categories

Major Federal Government Budget and Spending Categories	Billions of Dollars	Percent of Total	Mandatory Spending	Discretionary Spending
1. Social Security	612	20.5	612	No
2. Medicare and Medicaid	587	19.7	587	No
3. Other mandatory spending	411	13.8	411	No
4. Net interest expense on the national debt	253	8.5	253	No
Subtotal	1.863	62.5	1.863	No
5. National defense spending	592	19.8	No	592
6. All other discretionary spending	528	17.7	No	528
Subtotal	1.120	37.5	No	1.120
Grand Total Spending	2.983*	100	1.863	1.120

*This number is *$2.983 trillion*.

Source: President's Budget, Office of Management and Budget, Summary Table S-3 (published February 26, 2009)

The Federal Government will Soon Run Out of Borrowing and Spending Bullets in 2010-2014

Realistically and factually, the U.S. Congress and the past and present administrations are very good and successful at growing and expanding the federal government. However, they have *not* and *cannot* grow the U.S. economy or create any new net jobs. This is done in the private sector. The American people are going to be saying *no* to the U.S. Federal Government borrowing more and more money and spending more and more money and increasing the annual budget deficits and our national debt at the voting booths in November of 2010 and 2012 and beyond. These trends are irresponsible and are clearly *not* sustainable. Our federal government and the Federal Reserve Board will effectively run out of borrowing and spending *bullets* within the 2010-2014 time period. The American people and the markets will be effectively forcing our government to begin reducing its spending and committing to a balanced budget over the next five years and beyond. Bottom line, the federal government will have to finally begin living within its means, like consumers, families, businesses, banks and other lenders in America are now doing and will continue to do within the 2010-2014 time period and beyond.

It is clear that Congress and the White House must get serious about reducing spending. This means that at least five out of the total of six major categories of our federal government budget shown in Figure 9.14 must be reduced significantly over the next five to 10 years. The only major budget item that cannot realistically be reduced much is the interest expense on our national debt. To make real progress on reducing federal government spending, the amount of spending for Social Security, Medicare, Medicaid, and other mandatory items and for national defense must all be reduced substantially. Growing numbers of Americans have an *entitlement mentality* today regarding such spending, including the national (public option) healthcare and cap and trade socialistic ideas. If those attitudes are not reversed quickly, our country will soon become much more socialistic and will end up either going bankrupt, the worst case outcome, or at a minimum, losing our *U.S. Triple A credit rating*. This will mean much higher taxes, much larger and more expensive government, the loss of freedoms, a much slower growth economy, much higher than normal levels of unemployment and a reduced standard of living for most Americans for many years.

Out-of-control federal spending, our sharply increasing budget deficits and our unsustainable and rapidly increasing national debt must be seriously addressed soon. For the years 2009 and 2010, there is obviously no commitment by the U.S. House of Representatives, the U.S. Senate or the administration to seriously reduce federal government spending or to balance our government's budget. This was also true in the eight years of 2001-2008 by Congress and the past administration. The only real difference is that the degree of irresponsible federal government spending and budget deficits has gotten much worse in fiscal 2009 and 2010 than was the case in fiscal 2001-2008.

It is obvious that the majority of the members of Congress have *no* discipline or commitment to reducing federal government spending, annual budget deficits and taxes or balancing the federal budget. The only way this badly needed discipline will come is for the American people to replace many of the present members of Congress beginning in 2010 and to elect a new president through their voting power in 2012 and beyond. I believe this will happen because the majority of Americans today know that the course we are now on is not sustainable and will end up bankrupting our country. *I strongly believe that Americans are slowly waking up and getting mad, which will lead to doing the right things to take our country back.*

The combination of many Americans saying *no* to socialism and their deep and growing concern about the out-of-control federal government spending, massive budget deficits and rapidly escalating U.S. national debt, plus very painful, high and rising levels of unemployment across the United States, will very likely lead to the election of a new president and many new faces in Congress in 2012. I said in a speech I gave to the FC Store Fall Renewable Fuels Outlook Conference in West Des Moines, Iowa on September 18, 2008 *before* the 2008 national election, *"Because of what I see ahead for the U.S. economy over the next several years, whoever is elected President of the United States on November 4, 2008, will likely be a **one-term** president."*

Federal Government *Bailout, Economic Stimulus, Private Sector Investments* and *Too-Big-to-Fail* Programs and Policies Simply Do Not Work in the Bust Phase of the Long-term Business Cycle

Federal government *bailout, economic stimulus, bank and private company investments* and *too-big-to-fail* programs have very little positive and sustainable impact on economic growth, consumer spending, new job creation or the challenges of normal recessions and economic downturns, let alone during the *bust* phase of the long-term 60- to 80-year business cycle. Recent examples of these government policy failures include Bank of America, Citibank, JP Morgan Chase, AIG, General Motors, Chrysler Corporation, Freddie Mac, Fannie Mae and many others.

These have been major mistakes in federal government and Federal Reserve policy. *All* private sector businesses that become insolvent must be allowed to fail through the bankruptcy courts. *Rewarding seriously flawed business models, poor management and high risk financing with U.S. tax dollars is now and*

172

always has been a serious mistake. Success and failure are important parts of our capitalistic system. These same government programs and policies have virtually no positive and sustainable impact on economic growth, consumer spending and on new job creation when the U.S. economy goes through an economic depression. History is very clear on this point. For example, during the last depression in the 1930s, the federal government spent massive amounts of money on various *bailout* and *economic stimulus* programs when Franklin Delano Roosevelt was president. These spending programs basically did very little, if any, good. What did make a difference was the major government spending and the unification of America that resulted from the U.S. entering and winning World War II in the 1940s. World War II spending worked because the money was spent on manufacturing, which employed millions of men and women to work in factories and shipyards to make airplanes, battleships, destroyers, submarines, artillery equipment, guns, military clothing, munitions and other material. For example, my father was a medical doctor in the Army during World War II. My mother was a welder in the Navy Shipyards in San Francisco during the war.

Massive economic stimulus and government spending and bailout programs historically have not worked in Europe or Japan either. For example, during Japan's version of a serious modern day depression in 1992-2006, that nation spent massive amounts of money over 15 years on major bailout, economic stimulus and too-big-to-fail programs. *These Japanese government programs and policies did not work then and are not working today.*

The major reason why these programs did *not* work was because Japan was in the *bust* phase of its own long-term 60- to 80-year business cycle. Real estate values in Japan ended up declining **65%** to **75%** and their stock market declined **80%** from the high point to the low point. But the Japanese government and people at the time did *not* know they were in the *bust* phase of the long-term business cycle. So, when Japan tried to save banks and companies it thought too big to fail, their efforts failed and these policies significantly dragged out the painful process for a much longer period of time (for a number of years) than it would have taken otherwise.

We have had a very similar situation in the U.S. in 2008, 2009 and 2010. Our government and most Americans do not understand that our economy is now in the early stages of the *bust* phase of our own long-term business cycle or a *modern day* economic depression. Our government representatives believe today that these economic *stimulus* and *bailout* remedies will work or are working. But the programs are not working now nor will they work as expected or as advertised by government representatives and by most in the news media.

173

Any positive impact of these government efforts will at best be very minor and short-lived.

I strongly believe that U.S. economic growth, consumer spending, rising unemployment and asset deflationary forces will get significantly worse in 2010-2014 and particularly in 2010-2012. If I am correct in this forecast, as I believe I will be, most people will come to realize that our federal government *bailout, economic stimulus* or *too big to fail* programs did not work. Their surprise, disappointment and anger will result in even less spending and investing by consumers and even more saving by consumers. Most people will realize by the end of calendar 2012 that the U.S. is going through an economic depression and an extended period of economic stagnation.

Congress and the next president must commit to and follow essential conservative political and economic principles in order for Americans to take back their country and to say *no* to socialism, bigger government and higher taxes

I strongly believe that the majority of Americans today, regardless of their political affiliation, are concerned with the extreme far left and socialistic policies of the present administration and the actions of the U.S. House of Representatives and the Senate. Simply stated, most Americans do *not* like the socialistic and increasingly bureaucratic government and our massive and irresponsible budget deficits, our out of control spending and the sharply escalating national debt shown in Figures 9.1 through 9.4 and in 9.11 through 9.13. People understand that these excessive spending and budget deficit policies will result in much higher taxes for *all* Americans in the future. Americans generally know that it is wrong to live beyond our means as we have been doing the last 30 years and that it is especially wrong now. All Americans and all three party affiliations – Republican, Democrat and Independent – are to blame for the current mess and for the serious budget and spending problems we have today. The *blame game* will accomplish nothing. We as voting Americans must shoulder the responsibility. Below are the principles that must be committed and adhered to by members of Congress and by the next president in order for Americans to take back their country and say *no* to socialism, *no* to bigger government and *no* to higher taxes:

- Substantially reduce spending and benefits, including for Social Security, Medicare and for Medicaid.
- Reduce income and FICA payroll taxes and reduce the size and cost of government.
- Balance the budget in five to seven years.
- Reduce government regulations.
- Support a strong U.S. dollar and national defense.

- *Increase* the dependency on capitalism in the private sector. *Decrease* the dependency on socialism in the public sector.
- Depend on free market solutions. Depend on the American risk and reward, success and failure principles of capitalism.
- Increase freedom and liberty for all Americans and for America.
- Reduce America's dependency on foreign oil.
- Understand where the U.S. economy is now in the long-term boom and bust business cycle.
- Replace the federal government tax code with one that is the same as or very similar to the tax reform plan and proposal discussed below and summarized in Figure 9.15.

The U.S. Federal Government tax code and system is broken. It is in major need of being replaced with a better system that is much simpler, has a much broader and larger tax base and has much lower tax rates. The new system must substantially improve U.S. economic growth, new job creation, investment, saving by consumers, new capital formation, productivity gains and an improved standard of living for the American people. It also must tax income and capital only once as opposed to multiple times as is the case now, remain progressive, eliminate the IRS from the lives of all wage earners and transfer the power of taxation from the IRS and the U.S. Treasury to the U.S. consumer.

I have authored and worked diligently since 1984 to craft a very sound replacement to the present U.S. Federal Government tax code that indeed achieves all of the guiding principles outlined above. My proposed tax plan is called *The BEST Plan* and is summarized in Figure 9.15. *The BEST Plan* was introduced in the U.S. Senate as Senate Bill S.1921 on October 26, 2005 by senators Jim DeMint and Lindsey Graham. As of early January of 2010, S.1921 has not come out of committee and has not yet been acted upon by the U.S. Congress.

Figure 9.15

The "BEST" Plan

Americans For The BEST Tax Reform Plan

- The Broad Economic Simplification Tax (The BEST Plan), S. 1921, was introduced in the U.S. Senate by Senators Jim DeMint and Lindsay Graham of South Carolina on October 26, 2005. The lead sponsor is Senator Jim DeMint.
- The BEST Plan is not a Republican or Democratic idea or plan. It is a *people's* plan, not a *party* plan. It is a plan for all Americans. This new and much needed tax policy must be achieved on a bipartisan basis.

- The BEST Plan (when it is passed by Congress and signed by the president) will do significantly more for all of the American people, for our economy and for our competitive position in the global market place than anything that the U.S. Congress and our federal government has done in the last 100 years. The BEST Plan is a *homerun* economically and politically. It represents a truly *win-win* opportunity for all American wage earners, families, consumers, businesses and for our economy.
- The BEST Plan was authored by Bill Helming of Olathe, Kansas (economist and business consultant), along with valuable input from many people across the United States. Bill has been *fine tuning* the BEST Plan since 1984.
- The BEST Plan can be found at:
  govinfo.library.unt.edu/taxreformpanel/.../BBestPlanExecSumfinal42905.doc

Key points regarding Step One for the BEST Plan

- It initially (step one) replaces *100%* of all present federal government personal and corporate income taxes, plus all estate and gift taxes. The FICA payroll, excise, customs duties and all other federal government taxes remain in place. It replaces about *60%* of all present federal government taxes. Step two would replace all FICA payroll and all other taxes.
- It is a two-tiered revenue neutral tax system with a uniform tax rate of *8.5%*.
- *Tier One* is a business transfer tax. The *8.5%* business transfer tax rate is applied to all gross business annual wages. There is no withholding for wage earners relative to federal income taxes. All business capital purchases (including real estate), all purchased inputs and all purchased services (including contract labor costs), are deducted from gross domestic sales in calculating business profits that are also subject to the *8.5%* tax rate. There will be no depreciation from a tax standpoint as all business expenditures are deducted (expensed) in the year incurred via a cash basis of accounting. Interest expenses are not deductible for businesses, but interest income is also not included in domestic sales for businesses in calculating profits.
- *Tier Two* is a consumer sales tax on all consumer purchases. The sales tax is a uniform rate of *8.5%* on all consumer purchases of goods and services. However, all money put into *savings of any kind, all debt retirement, all purchases of stocks and bonds, all privately funded education and all charitable donations by wage earners, consumers and by families is done with **pretax dollars***.
- The total tax base is about one-third larger than the total tax base under the present federal income tax code. The reason for this is that all corporate, business, individual and family tax exemptions, tax breaks, tax subsidies and tax shelters are eliminated. Taxing imports also broadens the tax base

significantly from what it is now. In fact, the **8.5%** tax on all goods and services that come into the U.S. (imports) will account for about **11%** of all the tax revenues collected under the BEST Plan.

- The U.S. economy would double in **eight** to **12** years because of increased investment and savings. The power of taxation shifts from the IRS and the U.S. Treasury Department to the individual consumer, wage earner and to families. This truly represents freedom and liberty for all Americans.

- *Wage earners, consumers and families will have a major **incentive*** to (1) increase savings, (2) reduce debt, (3) invest in stocks and bonds, (4) buy more homes, (5) give to charities and (6) fund private education. The reason is that money put into the above items is all done in pretax dollars under The BEST Plan, which is just the opposite of the way it is done under the present federal income tax code.

- Wage earners will see their *take-home income go up overnight by **15%*** to **20%**. This is because there will be no withholding for federal income taxes.

- For all wage earners, consumers and families (for all non-business owners) the IRS will be completely gone from their lives. They will never again be required to file a tax return, report income or be subject to an IRS audit in the future.

- *Income and capital is taxed only once for individuals, families, consumers and for businesses.* Obviously under the present federal income tax code, income and capital are taxed multiple times. There will be no taxes paid on capital gains, dividends, interest and rental income and no estate or gift taxes under The BEST Plan.

- The BEST Plan is *very pro investment and pro new job creation. All businesses will be on a cash basis of accounting.* Businesses will account for about **57%** of all the income taxes paid to the federal government via the **8.5%** business transfer tax. *Wage earners, consumers and families* will account for the remaining **43%** of all federal government income taxes paid to the federal government via the **8.5%** sales tax on all goods and services purchased.

- *All IRS and Treasury Department **penalties*** now associated with tax deferred savings and investment programs, such as IRA, 401-K, Keogh and SEP programs, will be eliminated under The BEST Plan relative to tax policy. All of the money in these present tax deferred programs can be used immediately and for whatever purpose and with no penalties and with a maximum tax liability of **8.5%** under the BEST Plan, as opposed to a tax liability now ranging typically between **15%** and **38%**, depending on each individual tax paper's tax bracket under the present federal government income tax code.

- The BEST Plan *will result in many U.S. companies that have international manufacturing locations with a major incentive to come back home, stay*

177

home and hire U.S. workers. This is because exports of goods and services are not taxed, while imported goods and services are taxed at the *8.5%* tax rate. Since U.S. imports are not taxed now under our present income tax code, this encourages businesses to locate production outside of the U.S. and this also gives foreign firms a relative advantage in the U.S. market and abroad. U.S. imports typically far exceed U.S. exports as most people know. This by itself significantly *broadens the U.S. tax base,* helps keep the tax rate low at the *8.5%* rate and results in raising substantially more tax dollars for the federal government without penalizing U.S. taxpayers or our economy, compared to the present federal income tax code.

- The Best Plan is, by design, *transparent.* All businesses and all wage earners, consumers and families will know exactly what the cost of funding the federal government is relative to replacing the present federal income tax code. Under the present federal income tax code, it is very difficult if not impossible to know what the cost of the federal government is because the taxes are hidden in the costs of goods and services. With the *8.5%* business transfer tax (BTT) and the *8.5%* sales tax under The BEST Plan, all taxpayers will easily know what the cost of the federal government is for *tier one* and for *tier two* from California to New York and from Texas to North Dakota. This has many advantages.

- *Taxpayer collections and compliance will be substantially better under The BEST Plan,* compared to what taxpayer collections and compliance is under the present federal income tax code. It is widely acknowledged and understood that *there is substantial non-reporting and/or under reporting of income or the overstatement of expenses by individual, family and business taxpayers* under the present federal income tax code. With the elimination of about *141 million* or *95%* of all present tax returns (all non-business tax returns) under The BEST Plan, taxpayer collections and compliance for funding of the federal government will be significantly better than it is now under the present federal income tax code. *This will also save the non-business U.S. taxpayers collectively at least $170 billion a year!* Under The BEST Plan, all businesses and the self-employed will collect the federal government taxes and file tax returns with the IRS.

Chapter 10
Summary Outlook for 2010-2014
Major Lessons Learned
Recommendations of What to Do and
What Not to Do

I strongly believe that a *modern day depression* will occur in 2008-2014, when *average annual* U.S. economic growth will be much below normal. I expect the average annual GDP number for these seven years to be *1.5%* to *2.0%*. I continue to believe that 2010-2012 will be particularly painful and difficult for our economy, for businesses, for wage earners, for families and for the real estate, commodity and stock markets. Specifically, I expect the *eye* of the upcoming very serious and painful economic and financial *storm* will be within the second half of 2010 through the end of 2012 in the U.S. This *storm* will be significantly more severe and damaging than what we have already experienced in the years of 2008 and 2009.

I believe the U.S. economy will experience major price and asset deflationary pressures in these three years of 2010-2012, *likely starting during or shortly after the February-April period of 2010*. The specific timing is always the more difficult part. Consumer prices, measured by the average annual consumer price index (CPI), already have fallen *0.63%* below year-earlier levels in the first 11 months of 2009 compared to the same 11 months in 2008. The last time this happened was in the 1930s and briefly in 1949 and in 1955. I fully expect this general price deflationary trend to continue for most of the next 10 years and to become much more pronounced in the years 2010-2012. I expect the average annual year-to-year percentage change in the CPI numbers to be within the *1.0%* to *-3.0%* range over the next 10 years. Escalating inflation in 2010-2014 is highly unlikely, as we discussed in Chapter 7. I recommend that you plan instead on much lower than normal inflation, zero inflation and continued price deflation through at least 2014 and likely longer. The odds of this happening are *90%*.

Why all Americans are Now Facing a *Modern Day* Depression and More Serious Challenges in 2010-2014 in a Nutshell

I sincerely hope I am wrong about my economic and financial expectations and forecasts for 2010-2014 as presented in this book and in this chapter. However, I believe the odds are *90%* that the primary economic and financial market forecasts and expectations presented herein will turn out to be correct. The basic economic and financial market forecasts for 2008 and 2009, which I originally made beginning in 2007, did turn out to be correct. Those who take these conclusions and recommendations seriously and act upon them in preparation for the 2010-2014 time period will find them to be very helpful whether or not my forecasts for 2010-2014 prove to be accurate.

During late December, 2009 and early 2010, the bullish and positive sentiment forecasts of most U.S. stockbrokers, financial advisors, economists and news media sources was running at very high levels regarding an expected return of the U.S. economy to normal and stronger economic *boom period* growth, further significant increases in stock market values and sustained new job growth. When these same people and the American public, business owners and managers in general find out that these positive expectations are not being realized, this will come as a major surprise, shock and disappointment to everyone. I feel very comfortable in having a contrarian outlook and viewpoint relative to what is likely going to happen in the 2010-2014 time period and beyond regarding the U.S. economy.

Most Americans and our U.S. economy very likely will go through a lot of financial, economic and emotional pain because many consumers, families and businesses still have far too much debt. Much of this private sector debt is bad debt and will not end up being repaid. Therefore, much of this unpaid debt will be written down and written off, resulting in major U.S. and global credit default bubbles bursting over the 2010-2014 time period. This will be an important part of the necessary private debt deleveraging process that is now already underway. These developments will result in major further losses of real estate, commodity and stock market equity and wealth. This will result in major and persistently high levels of price and asset deflationary pressures over the next five to 10 years in the United States.

The write-down, write-off and deleveraging of massive amounts of bad private debt, which will be highly deflationary relative to real estate, commodity and financial market assets (stocks) within 2010-2014 is absolutely necessary *before the bust phase of the long-term business cycle* can end. There simply is no easy, quick fix or short cut measures by government or within the private sector that can be successfully implemented to prevent this deflationary process from running its course over the next several years. That is the bad news. The good news is that this very painful deflationary and private debt deleveraging process in 2010-2014 will end up being positive and bullish on a longer-term basis for our U.S. economy, for Americans and for the U.S. dollar once we get by the 2010-2014 time period. Bottom line, consumers will be spending less and saving more during 2010 to 2014 and likely longer. Average annual U.S.

economic growth will be much slower than normal and unemployment will be much higher than normal during the bust phase of the long-term business cycle during 2010-2014.

★ ★ ★

Many economists, stockbrokers, financial advisors and others today believe that the recession is over. **It is not over**. Positive U.S. economic growth in the third quarter (*2.2%*) and some positive economic growth in the fourth quarter of 2009, which I have been forecasting since early in 2009, does *not* mean the U.S. economy is off to the races. *The rate of U.S. economic growth will start slowing down substantially and will be at levels much less than normal within the second half of 2010 through at least 2012.* Remember that the U.S. economy *grew* at an average annual *1.32%* rate during the *10* years of the Great Depression, which was the last *bust phase* of the long-term business cycle. But economic output, measured by the gross domestic product, or GDP, grew nearly three times faster at a *3.82%* rate, on an average annual basis, during the *68* years of 1940-2007, which represented the last *boom phase* of the long-term business cycle.

Both GDP numbers were positive, yet the low *1.32%* growth was too meager to overcome deflationary forces, high unemployment and other symptoms of an economy in the *red light zone* of a depression. The stronger *3.82%* rate fueled good economic times, general asset class inflation and appreciation for homes and other real estate, rising stock market values, rising incomes, more new jobs and an increasing standard of living for most Americans.

The *1.32%* average annual rate of GDP growth in the 1930s was closely associated with an **L**-shaped economic downturn and recovery period lasting, in this case, for 10 years from 1930 to 1939. There were downturns during the 68-year boom that followed the Great Depression too, but the overall *3.82%* average annual rate of GDP growth kept them short, which made the fall and rise more **V**-shaped. The *11* such U.S. recessions that happened between 1940 and 2007 lasted *10.2* months on average and average annual rates of unemployment reached only *5.9%*.

We are now in an **L**-shaped downturn and economic recovery period, which I have been forecasting and discussing starting in 2007. I strongly believe that the economy will grow no more than at an average annual rate of *1.5%* to *2.0%* for the seven years of 2008-2014. Average annual GDP growth will be positive, but much less than normal. Unemployment levels, which were at *10.0%* in November, 2009, will go higher and stay painfully high over at least the next three to five years. I do not expect the level of U.S. *standard* unemployment to peak until sometime in 2012 at close to *12%*.

The November, 2009, *standard* rate of unemployment of **10.0%** represents **15.4 million** men and women who lost their jobs. More accurately, **17.3%** of America's workers *or* **26.8 million** were out of work, had given up trying to find work, or were substantially under-employed, according to what the U.S. Department of Labor calculates as the *real* and effective rate of unemployment in the U.S. for November of 2009.

By the fall of 2012, I expect the standard rate of unemployment in the U.S. to reach the **12.2%** level, representing about **18.6 million** men and women who will have lost their jobs. I also expect that the higher, real and effective unemployment rate will reach **20.0%**, representing about **32.2 million** workers within the year of 2012. But, the rate and level of unemployment in the U.S. in 2010-2012 could easily be higher than that, too.

Many people say today that the *recession is over* or the *recession is behind us* and believe our economy is now experiencing a **V**-shaped economic recovery. I strongly believe these people will end up being wrong. *I believe the worst is yet to come within the 2010-2012 time period.* The economy will get worse before it bottoms out and before it stabilizes and slowly begins to get better. *Remember, we are in a depression, not a normal recession.* Depressions last for years, not months, during the *bust* phases of the long-term boom and bust business cycle. We are now in a *bust* phase that began in 2008 and will likely not reach bottom until we get through the 2010-2012 time period.

Our Most Painful Financial Storm is Just Ahead

Prepare for the second half of 2010 and for the two years of 2011-2012 to be substantially more painful and difficult economically and financially. Unemployment will be higher than we saw in 2008-2009. Economic growth will be slower. Real estate and stock market values will fall and more wealth will be lost. Prices and the value of our assets and commodities will fall, our incomes, wages and benefits will be reduced, loan delinquencies and defaults will mount, more homes will be lost and more banks will fail. The economic and financial storm ahead of us will be significantly more painful than we felt in 2008 and 2009 and the losses will be global, not just national.

I believe the next and serious economic and financial market downturn will **begin** *during or shortly after February-April of 2010.* It may start slightly after this period. I believe this major and serious downturn will be very surprising to most people and will very likely continue through most of 2012. Here are some specific changes I urge you to plan for:

- **Consumer Spending will Contribute Significantly Less to Future GDP Growth Moving Forward** – Consumer spending accounted for **70%** to **71%** of GDP economic growth in 2007 through 2009. For many reasons we've already discussed, I believe consumer spending will decline and moderate significantly in the next 10 years and that the rate of consumer savings will increase substantially. I believe strongly that by 2020, consumer spending will account for no more than *62% to 64%* of our GDP economic growth. Those would be the lowest levels since consumption expenditures accounted for *61.9%* of GDP growth in 1966, the year Bank of America issued the nation's first general purpose credit card. Average annual consumer expenditures, as a percent of GDP growth, accounted for *65.72%* of GDP growth for the 53 years of 1957-2009. Reduced spending and increased saving are two key trends that will result in average annual GDP growth being *1.5%* to *2.0%* for at least the 2008-2014 time period, the current bust phase of the long-term 60- to 80-year cycle, and perhaps longer.

- *Economic Growth will Slow* – U.S. economic GDP growth will be much less than normal and we will see some more quarters of negative economic growth within the 2010-2014 time period. Average annual GDP growth will be *1.5%* to *2.0%* per year during 2008-2014. This relatively slow rate of growth will be much closer to the *1.32%* Great Depression annual average GDP growth rate in 1930-1939. These much slower than normal growth rates are in direct contrast to the *3.82%* average annual rate of GDP growth rate during the 68-year boom period extending from 1940 through 2007.

- *Consumer Spending will Significantly Moderate and Consumer Saving Rates will Increase Further* – Much slower than normal GDP growth, rising and relatively high unemployment rates, declining equity and wealth, reduced consumer borrowing capacity, reduced lending by banks and other lenders, plus reduced spending by *78 million* baby boomers for at least the next 10 years, all will cause a significant reduction in consumer spending. Those same changes also very likely will raise the U.S. consumer savings rate to at least the *10%* to *12%* level by 2012-2014 or about double the *5.3%* savings rate expected for 2009 and much higher than the *1.4%* actual consumer savings rate in 2005.

- *The Home Real Estate Market will Continue to Drop* – Average U.S. home values will have declined by *45%* to *55%* by 2012 from the high point in July of 2006. Within the year 2012, owners of *50%* to *60%* of all homes with mortgages will be *underwater* and they will owe more on those mortgages than what their homes will be worth. Foreclosures and delinquencies will reach record high levels in 2010-2012.

- *Commercial and Industrial Real Estate Values also will Fall* – By 2012-2014, average hotels, motels, office buildings, strip malls, shopping malls, warehouses and industrial real estate property values will have declined **50%** to **60%** from their October, 2007 high points. Foreclosures and delinquencies will also reach record levels in 2010-2012.

- **Farm and Ranch Real Estate Values will also Fall** – Average farm and ranch real estate values will decline by **25%** to **40%** from the high point in early 2008 to their low point in about 2012-2014. Farm lenders will encounter major loan servicing and debt-to-equity (loan to value) issues during the next five years and serious problems will arise with a good many farm and ranch real estate loans.

- **Commodity Market Values will Fall** – I am bearish on almost all commodity market values in 2010-2012, beginning generally during or shortly after the February-April period of 2010, but beginning no later than within the second half of 2010. The trend in commodity prices generally will be lower through the three years of 2010-2012. Crude oil prices, for example, will fall to the **$25** to **$35** per barrel level between now and 2012 and may decline temporarily to the **$10** to **$15** per barrel level before bottoming out. Overall price and asset value deflation and a permanent loss of demand in 2010-2012 will be major driving forces behind the general trend of lower commodity prices over the next three years for crude oil, natural gas, gold, silver, other metals, grains, livestock, poultry and milk prices.

- **The Stock Markets will Fall and will Remain Volatile** – I continue to believe the U.S. stock market Dow Jones Industrial Average index will fall to early 1995 levels and reach **3,500** and **4,500** in 2010-2012 and that the Standard & Poor's 500 index will drop to the **450-550** level. I believe the Dow could go to the **10,800** to **11,500** level before turning sharply lower beginning in or shortly after February-April of 2010. I do *not* expect the U.S. stock market lows to be reached until 2011 or 2012.

The U.S. stock markets ended up declining and closing significantly lower at the end of calendar year 2009, compared to the end of calendar year 1999. In this *10*-year time period, the Dow, the S&P 500 and the NASDAQ stock markets were about **8.3%**, **23.2%** and **43.7%** *lower*, respectively, as of January 1, 2010, compared to January 1, 2000. The buy and hold stock market investing strategy obviously did not work very well during this 10-year period. There was, of course, major up and down stock market volatility during this same 10-year period. You can expect continued major U.S. stock market volatility over the next 10 years.

- **These Asset Bubbles were Created by Excessive Easy Credit, Excessive Growth of Debt and Credit and Excessive Leverage** – The present bust phase of the longer-term business cycle was created by the private sector of our economy living far beyond its means for many years. This took the form of excessive easy credit terms, excessive growth of debt and credit and excessive leverage. Much like what took place in the 1930s in the U.S. and what happened in Japan in the 15 years of 1992-2006, these financial excesses always result in the various asset class bubbles bursting, including the credit default bubbles bursting. These bubbles were created by *excessive credit inflation* and *growth* over many years. The Japanese economy, presently the second largest economy in the world, continues to seriously struggle as of early 2010. This deleveraging and deflating process takes years to run its course in the U.S., in Japan, in Europe and elsewhere and to find an equilibrium point. Much of this deflating and deleveraging process is still ahead of us for the United States within the years of 2010-2014.

- *A Lot More Air Will Come out of the Asset Bubbles* – These are the real estate, commodity market and stock market asset classes that will decline significantly further in value over the next three to five years. This is well illustrated in Figure 4.1. As discussed above, I expect the year-to-year average annual rate of CPI inflation/deflation to be within the *1.0%* to *-3.0%* in 2010-2012 and for this general trend to likely continue for the next 10 years.

- *Major Loss of Equity and Wealth will Occur as Bubbles Continue Bursting* – By the time we get to 2012-2014, the total loss of equity and asset wealth in America will be very nearly *$27* to *$30 trillion* resulting from the decline of real estate, commodity market and stock market values from their high points in 2006, 2007 and early 2008 as shown in Figure 5.4 in Chapter 5. This represents a *loss* of *50%* to *60%* of the total asset wealth in the United States. This will be a serious development and I expect most of it to happen in 2010-2012.

- *The Bursting of the U.S. Credit Default Bubble will be a Major Development in 2010-2014* – Trillions of dollars of private debt will be written down and/or written off by the time we reach 2012-2014. These developments will have serious implications on reducing significantly further the lender's lending capacity and the borrower's borrowing and spending capacity during the next five years. This is now and will continue to be a very serious problem for millions of small and medium sized businesses in America.

- *Major Commercial Bank Failures will Occur* – Be prepared for 800 to 1,200 U.S. commercial bank failures in 2009-2014. The collateral values on the balance sheets for many banks, I believe, are realistically overstated by *25%* to *50%*. The day of truth and reckoning is coming in 2010-2012. Many banks are very vulnerable to becoming insolvent and having too little capital to *shore up* their balance sheets over the next

185

three to five years. These banks will be deleveraging private debt, which will result in sharply reducing credit growth. This will, therefore, have the net result of credit deflation in the U.S. over at least the next five to 10 years, i.e. banks and other lenders will be loaning significantly less money to consumers and businesses over most of the next five to 10 years, compared to the 1990-2007 time period. This is one of *two key reasons* why commercial banks and other lenders are not now making new loans to consumers and to businesses in the U.S. anywhere close to the same pace that occurred between 1990 and 2007.

The other major reason many commercial banks and other lenders are *not* making new loans to consumers and businesses, particularly small and medium-sized businesses, is that many banks and other lenders are borrowing money from the Federal Reserve at essentially zero interest rates and using the money to buy U.S. Government one-year, five-year and 10-year Treasury Notes, Treasury Bills or Treasury Bonds. These banks thus receive an interest yield of *1.5%* to *4.5%* with essentially no financial risk. This eliminates or at least substantially reduces the amount of capital these lenders can and/or or will be willing to lend to businesses and consumers. In short, U.S. commercial banks and other lenders are financing our out-of-control and rapidly growing national debt at the expense of American consumers, families and businesses that need additional financing in the form of new loans.

These developments and trends are now and will continue to contribute to much-slower-than-normal rates of GDP growth, reduced consumer spending, increased consumer savings and much higher-than-normal levels of unemployment in the U.S. during 2010-2014 and beyond. However, these trends and developments are also part of the overall financial deleveraging process that is well underway in America and globally and that will take at least five to 10 more years to run its course.

- *I am Bullish on the U.S. Dollar Longer Term* – I am now and particularly once we get past February-April of 2010, bullish on the U.S. dollar for at least three to five years for a number of good reasons that were discussed in Chapters 8 and 9. Most people are bearish on the U.S. dollar today and for the longer term. I am confident the U.S. dollar will remain the reserve currency of the world for many years into the future.

- *Interest Rates will Remain Low* – I believe U.S. interest rates will remain close to historically low levels for the next three years. I believe the Federal Reserve will keep the fed funds rate at or near zero for all or most of 2010-2012. *If* the Federal Reserve increases the fed funds rate slightly sometime in 2010 and *if* interest rates on U.S. Government 5, 10 and 30-year Treasury Bonds and on U.S. Government Treasury Notes also increase slightly in 2010, such increases will be temporary, and will go back down again within the second half of 2010 through the 2012 time period. I recommend that you plan accordingly. Economic and financial market trends, conditions and deflating prices and assets provide little other choice. I believe the difference between short and long-term interest rates will narrow within the next **36** months as more people realize that escalating inflation is not and will not become an issue in 2010-2014, and when these same people start to adjust to major asset deleveraging and credit default deflationary forces over the next five to 10 years in the U.S.

I continue to strongly recommend that you borrow *all* money on a monthly floating and variable rate basis. Do *not* fix rates now or in 2010-2012 for borrowed funds of any kind relative to term debt.

- *Cash is King and Reduce Debt* – I continue to recommend that you make every practical effort to reduce debt and, if possible, get completely out of debt. Cash will truly be king and will present some *chance of a lifetime* opportunities for you, your family, your employees and your business over the next five years.

- *Be Patient* – For many people, it will be very tempting to purchase assets, commodities, stocks, real estate and other assets because they do now or will soon look very attractive. *My strong advice is to be cautious, conservative and patient.* In the present and coming deflationary environment, good deals in many cases will get much better than you ever thought possible. There are going to be some *buys of a lifetime* coming up that will present some great opportunities if you are patient.

- *Federal, State, and Local Government Spending and Budget Deficits are Out of Control* – For example, for the 53 years of 1957 to 2009, the average annual year-to-year combined percentage rate of change in federal, state, and local government spending was *8.1%* per year as shown in Figure 9.2. Be sure to review Figure 9.8. This compares the average annual year-to-year percentage change in (1) U.S. population growth, (2) GDP growth, (3) CPI growth and (4) federal debt as a percent of GDP of *1.4%*, *3.2%*, *4.0%* and *4.3%*, respectively, with the average annual year-to-year percentage rate of growth in federal, state, and local government spending of *8.1%* per year.

The majority of the American people are going to register their growing concerns about the federal government's out-of-control spending in 2010 and 2012 and beyond by voting for candidates who make a firm commitment to reduce spending, reduce taxes and balance the budget over the next five to seven years. The American people are going to start waking up and start saying *no* to socialism, *no* to higher taxes, *no* to irresponsible budget deficit spending and *no* to an unsustainable and out of control rising national debt in the years ahead as discussed in Chapter 9.

Lessons Learned

The most important lesson learned by those who have read this book is that there is both a shorter-term and a longer-term business cycle. The shorter-term business cycle relates to periodic economic recessions via the *yellow light zone*. U.S. recessions typically last for months and for less than one year. We have had *11* recessions from 1940 through 2007. The average length was only *10.2* months. Most of these recessions were relatively mild, but some were rather painful, like the 1981-1982 recession. Almost everyone is aware that the U.S. economy has periodic recessions or *bumps in the road*. These periodic recessions are part of an otherwise longer-term boom cycle that typically lasts for 60 or more years. The last boom cycle in the U.S. lasted *68* years from 1940 through 2007.

The 60- to 80-year long-term business cycle is the one that most people are *not* familiar with. Most people just don't think about our economy in terms of a long-term business cycle. About every *60* to *80* years, the U.S. does have occasional depressions via the *red light zone*. Specifically, there have been *three* economic depressions in the U.S. since 1800 as discussed in Chapter 1. Two of these depressions were in the 1800s and the last depression was the one we are all the most familiar with that occurred in the 1930s, the Great Depression, which lasted *10* years. It has been about *80* years since that depression. Economic depressions typically last for seven to 10 years and are the *bust phase* of the long-term 60- to 80-year boom and bust business cycle.

Most people have fortunately experienced none or only one economic depression in their adult working lifetimes. The period of time between economic depressions is close to 60 to 80 years. During this relatively long period of time, most of us have forgotten or think that *things are different now*. We also think that *another U.S. depression is impossible because we live in such an enlightened and technologically superior age*. This is very understandable and a predictable part of human nature.

Most Americans have *not* experienced the difficult economic and financial market conditions associated with a depression in their lifetime. The 2008-2009 *Great Recession* is by far the most painful and longest lasting downturn since the 1930s. Most Americans alive today are used to the long-term *boom* phase of the long-term business cycle with its generally good economic times and conditions. They have experienced generally good jobs, higher incomes, increased asset and wealth appreciation and an increasing standard of living. This is what most people have known during the past *60* to *70* years and this is what they expect to continue in the years ahead.

In America we generally do not believe that another depression could happen. Americans in late 2009 and early 2010 believe the U.S. had a major, serious and much longer lasting than normal recession in 2008 and 2009 and that this recession is basically behind us. Most people believe that we will soon get back on track and return to *normal* employment and a relatively strong economic growth pattern, or basically an economic *green light zone*. Most people are *not* planning on or prepared for the *bust* phase of a long-term business cycle.

By definition, the *bust* phase is an economic depression that lasts for a period of years. This phase is characterized by very painful and much slower than normal five to 10 years of economic growth, reduced consumer spending and sharply higher than normal unemployment. Deflating prices and assets result in the loss of massive amounts of equity and wealth by consumers, families and business owners.

During the *bust* phase of the long-term 60- to 80-year business cycle, economic depressions occur because of financial excesses. As a nation, we borrowed our way to prosperity and we lived far beyond our means for many years. We used major amounts of excessively easy credit to create excessive growth in private debt and leverage. This created massive bubbles that finally have begun to burst. The bursting of these bubbles takes years and causes major price and asset deflationary forces to set in and run their course.

The primary purpose for writing this book is to help you better understand and to be better prepared for a serious *modern day* economic depression within the 2008-2014 time period. It will be very painful for all Americans, consumers, private sector employees, families, retirees, business owners and for all politicians and government workers. *The 68-year party of good economic times ended in 2005-2007.*

Between 2010 and 2014, the most serious and damaging impact of the next U.S. economic depression and bust period will likely have happened. What I hope is that *all* Americans in both the private and public sectors of our economy will start seriously planning for and getting better prepared for both the 2010-2014 depression and also for the *next* economic depression *60* to *80* years from now. The next U.S. economic depression and bust phase will likely occur sometime between 2070 and 2090. Economic history will continue to repeat itself over time. This is the nature of our capitalistic system in America. *The period of 2010-2014 will be a major, once in a lifetime, serious bump in the road for most people.*

I strongly encourage you to plan and prepare accordingly by educating your children, friends and employees about the historic inevitability of long-term economic boom and bust business cycles, as we've seen in Europe, Japan and for United States and as presented in this book. *Bottom line, the short and longer-term boom and bust business cycles have not been repealed. They will not be repealed in the future. History is repeating itself once again because we cannot seem to get away from creating and building major financial excesses and bubbles over time.*

What to Do
Where to Consider Investing or *Parking* your Available Cash Funds During the 2010-2014 Storm

Assuming the U.S. stock markets decline significantly, which will likely begin during or shortly after the first four months of 2010, I am recommending the steps listed below. This is the financial path I will be taking between now and 2014. I am *not* a stock broker or a professional financial or investment advisor. Therefore, I encourage you to simply seriously consider the following recommendations and to also share them with your financial and investment advisor, stockbroker, family members, friends, employees and business associates:

1. *FDIC Bank Certificates of Deposit (CDs)* – For a period of at least three years (2010-2012) and very possibly longer, *park* significant funds in bank CDs insured by the Federal Deposit Insurance Corp. The goal should *not* be to maximize the return on your cash funds, but to *safeguard your available cash funds* for the next three to five years. Longer term, after 2010-2014, you can and should seek higher returns by again buying selected stocks and making other carefully considered investments. I feel very comfortable personally taking this action.

2. *Long-term U.S. Government Treasury Bonds* – I believe 30-year U.S. Government Treasury Bonds also represent a very good place in early 2010 to park and invest your available cash funds for 2010-2014. The interest yield on these 30-year bonds in early January of 2010 was about *4.3%* to *4.5%*. I fully expect the 30-year Treasury Bond interest yield will decline to *2.50%* to *3.0%* in 2010-2014, which means that the redeemable market value and market appreciation of these same bonds will go up at least *20%* to *25%*. If, as I expect, this happens over about a 24-month period, the value of the bonds will increase the equivalent of *10%* to *13%* per year, plus the interest yield of *4.4%* per year will create a total combined and conservative return of *14.4%* to *17.4%* per year on your money over a two or three-year period.

U.S. Government 30-year Treasury Bonds are a safe place to park your available cash investment funds in a slow growth and a general price deflationary economy in early 2010. These bonds presently represent the best credits in the world. I believe this will continue to be the case. They are also very liquid. In addition, the U.S. Treasury cannot call these treasury bonds. Thus, the return on your money is very good with relatively little risk. This assumes, of course, that I have correctly predicted that the interest yield on these 30-year government Treasury Bonds will go down from about *4.3%* or *4.5%* in early January, 2010 to *2.50%* to *3.0%* within the 2010-2014 time period.

I am confident in this forecast, but obviously it does not represent a guarantee. I feel very comfortable taking this action on a personal basis.

3. *Investment Grade and High Quality Corporate Bonds* – For the 2010-2014 time period, I recommend that you seriously consider placing some of your available cash funds into selected, high quality and relatively low risk investment grade corporate bonds, beginning early in 2010. These should be well established companies with strong balance sheets and that have very positive free cash flow numbers. I feel comfortable taking this action on a personal basis.

4. *Fixed Rate Annuities* – For the 2010-2014 time period, I also recommend that you seriously consider investing some of your available cash into highly selected fixed-rate three, five or 10 year insurance company annuities. This represents a good and sound investment option providing you are very selective and careful about which insurance companies from which to buy these fixed-rate annuities. These investments do have a financial risk.

The fixed simple annual interest rates, as of early January, 2010, that the companies listed below generally pay investors vary significantly depending on (1) the company, (2) the length of time you invest in the fixed-rate annuity and (3) on the total amount of money you invest. For example, the three-year fixed interest rates typically range between *1.3%* to *1.85%* per year for a three-year term and *2.3%* to *3.05%* per year for a five-year term as of early January, 2010. For a 10-year or longer term, the fixed interest rates are typically significantly higher. Annuities are not guaranteed safe or backed by the federal government or by FDIC, so buying from a financially sound insurance company is critical.

There are many U.S. insurance companies to select from. Following below are six U.S. life insurance companies that I feel comfortable investing in on a personal basis, relative to purchasing fixed-rate annuities:

- John Hancock Life Insurance Company
- Lincoln Life Insurance Company
- Hartford Life Insurance Company
- Protective Life Insurance Company
- Northwestern Life Insurance Company
- State Farm Life Insurance Company

5. *Selected Public Utility Stocks Paying Relatively Good Dividends* – As discussed above, I believe that the U.S. stock market is considerably overpriced in early 2010 and that the prices of many stocks are far too high compared to their companies' future earnings to be sustained. I also believe the prices for most stocks will begin declining substantially after February-April, 2010 and sometime before the end of 2012. Again, I expect the Dow to end up reaching the **3,500** to **4,500** level and the **S&P 500** to reach the **450** and **550** level. These levels will represent a loss of **62%** and **55%**, respectively, within the 2010-2012 time period.

    In the much slower than normal growth economy and within a major price deflationary environment that I foresee, you may want to consider, early in 2010, buying stock in selected public utilities and take advantage of the generally good cash dividends these typically conservative shares provide. On a personal level, however, I favor CDs, Treasuries, high-quality corporate bonds, fixed rate annuities and the U.S. dollar during the 2010-2012 time period and allowing the U.S. and global stock markets to go through their major downward corrections before purchasing any selected stocks again on a longer-term basis.

6. *Go Long the U.S. Dollar* – I am bullish on the U.S. dollar, particularly during 2010-2014. I recommend that you go long and purchase the U.S. dollar index, U.S. Treasury securities or purchase ETF's, as discussed below, beginning in early 2010. I feel comfortable taking this action on a personal basis.

7. *Consider Exchange Traded Funds (ETF's)* – ETF's provide individual investors a very good, low fee and targeted alternative way to invest available cash funds. For example, while I am recommending that you get **100%** out of the U.S. stock markets by no later than February-April, 2010 and stay out through most of the 2010-2012 time period, I recommend that you seriously consider using ETF's to buy and go long the U.S. dollar starting in the January-April period of 2010. As you know and as discussed in Chapter 8, I am generally bullish on the U.S. dollar for at least the 2010-2014 time period.

What Not to Do
Key Categories Where I Recommend that Americans Not Invest their Available Cash During All or Most of 2010-2014

- Get *100%* out of the U.S. and global stock markets in February-April of 2010. This includes getting out of any stock allocations in your 401(k) plan portfolios and, if necessary, rolling over those funds into Individual Retirement Accounts (IRA's) that allow you to more easily buy CDs, Treasuries or other relatively safe investments discussed above. Stay out of the U.S. stock markets until the Dow and **S&P 500** Indexes decline to at least the *3,500-4,500* and *450-550* levels, respectively. Plan on the stock markets recovering slowly and with considerable volatility after they bottom.

- Be very patient about buying and investing in any kind of real estate during 2010-2014. This includes homes, commercial and industrial real estate and farm and ranch real estate. Real estate values will generally continue to decline further because of the significant deflationary, credit default and debt deleveraging forces dominating the economic and financial landscape over this period of time.

- Stay completely away from investing in any corporate *junk bonds* during 2010-2014. Also, be very careful about investing in tax-free municipal bonds over this period. There will be many risks in both of these sectors in the next several years.

- Be very careful and selective in investing in banks and other lenders during 2010-2014.

- If you have invested in and own *gold*, I recommend that you sell all of it within the February-April period of 2010. If you have purchased gold as a hedge against potential coming and escalating U.S. inflation, you will be disappointed. Instead of inflation, the U.S. overall economy will be experiencing general and major price and asset deflation. I fully expect the market value of gold to decline by at least *50%* from the levels seen in the February-April period of 2010 within the 2010-2014 timeframe.

- *Expect and plan on persistent and significant year-to-year general price CPI deflation over most of 2010-2020.* I believe the year-to-year percentage average annual change in the rate of CPI inflation/deflation will be a *1.0%* to a *-3.0%* per year for the next five to 10 years. Businesses and producers of goods and services during those years are going to generally find that their products will be selling for lower prices. Therefore, these same people and businesses will be paying generally less for what they are buying. *The transition from inflation to deflation will be a major and fundamental change for nearly all*

Americans, who experienced nothing but general price inflation in their lives.

What Goes *Down* Eventually Comes Back *Up* Again

I want to emphasize and end this book with the thought that the U.S. economy, the price and asset deflationary pressures and the stock markets will very likely bottom out within the 2010-2014 *modern day* depression time period that is extensively discussed in this book. The recovery will generally be slow and uneven but what goes down will eventually bottom out and then indeed begin going back up again as shown in Figure 10.1. You should plan accordingly. However, your patience will be severely tested and well rewarded. Once we get past the 2010-2014 time period, the U.S. economy overall will begin to recover relatively slowly until we get to 2020-2025. From about 2023 forward, the U.S. economy will very likely experience the beginning of another major *60-* to *70-year* **economic boom period.** Like the *68* years from 1940-2007, this new boom will include periodic **V**-shaped downturns and recovery recessions that typically will last for less than one year. Yes, we are now facing a *modern day* depression in 2010-2014 that began in 2008 and 2009 via the *red light zone.* However, in time and after we get past 2010-2014, economic and financial market conditions and trends in America will slowly start getting much better once again for most Americans. *You should plan accordingly.*

Keep Smiling

Figure 10.1

What Goes *Down* Eventually Comes Back *Up*
*Hard and Financial Asset Values Deflate and Burst over Time and Then
These Same Asset Values Begin the Gradual Inflating Process Again*

*This is What Likely will Start to Happen During the 2020-2025 Time Period
for Another 60- to 70-Year Boom Period*

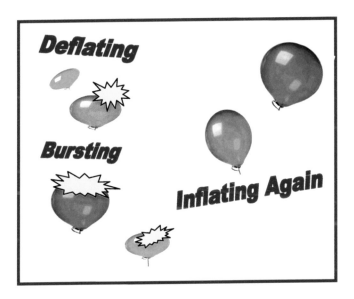

If you would like to order more copies of this book and/or become a subscriber to Bill Helming's quarterly economic and ag sector newsletter, *AS I SEE IT,* please use these convenient perforated order forms. Fill out the form(s) and mail along with your check made payable to Bill Helming Consulting Services to the address below:

**Bill Helming Consulting Services
10640 South Glenview Lane
Olathe, Kansas 66061**

Thanks for your interest and your business!

For copies of the book, *What Goes Up Eventually Comes Down*

NOTE: Each copy of the book will be autographed and dated by the author. Book(s) will be mailed to the address provided below by first class or priority U.S. mail service within three business days of receipt of payment. This book is self-published by the author.

A. MAIL BOOKS TO: _____

_____

_____ ZIP CODE: _____

B. DAYTIME CONTACT NUMBER: (_____) _____

C. PRICING AND SHIPPING COST: The price for one to four copies of this paperback book is $45.00 per book, plus $5.00 for shipping and handling per book. For five or more copies, the price is $35.00 per book, plus $3.00 shipping and handling per book. The shipping and handling fee is only for books that are mailed.

D. NUMBER OF BOOKS:

One to four books @ $45 per book
No. of copies: _____ x $45/book $_____
Shipping & handling: _____ x $5/book $_____
Total payment $_____

Five or more books @ $35 per book
No. of copies: _____ x $35/book = $_____
Shipping & handling: _____ x $3/book $_____
Total of payment $_____

Please complete this form and send with your check made payable to *Bill Helming Consulting Services* to the **Order Form Address** at the beginning of this section. If you have questions, call **(913) 768-6540**. Have a great day and week.

To subscribe to Bill Helming's quarterly economic and Ag sector newsletter, *AS I SEE IT*

Bill has been writing and publishing this newsletter since 1975.

Complete the order form below and send it along with your check made payable to Bill Helming Consulting Services to the *Order Form Address* at the beginning of this section.

A. MAIL QUARTERLY NEWSLETTER TO: _____

_____

_____ ZIP CODE: _____

B. DAYTIME CONTACT NUMBER: (____) _____

C. ANNUAL SUBSCRIPTION COST: The subscription cost for this quarterly newsletter is *$350* per year. This cost includes periodic phone access to Bill Helming to discuss the U.S. economy and the ag sector.

Please complete this form and send with your check for $350 made payable to *Bill Helming Consulting Services* to the *Order Form Address* at the beginning of this section. If you have questions, call **(913) 768-6540**. Have a great day and week.

D